IMAGES
of America

GLADWIN COUNTY

On the cover: This camp probably served as a lumbering camp and farming homestead in section 26 of Gladwin Township around 1905. Their expressions exemplify determination and the spirit to thrive. From left to right are (standing) Charlotte (Lottie) Koontz, her daughter Alice Koontz, Gilbert Koontz, Mable Koontz, and Ben Hetherington; (seated) Elmer Koontz and Wilburt Hetherington. The image was restored by Robert Frei. (Courtesy of Gladwin County Historical Society.)

IMAGES
of America

GLADWIN COUNTY

Rick Sigsby

ARCADIA
PUBLISHING

ISBN 978-0-7385-5247-7

Published by Arcadia Publishing
Charleston, South Carolina

Printed in the United States of America

Library of Congress Catalog Card Number: 2008922971

For all general information contact Arcadia Publishing at:
Telephone 843-853-2070
Fax 843-853-0044
E-mail sales@arcadiapublishing.com
For customer service and orders:
Toll-Free 1-888-313-2665

Visit us on the Internet at www.arcadiapublishing.com

To Tom Barthell, a true historian, and Dottie and Ann Sigsby, who have always helped to keep the dream alive.

Contents

ACKNOWLEDGMENTS

Gladwin County is fortunate to have two active historical societies.

The Gladwin County Historical Society began developing a historic village in the 1980s. The complex has grown to six buildings, including the old Gladwin railroad depot, a church, and a schoolhouse. In 2007, a new event, led by current president Tom Cummins, began called the Carriage Festival featuring horse-drawn carriages of all types with a weekend of activities. An exciting new endeavor unfolded in 2008, as a downtown building was donated to become the county historical museum.

The Beaverton Historical Society, led by Bob Frei, has been active promoting several events including its own Fourth of July History Day, Good Ole Days, and the Beaverton Classic Auto Show. They also are continuing to add more farms to the Centennial Farm project.

As a columnist for the local newspaper, I have had an opportunity to meet many of the historically significant people in the county. With a natural sense of curiosity, the chance to dig deep into the who, what, and how of Gladwin County was an exciting proposition.

Both historical societies have been instrumental in assisting with this book. The Gladwin City Council and Gladwin District Library have also been helpful in seeing this project through. A special thanks to the *Gladwin County Record and Beaverton Clarion* for providing advertising, office space, and materials to inform the public and invite their participation.

Each historical society graciously opened their photograph archives to me. If any photograph is not specifically credited, it came from those sources. The following people shared their personal photographs: Nadine Saiki, Karen Mack, Don Hetherington, Stan Smith, Nancy Nakkula Prescott, Janet Whitmer, Inez Soldan, Ben Ball, John Blades, Tom Winarski, Ken Thurlow, Virginia McCulloch, Julie Ellis, Fran Seebeck, Greg Stryker, and Marie Plude.

In pursuit of writing, I have had considerable assistance and mentorship from Dean Hoffman, Mike Drey, Chris Zimmerman, Eldrick Wilson, and Jack Westbrook.

This project would not have been possible without the contributions of the following three people: Bob Frei, John Rhode, and my wife, Ann. All three were invaluable.

INTRODUCTION

Henry Gladwin most certainly never set foot in the county that bears his name. Unlike many Michigan landmarks, cities, towns, and counties, Gladwin is not a Native American name. However, it was primarily due to Native American activity that this area became known as Gladwin County

Originally a part of the neighboring counties of Midland and Saginaw, Gladwin County was surveyed in 1831 and named after the British major Henry Gladwin, who commanded Fort Detroit, the only fort in the Midwest to withstand Chief Pontiac and the Chippewa Indians resistance to the white man's attempts to gain toehold settlements in Michigan.

The first settler in the area was Marvil Secord in 1861. He came by canoe up the Tittabawassee River and set up residence not far from where the Hetherington farm and city of Gladwin are today.

Gladwin's location on the Cedar River was originally named Cedar until it was discovered from the disappearance and delay of mail that another town already existed by that name. There was also an area known as Gladwin City nearby, which created even more confusion. After some political maneuvering, a county seat was chosen and people began calling their new location on the Cedar River the village of Gladwin.

At the time, virtually all of the 550 square miles of Gladwin County were covered with white pine forest. This prompted lumbermen to head here from the Saginaw Valley in the 1870s. The county's vast river system provided a natural highway for millions of board feet of timber to be delivered efficiently to numerous sawmills in the area.

The railroads were eager to push north to provide a rapid exit of logs to the bigger mills downstate. But it took a bribe for the last few miles to be completed. After the forests disappeared, Gladwin began a new phase, converting from the lumber era to agriculture. This time, farmers came north by rail to buy cheap acres of stump land. In many cases, the farmers bundled up and headed back into the woods in wintertime. Money that could be made as a lumberjack paid for the things they could not grow or barter for.

Vast tracts of land in Gladwin County are now state forest. This is primarily due to two reasons. Many of the large logging companies walked away after lumbering off thousands of acres without paying back taxes. Seizing the opportunity, many people made an effort to farm the land. Bumper crops were reported in the first few decades of the 20th century. But draining the swampland, fires, and lack of fertilization forced many farmers to quit. There is a ghost town called Hard Luck in Grim Township nearby.

Oil was discovered not far from the town of Beaverton in the 1930s. At one time, Gladwin County was the largest producer of oil in Michigan. However, that period was short-lived and typical of the "boom or bust" oil industry. Several times since, there have been brief periods of renewed activity due to improvements in the recovery process.

Beaverton was originally known as Grand Forks because of the convergence of the Cedar and Tobacco Rivers forming the Tittabawassee River. Founded by the Ross family, they later renamed the town in honor of their hometown of Beaverton in Ontario, Canada.

The 1950s brought about another reinvention with the rise of a relatively new creation called plastic. Gaylord Brown started from a small workshop that eventually evolved into Brown Machine Company. Multiple businesses were spawned and Gladwin County became the thermoforming capital of the world.

With the abundance of rivers and lakes in the county, recreation and tourism has been an intricate part of the economy. Many of the early cabins and cottages became homes, while old lumber camps and boomtowns have survived as resort areas.

An extensive dam system was established to meet the needs of the lumber industry and later to meet the energy demands of the increasing population. Wolverine Power Company's ambitious projects created several major backwater lakes, including Sanford, Wixom, Albright Shores, Smallwoods, and Secord, which all are lined with resort areas and year-round residents. Dams created two large communities, Wiggins Lake from the Chappel Dam and Sugar Springs Resort with Lake Lancer and Lake Lancelot from the damming of the Sugar River.

One of Gladwin's early celebrities was the first Miss Beaverton in 1929, Lorraine Budge. She went on to be named Miss Michigan and competed in the Miss America pageant. The second Miss Beaverton, Virginia Evans, is still a celebrity of some note today. A few years after winning the beauty contest, Evans married Willis McCulloch, who was named State Farmer of Michigan and the National Future Farmer of America in 1933. They both worked in the McCulloch Riverside Dairy during the Depression, making one-pound blocks of butter to be sold at local grocery stores. In 1969, the year a man walked on the moon, she went back to college at age 56. Now a great-great-grandmother and in her 90s, she is just one of many fascinating people who call Gladwin County home.

Each resident has roots that run deep and their reasons for living here weave an interesting theme. Gladwin people have overcome economic hardship, made the most of their situation, and have thrived.

Gladwin County has been blessed with a treasure trove of natural resources. It has survived by reinventing itself through the development of those resources, and it is a prime destination point in the heart of Michigan.

One

PATHWAY TO THE PINES

The county of Gladwin was named after British commander major Henry Gladwin, who was born in Derbyshire, England, in 1732. He worked his way through the ranks of the English infantry to eventually become the third commander of Fort Detroit under British rule in 1762. Much of his time there was spent defending the fort during the siege waged by Ottawa Indian chief Pontiac. Gladwin left Fort Detroit in 1764 and returned to England where he died in 1794. It is not known whether he ever returned to America. Almost 100 years later, an area several hundred miles north of the fort now bears his name. The first settlers were Native Americans of the Ojibway, Menomine, and Sauk tribes. John Holland completed a painting of the major. A former resident of Gladwin, M. J. Hiscosck made a copy of the original and presented it to the county in 1924.

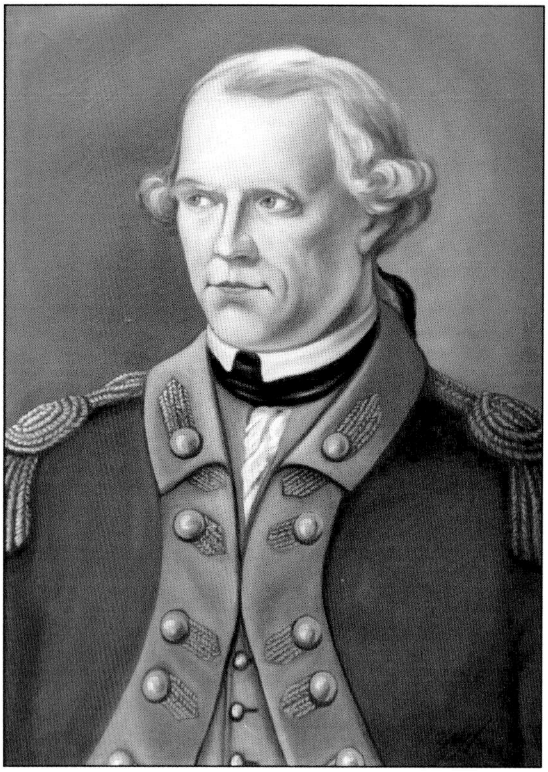

Pictured here is the portrait of Maj. Henry Gladwin as painted by John Holland. (Courtesy of Gladwin County Historical Society.)

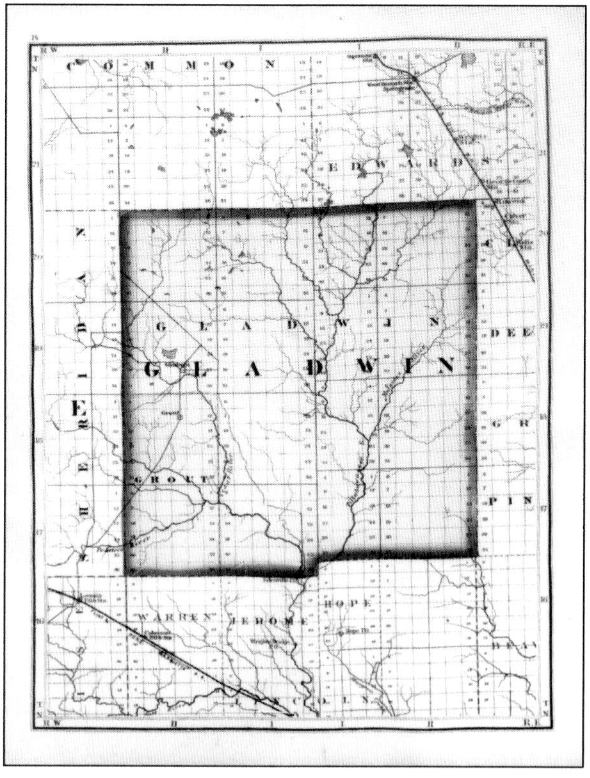

The area known as Gladwin County was originally a part of Midland County as Gladwin Township in 1860. This 1873 H. F. Walling Michigan atlas shows two townships, Gladwin and Grout. The county was eventually organized into three townships in 1875–Gladwin, Grout, and Billings.

Marvil Secord is known to be the first white settler in the Gladwin area. He was originally from Brantford, Ontario, but moved to Michigan at an early age and lived in the Detroit area. In September 1861, Marvil and his son Jerome set out on an expedition up the Tittabawassee River. Secord died of a self-inflicted tomahawk wound in 1886 at the ripe old age of 84. (Courtesy of Gladwin County Record and Beaverton Clarion.)

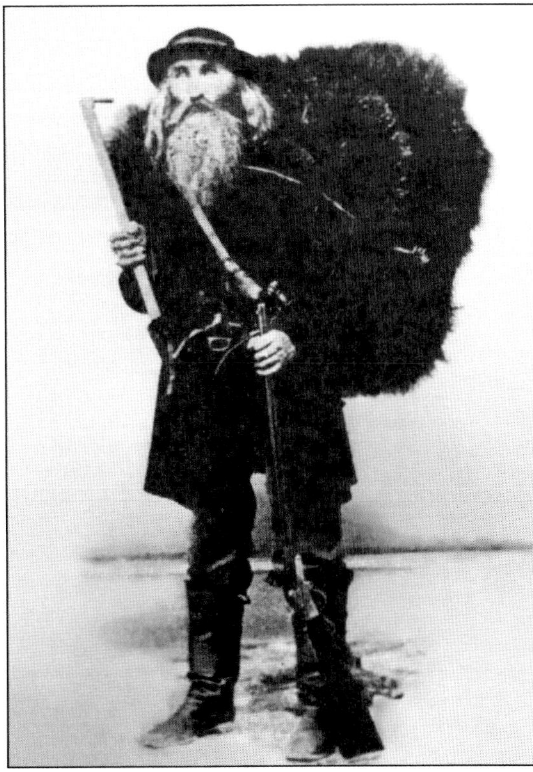

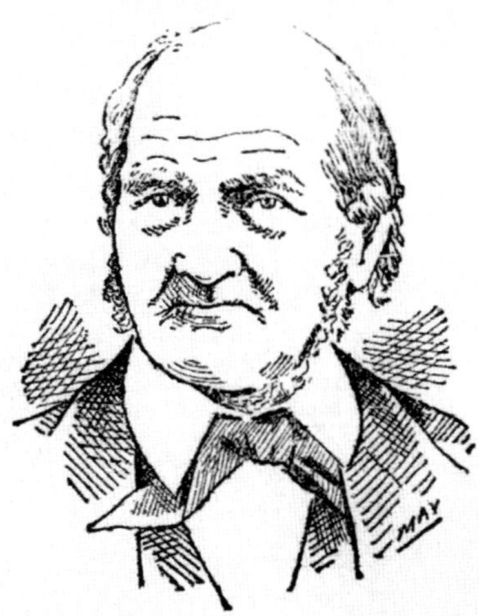

Willard Grout

Early settler, farmer and influential leader in the earliest days of Gladwin County and namesake of Grout Twp.

Willard Grout established the first homestead in what was to become Grout Township, which separated from Gladwin Township over some financial disputes in 1871. That year, he was appointed justice of the peace, and in 1874, he became the first postmaster with an office named Grout, which operated until 1880. The county seat was established in 1875 on the east bank of the Cedar River, and the town took the name Cedar. Grout owned a lot of land on the west bank of the Cedar River; his son owned the land on the east bank. That area eventually became the city of Gladwin.

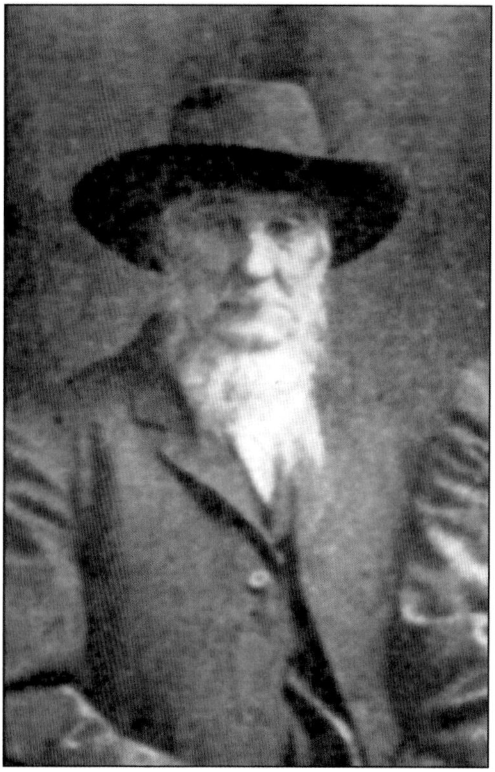

Benjamin Teeple came from the London, Ontario, area and moved to Michigan in 1852. He enlisted in the U.S. Army in St. Clair County and served in Company K of the Second Michigan Cavalry. In 1863, Teeple came to mid-Michigan by foot and later moved his family to Grout Township in Gladwin County. While cutting a bag of hay for his horse, he dropped dead near his home at the age of 80 in 1912. This is a photograph of Teeple from the August 1911 *Gladwin County Record.*

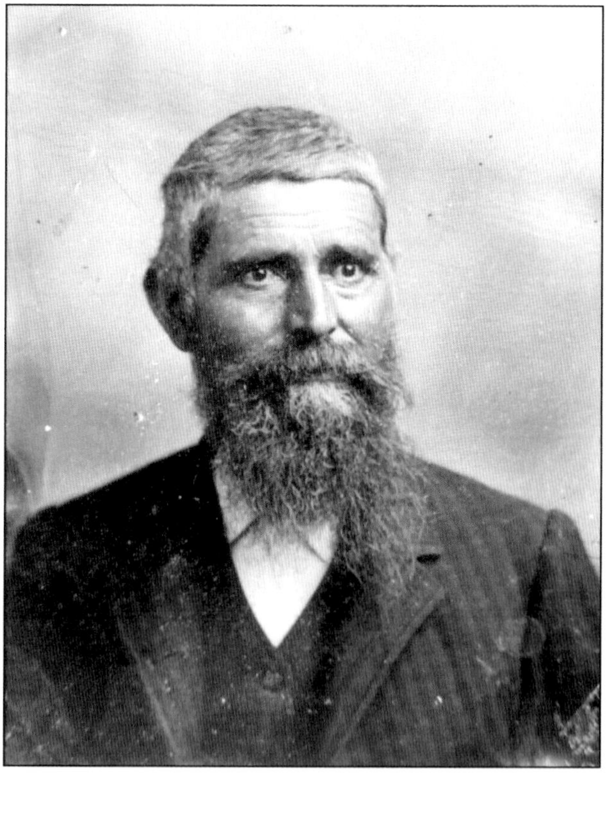

One of the earliest settlers was Christopher Columbus (C. C.) Foutch, a lawyer and merchant who came to Cedar (city of Gladwin) from the town of Farwell in nearby Isabella County. Foutch immediately constructed several buildings and soon brought his sister Minnie and brother David to establish one of the foundation families. C. C. plotted out much of the south end of the city, and the streets were named after his children, May, June, Jay, Columbus, and Squire. He died in 1900 and is buried in the Highland Cemetery.

Two

Lumbering on the Rails

Although Gladwin County has abundant rivers and was covered with large stands of white pine and hardwoods, the lumber industry did not thrive until the late 1800s. The Saginaw Valley had one of the largest concentrations of sawmills in the country, but most of Gladwin County was inaccessible. By 1883, there were only two public roads in the county. That all changed when the railroad came in the late 1870s. Soon narrow gauge railroad spurs sprang up throughout the county, cutting deep into the forest allowing lumberjacks to bank the timber for short trips to the nearest rollway along the rivers. Those rivers were choking with logs each spring on the way south to the mills in Saginaw. Lumber camps began appearing at strategic locations, including places like Hard Luck, Bowmanville, Smith Creek, Highwood, and Secord. The woods were swarming with men from Canada and Scandinavia; many of them were farmers who worked the winters to make ends meet. Hundreds of millions of board feet were eventually taken from Gladwin County. That figure reached over 160 billion statewide by the dawn of the 20th century.

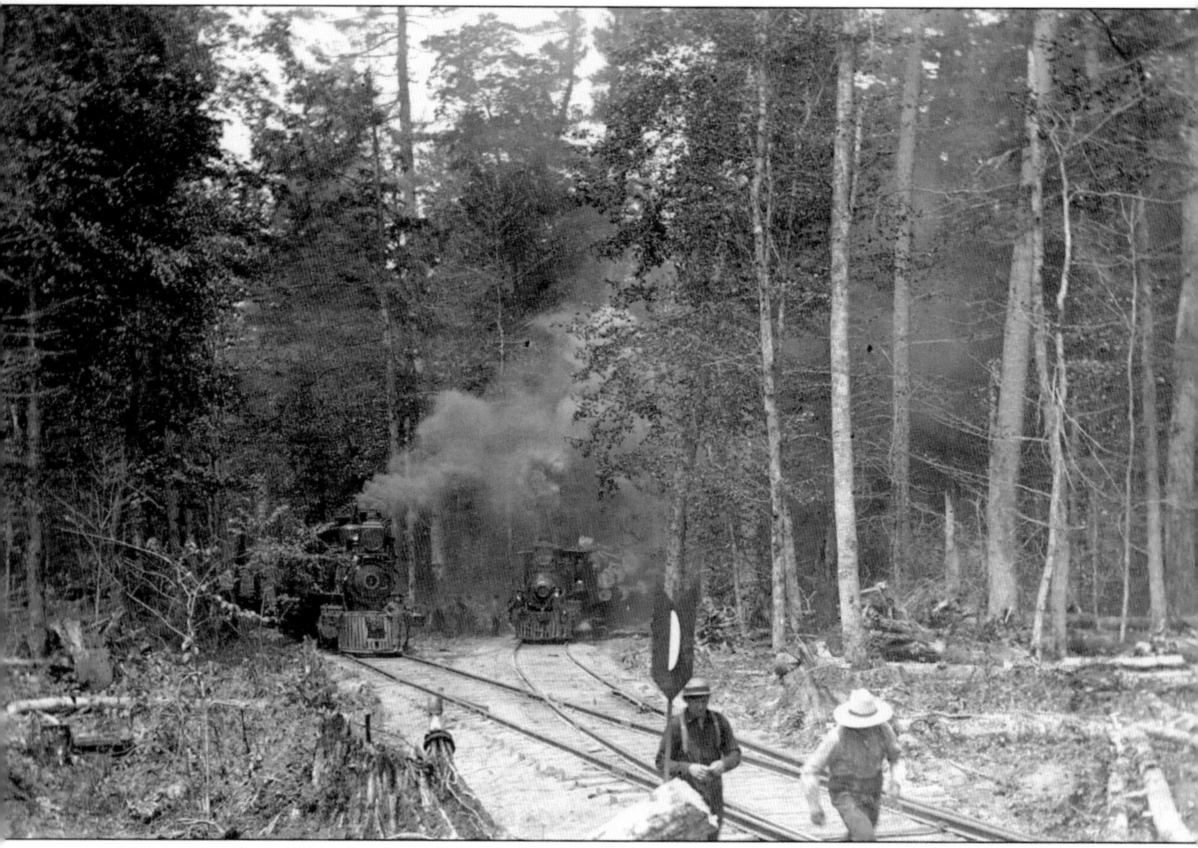

The railroad makes its way to Gladwin in the late 1880s. This photograph shows how the men laid track right through the woods.

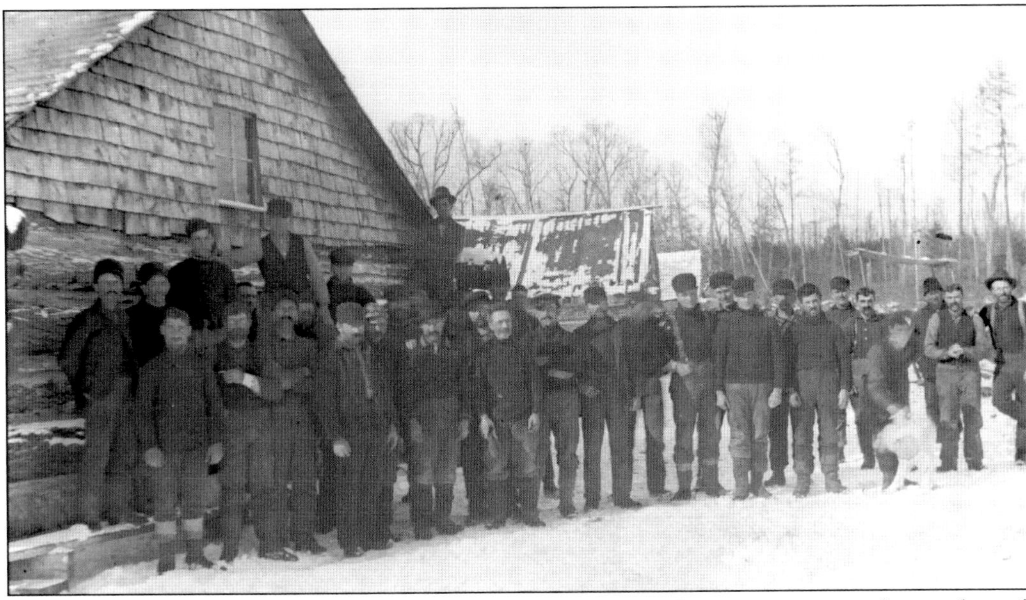

This is a picture of the Bowmanville lumber camp. George W. Bowman came up the east branch of the Tittabawassee River in the early 1870s and founded the Bowman Lumber Company. In addition to operating a sawmill and shingle mill, he was also general manager of the company store. Lumber was shipped out on the Bowmanville line of the Michigan Central Railroad. Florence Swanton became the first postmaster in April 1906. The lumber company closed in 1910, and the train line was abandoned the same year.

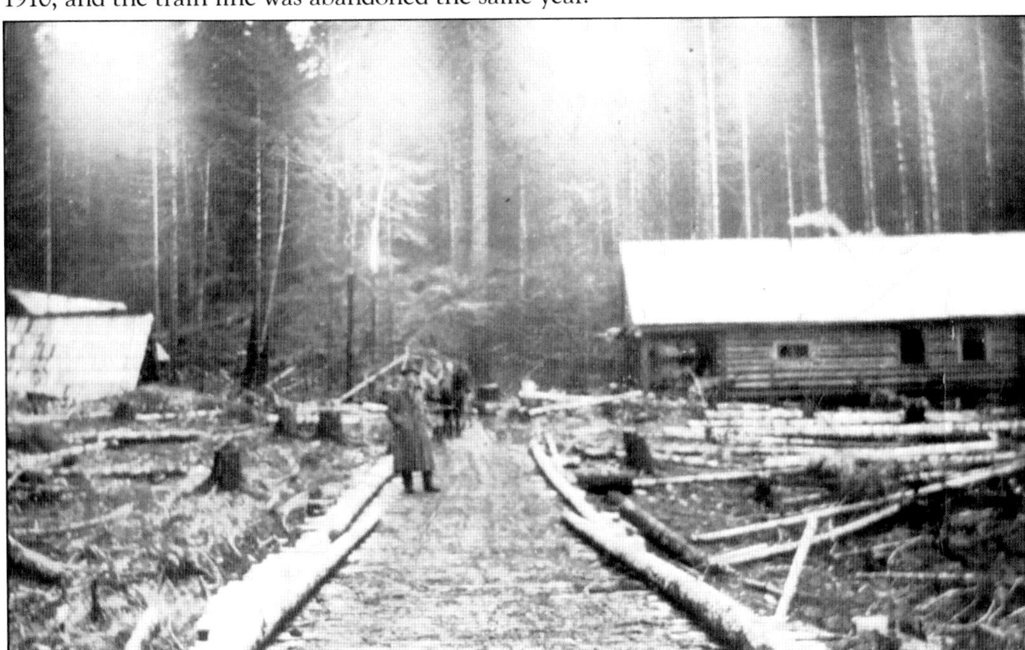

Lawrence Calhoun came to Grout Township from St. Joseph. He bought 160 acres of woodland with the intent of logging off the timber and establishing a farm. Notice the plank road in the picture of the Calhoun camp. Logs were hewed on two sides and fastened to other logs that ran along both ends to hold it all together. (Courtesy of Janet Whitmer.)

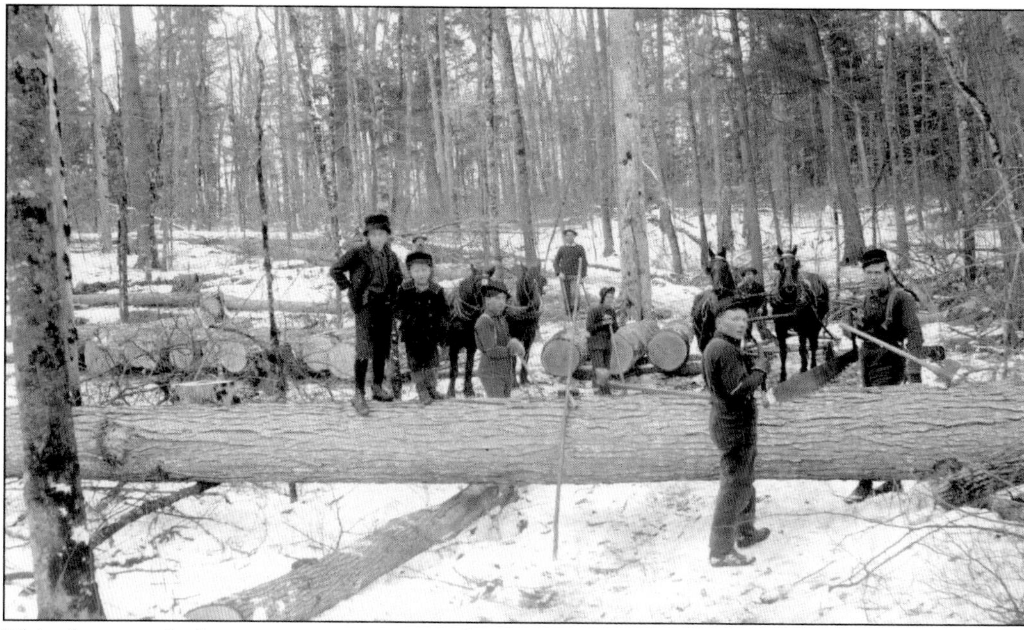

This photograph shows men crosscutting a log using a two-man saw. Depending on the diameter of the felled trees, the lengths were as small as eight feet and as long as 18 or 20 feet. The rod in the middle was used to measure the lengths. Sometimes a cheat stick was used, which also determined the amount of board feet each log contained.

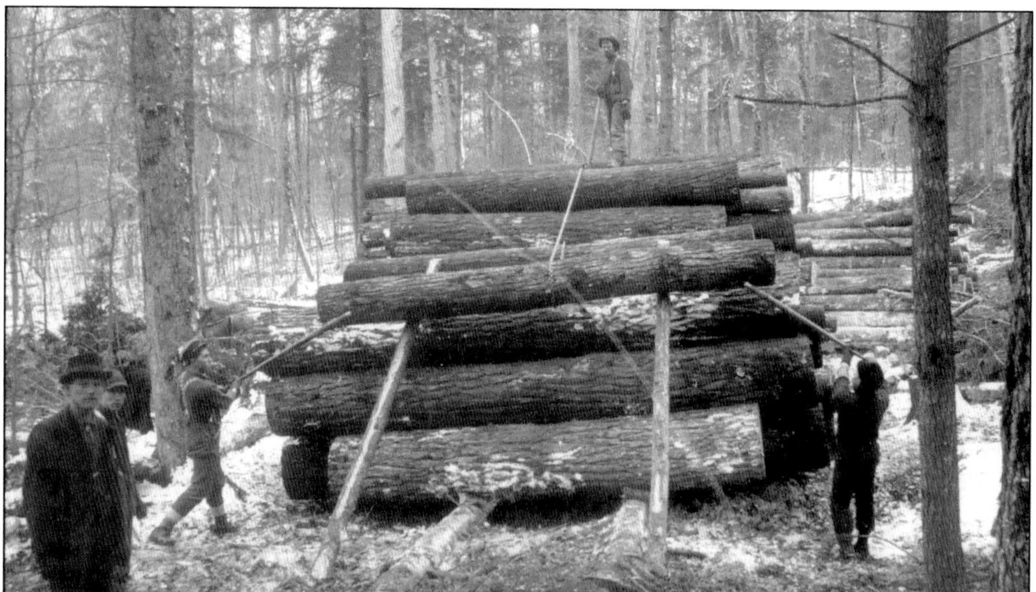

When horses were not available, manpower was used. Here the lumberjacks are banking logs, using inclines, ropes, and brute force. Also notice the logs in the ground that helped move the logs on top along to a designated staging area where they were put on sleds at a later time. The lumberjacks probably used a cant hook (a three-to-six-foot pole with a dangling iron hook near the working end) or a pike pole (a long, wooden pole that was spiked on the end and used to push logs along on the river).

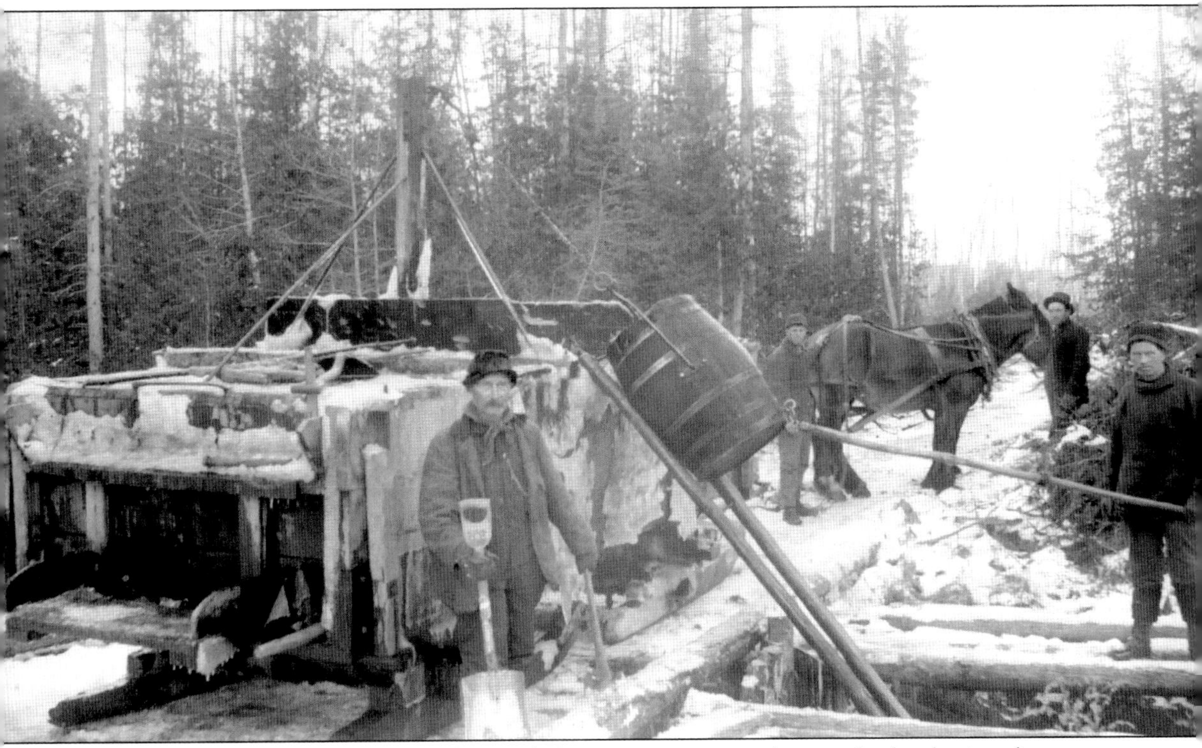

The hazards of traveling on icy roads in Gladwin are numerous, but in the lumbering days, an important job was to keep the roads icy. Here the workers are loading water from a stream into a makeshift water tank that kept the roads iced. This in turn made it much easier for the horse teams pulling the sleds loaded with logs. The horses were shod with special caulked or spiked shoes to assist them with traction.

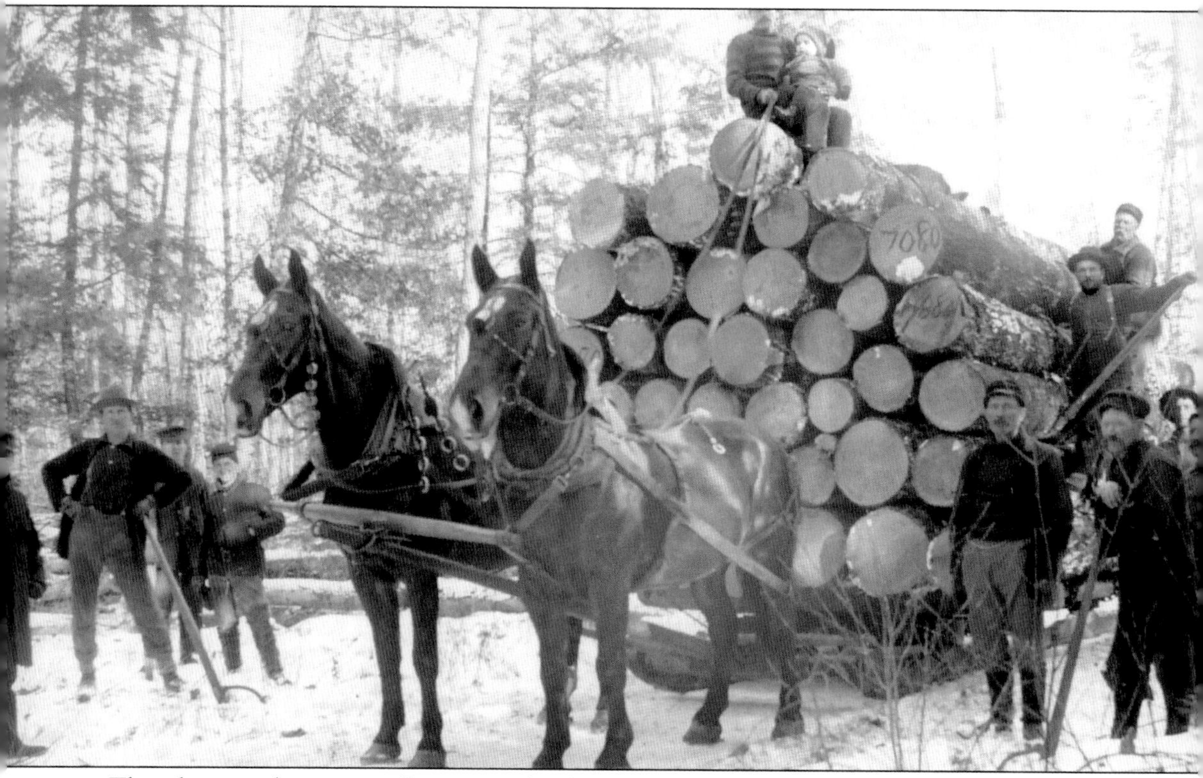

This photograph is an excellent example of early horsepower. Teams of horses were used to haul logs out of the woods to the banking area or railroad. Whenever a photographer was around, the loggers went out of their way to build up a monster load. This team, Cube and Jim, was quite famous for hauling large loads and was used to put a derailed train engine back on the tracks. (Courtesy of Clarke Historical Library, Velma Ross Damouth collection.)

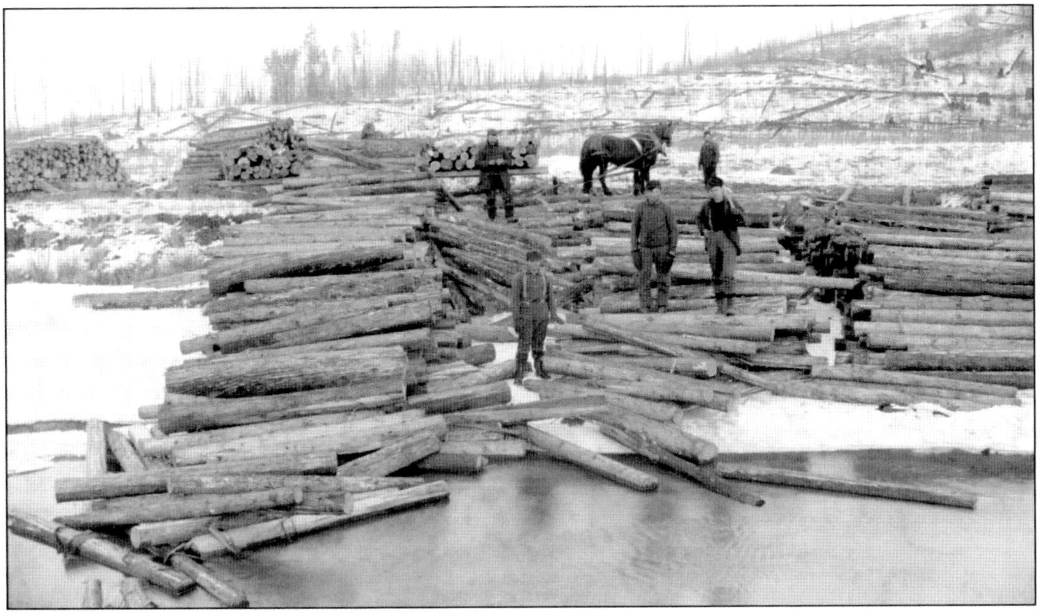

The horse teams or railroads took the logs to a banking ground or rollway that was located along the closest major river. The logs were then stockpiled for the remainder of the winter until springtime and high water levels. Then the river hogs rode the logs downstream to the booming grounds where the timber was sorted according to each company's log mark.

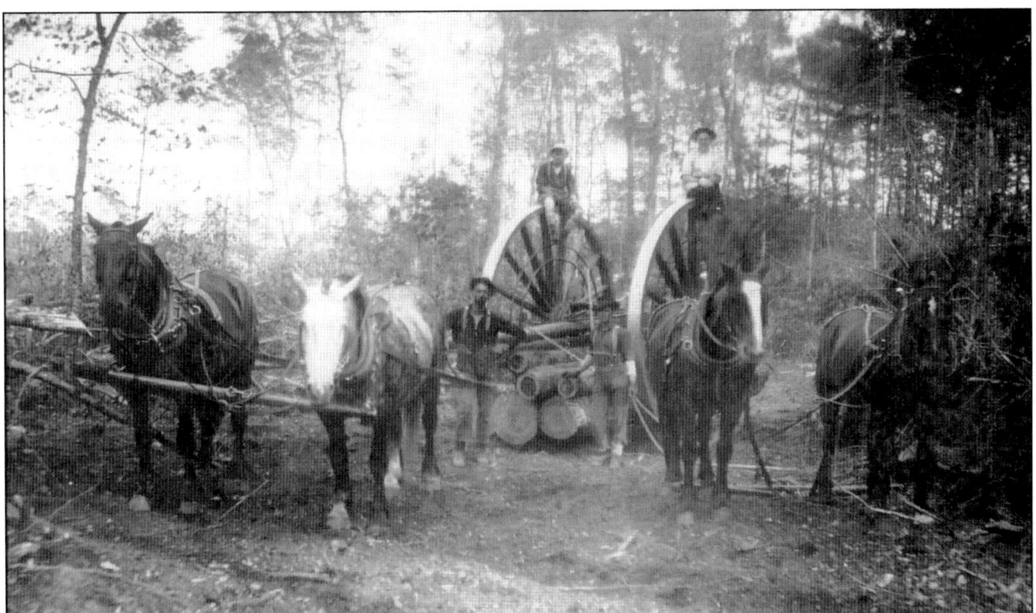

Although the automobile was many years away, the big wheels were used extensively in the woods. By chaining or roping a log or logs between the wheels, a team of horses could maneuver a very large load through the woods. The going was obviously rough and in many cases swampy, but the big wheels made it much easier.

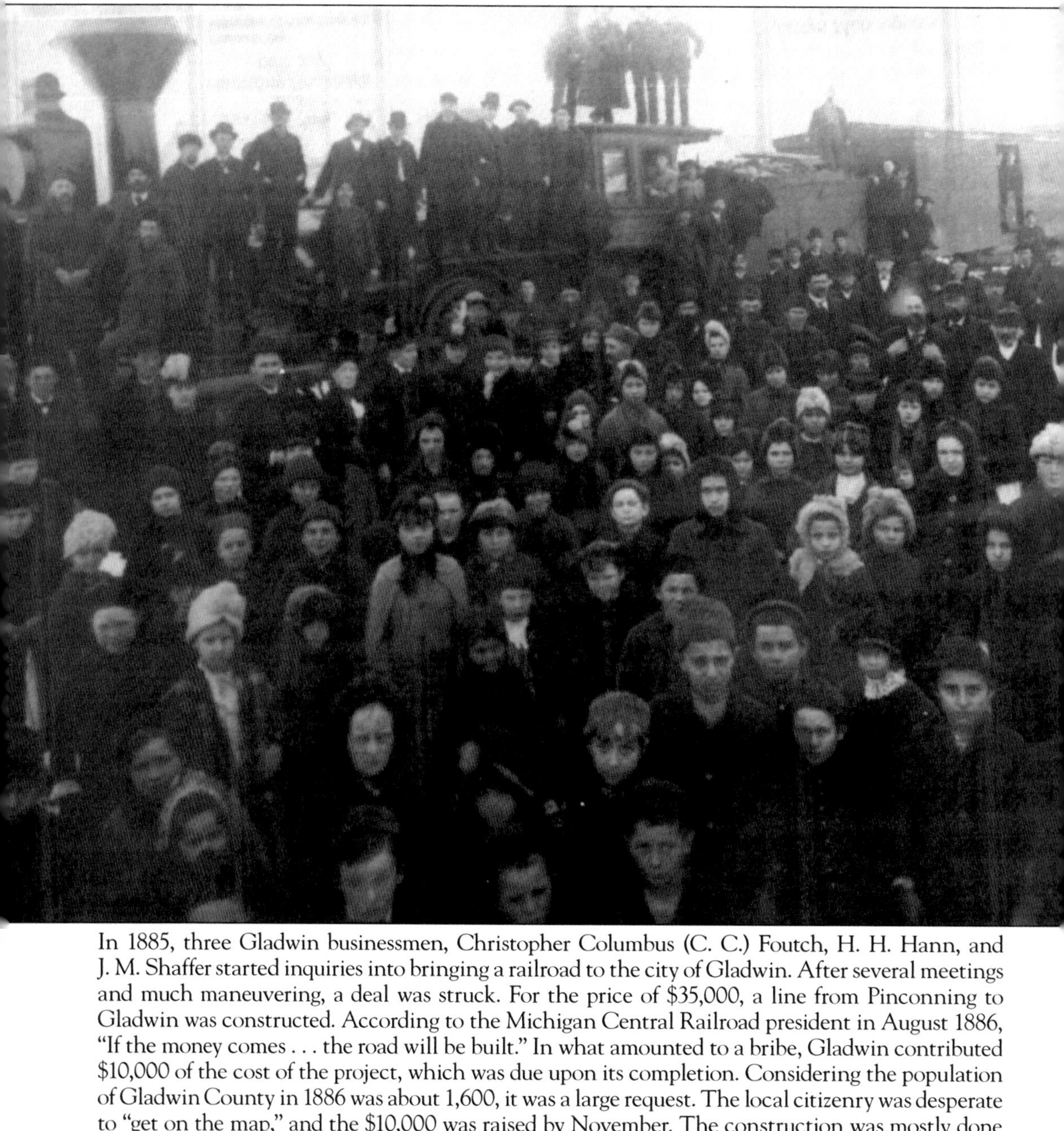

In 1885, three Gladwin businessmen, Christopher Columbus (C. C.) Foutch, H. H. Hann, and J. M. Shaffer started inquiries into bringing a railroad to the city of Gladwin. After several meetings and much maneuvering, a deal was struck. For the price of $35,000, a line from Pinconning to Gladwin was constructed. According to the Michigan Central Railroad president in August 1886, "If the money comes . . . the road will be built." In what amounted to a bribe, Gladwin contributed $10,000 of the cost of the project, which was due upon its completion. Considering the population of Gladwin County in 1886 was about 1,600, it was a large request. The local citizenry was desperate to "get on the map," and the $10,000 was raised by November. The construction was mostly done by more than 200 Italian workers for wages up to $2.50 a day plus room and board. The first construction train pulled into the city on November 1, 1887. On December 7, a free excursion was arranged after the company was assured the $10,000 was paid.

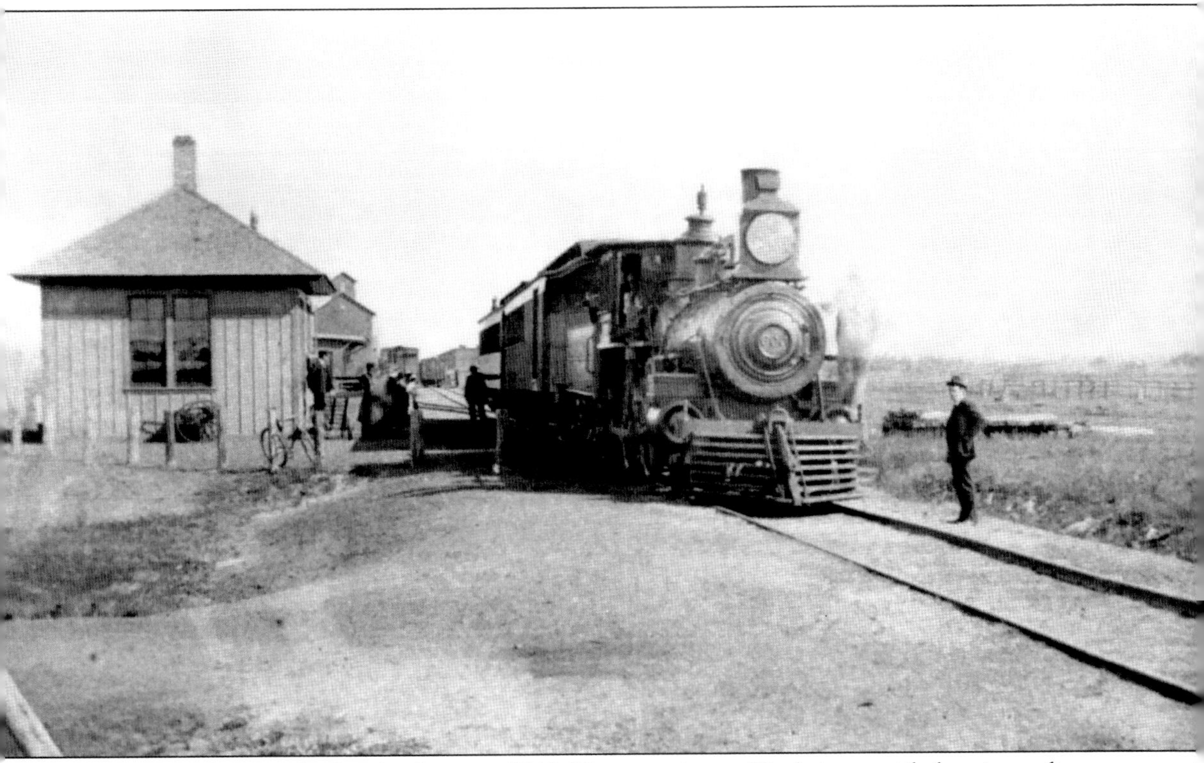

The picture above is the freight depot in 1900. Train service to Gladwin provided an immediate economic boom. This made transportation of lumber industry products such as logs, shingles, railroad ties, cedar posts, and telephone poles much more profitable. Another huge benefit was the confidence it gave the people that Gladwin County was going to survive. It became a destination point and brought the outside world to Gladwin on a regular basis. During the railroad's peak time serving the city, five trains arrived and left daily. As the forests disappeared, so did the number of scheduled trains. By 1906, it was down to only one train daily, and by 1937, passenger service was no longer offered and only one freight train served Gladwin weekly. On January 2, 1962, Michigan Central Railroad filed notice with the Interstate Commerce Commission their intent to abandon the Pinconning to Gladwin line.

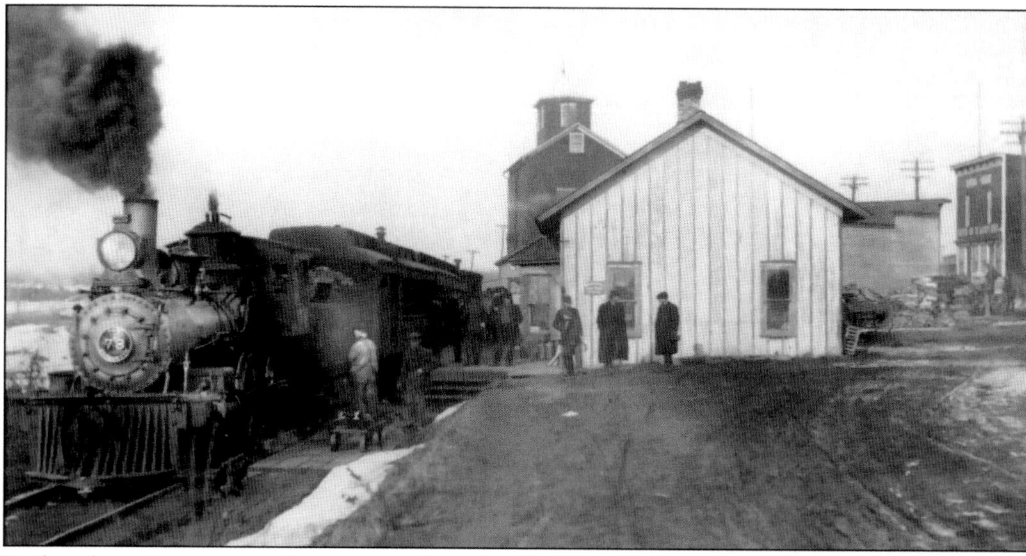

Railroad service came to Beaverton when the Flint and Pere Marquette Railroad built a line from Coleman to the Ross Brothers Company sawmill in 1890. The picture shows the Beaverton depot with the Ross elevator in the background and the Opera House (right), which burned in 1939 and later became the W. H. Hall and Son Lumber Company. This train station was destroyed in an explosion and fire in September 1909.

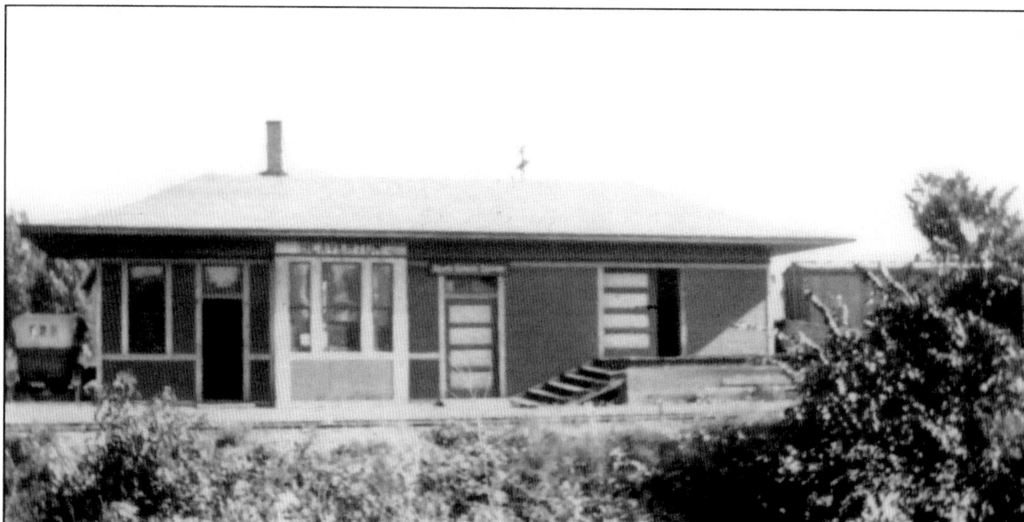

After the destruction of the first depot, a second depot was constructed just west of the current Beaverton Library on Saginaw Street. Train service continued to Beaverton from Coleman until 1943. With the shortage of steel, the tracks were torn up shortly after the last train came to town. In many places, the old railroad bed is still clearly visible today.

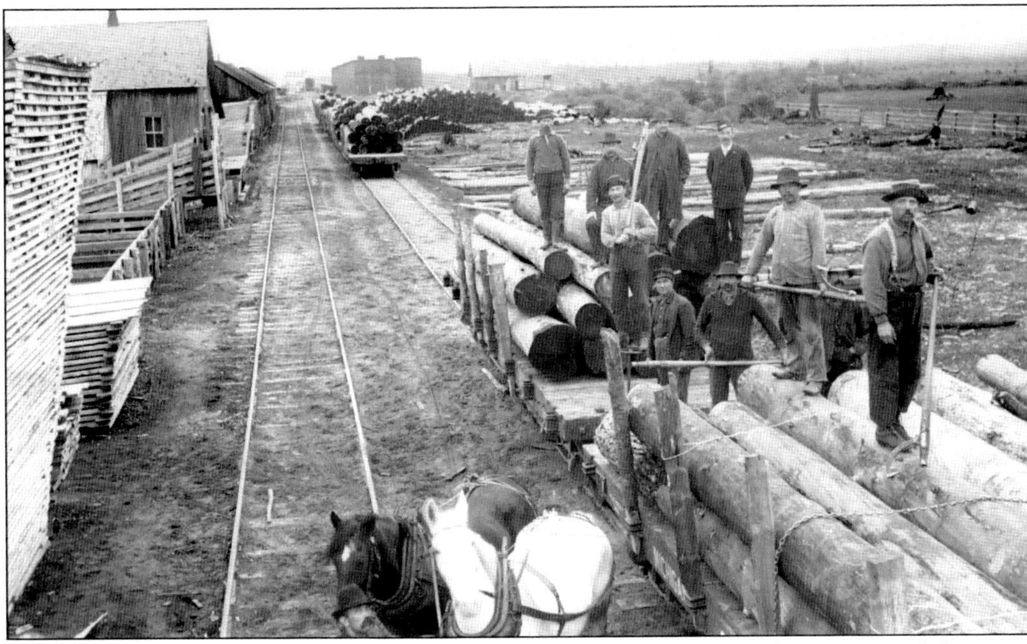

The railroad provided a much less time-consuming way to transport logs to one of the many sawmills throughout the county or down to the city of Saginaw. This picture of the Gladwin loading yard in 1902 shows three stages of lumbering, including raw logs, cut to board, and the buildings that were used for storing wooden shingles. Even the horses pose for this photograph.

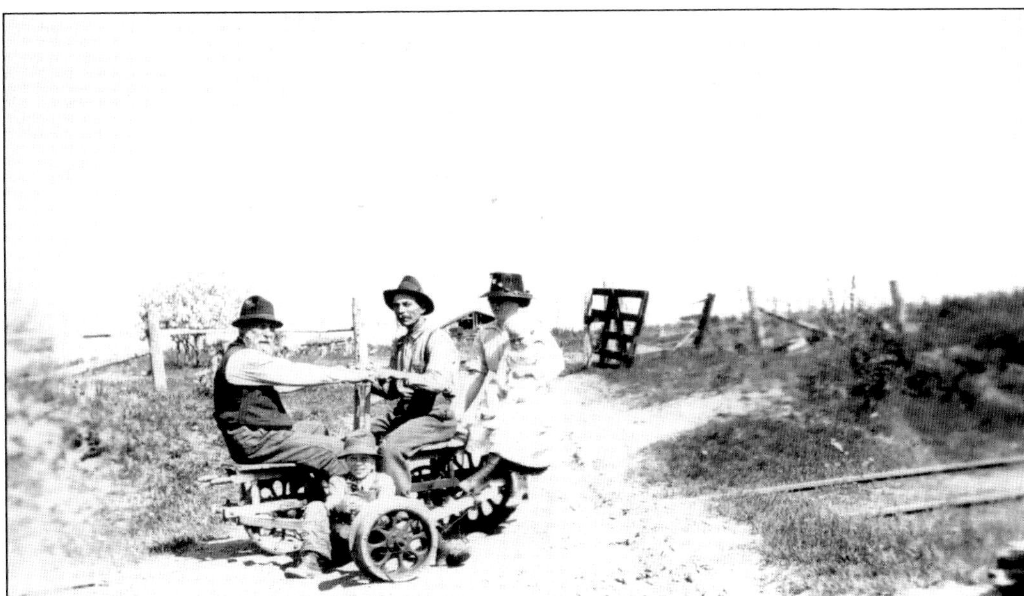

An inspection car ran the rails in front of the trains on a regular basis. This photograph shows one of the hand-operated models. Some had little gas motors attached for easier going. They were necessary because, unlike today's railroad with heavy-gauged steel rails laid on thick timber, most early-20th-century rails were laid over cedar logs. This required constant inspection and repair. (Courtesy of Inez Soldan.)

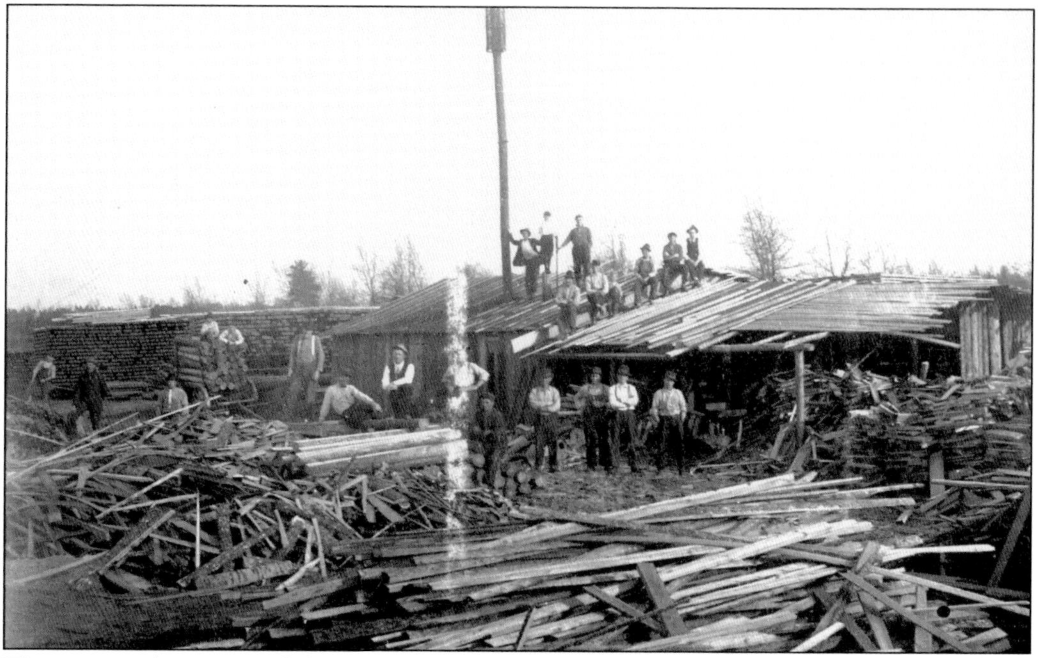

This picture shows one of the portable sawmills in Highwood. Many of the smaller operators set up a site mill to cut boards to ship out instead of sending the logs downriver to the big mills. Mill hands made $1.15 per day for a 10-hour day. Lumberjacks made as much as $26 per month. Having the most dangerous job, river hogs made $2.40 per day.

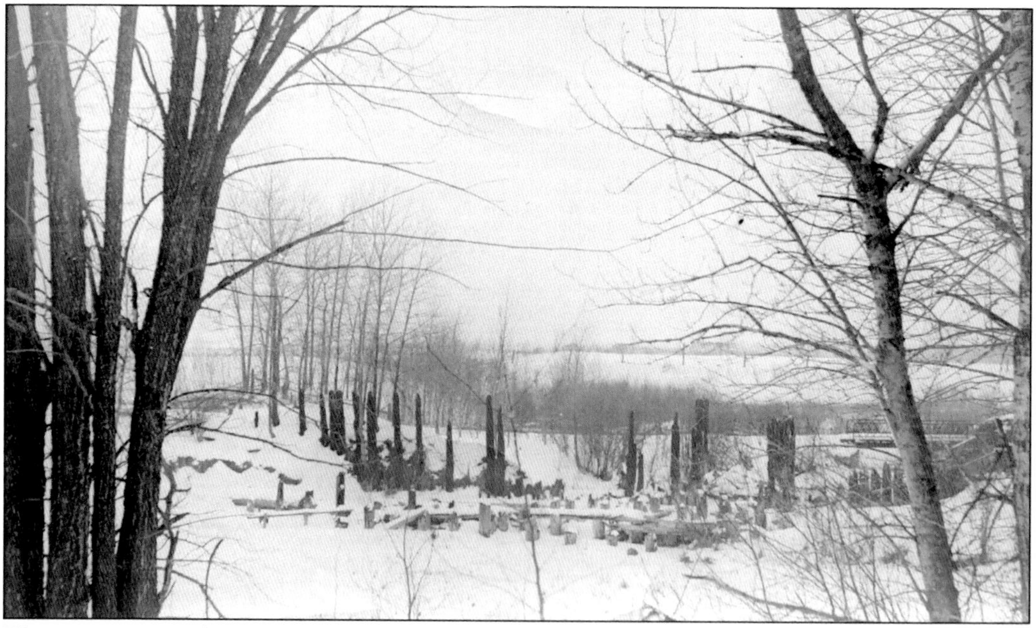

This picture is a glimpse of the devastation left by the lumbering era; the charred remains of a logging dam. Forest fires ravaged Gladwin County and much of Michigan on many different occasions. The lumber companies immediately rushed to a burned area because they had a limited time to salvage the timber, possibly a year or less, before the wood began to rot or become insect infested. (Courtesy of Inez Soldan.)

Three

From the Woods to the Fields

Agriculture has been a part of everyday life in Gladwin from the very beginning. Much of the available land that was not covered in forest was bought by large lumber companies and used for grazing cattle. The A. W. Wright Lumber Company had the largest farm in Gladwin County with over 1,600 acres of cleared land. They also boasted of having the largest barn in Michigan. It was 80 feet from the basement to the crown. Extension work began in the county in 1914. Farmers institutes sponsored by the U.S. Department of Agriculture held two-day seminars on such subjects as growing alfalfa, feeding the dairy cows, and modern agricultural education. Soil quality has always varied. Many farmers experienced bumper crops after the logging days, but years of erosion and lack of fertilization caused many farms to go under for back taxes. Oats, wheat, barley, and corn were always the staples, but farmers in Gladwin have always been willing to experiment. Sugar beets, potatoes, and fruit trees have all thrived at times. There was even an attempt to grow peppermint. Now agriculture makes up less than seven percent of Gladwin's economic base. Many of the farms are still family owned, but most farmers today work elsewhere and only farm on a part-time basis.

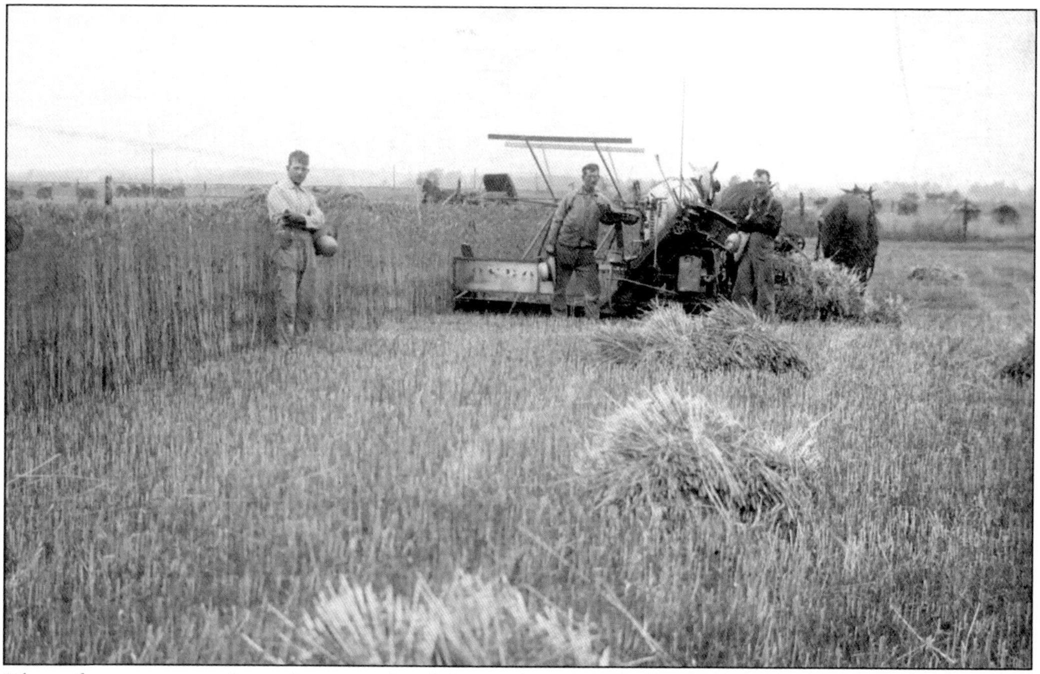

These farmers pause for a photograph while working on the harvest.

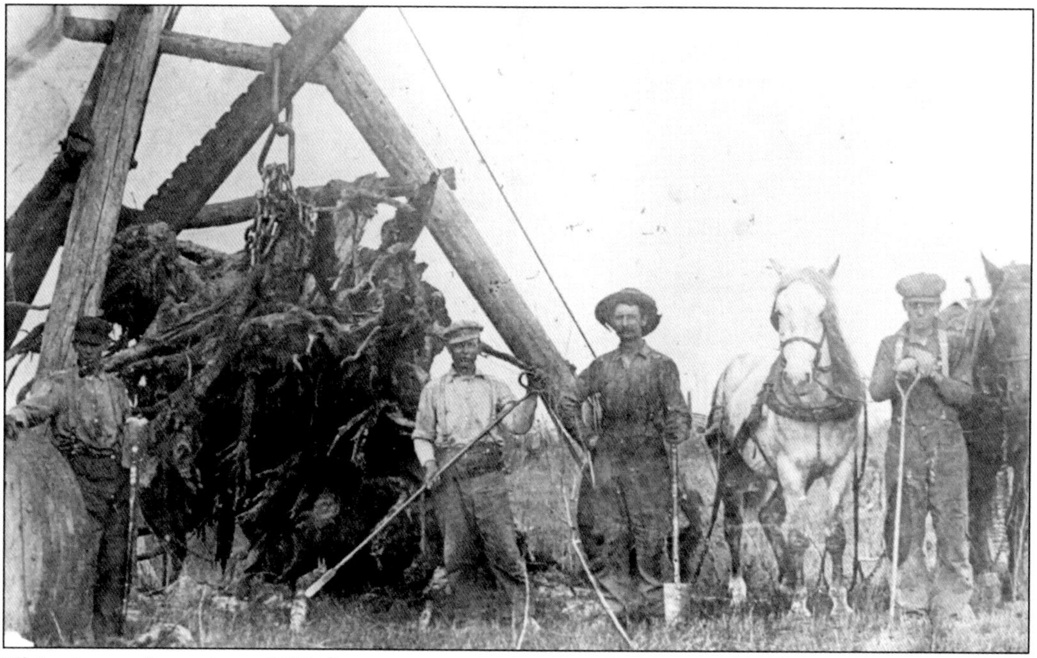

This picture from about 1910 shows a monstrous piece of equipment called a stump puller. The arduous task of removing stumps required many man-hours of labor even with the assistance of a stump puller and horses. The primary task of most landowners was to immediately clear enough area to establish a garden. This could take weeks. Henry Bard is pictured just to the left of the white horse.

L. V. Soldan moved from Butman to Lyle when he bought the store there from Austin Fowler in 1920. Because using the stump puller was so labor intensive, the preferred method of removal was dynamite, but it was expensive. From the size and number of stumps in the picture, it is no wonder Soldan's daughter Inez said, "My dad used dynamite whenever he could afford it." (Courtesy of Inez Soldan.)

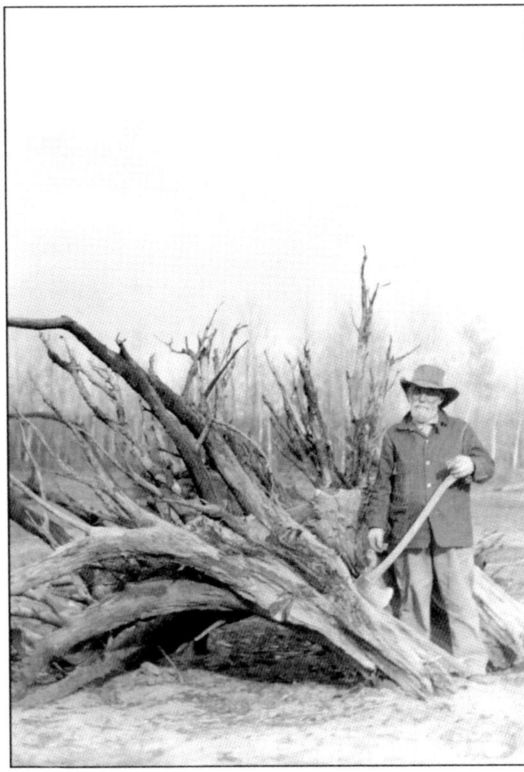

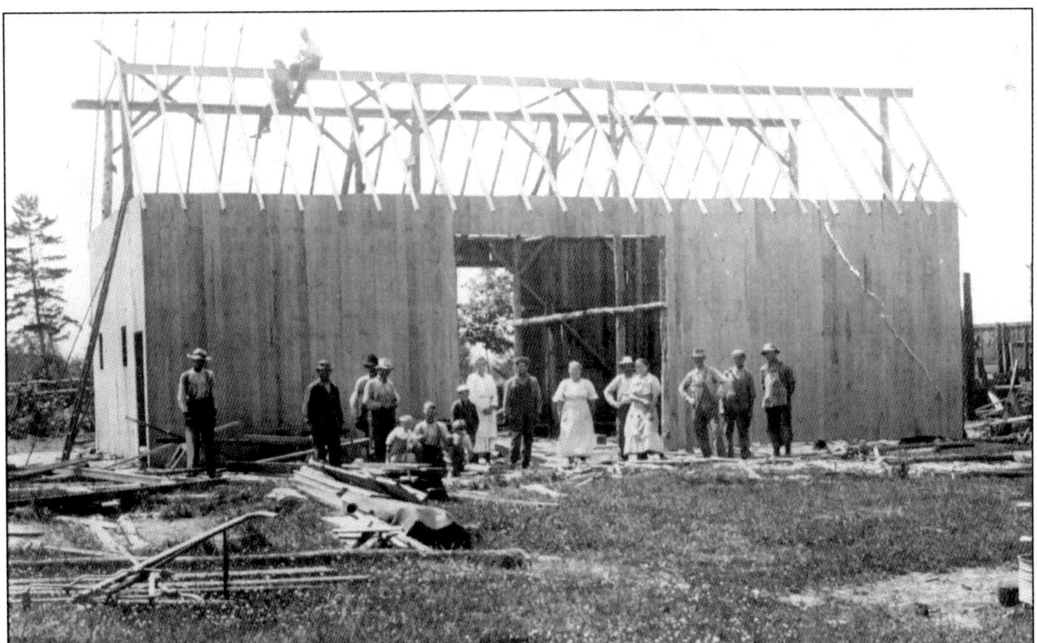

The lumber cut on Lawrence Calhoun's 160 acres was used to pay for the land and build a farm. The barn and homestead were built approximately a mile from one of only two public roads in Gladwin County at the time—the road from Loomis to Grout Township. The path carved out to his property was later named Calhoun Road in his honor. (Courtesy of Janet Whitmer.)

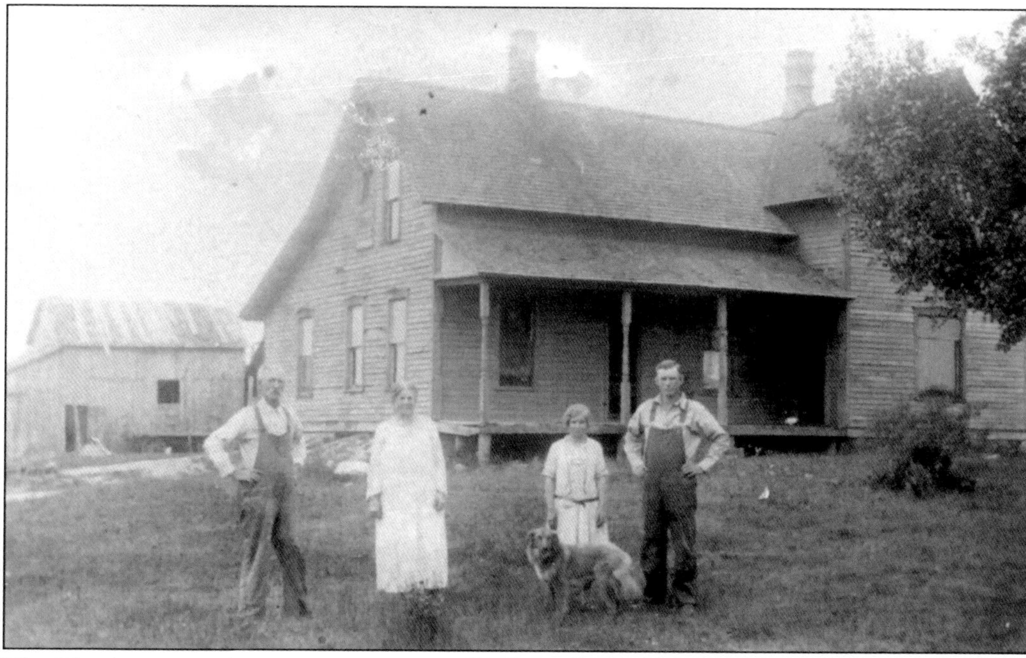

The Thurlow name is very prominent in Gladwin County. Here is the homestead farm with James Thurlow and his wife, Nellie, around 1899. They came from Ontario, Canada, and purchased 120 acres five miles north of Cedar (Gladwin). The paperwork was not official until 1901. Prior to purchasing the farm, James worked in the Ross Shingle Mill and Nellie ran the Beaverton Hotel. (Courtesy of Ken Thurlow.)

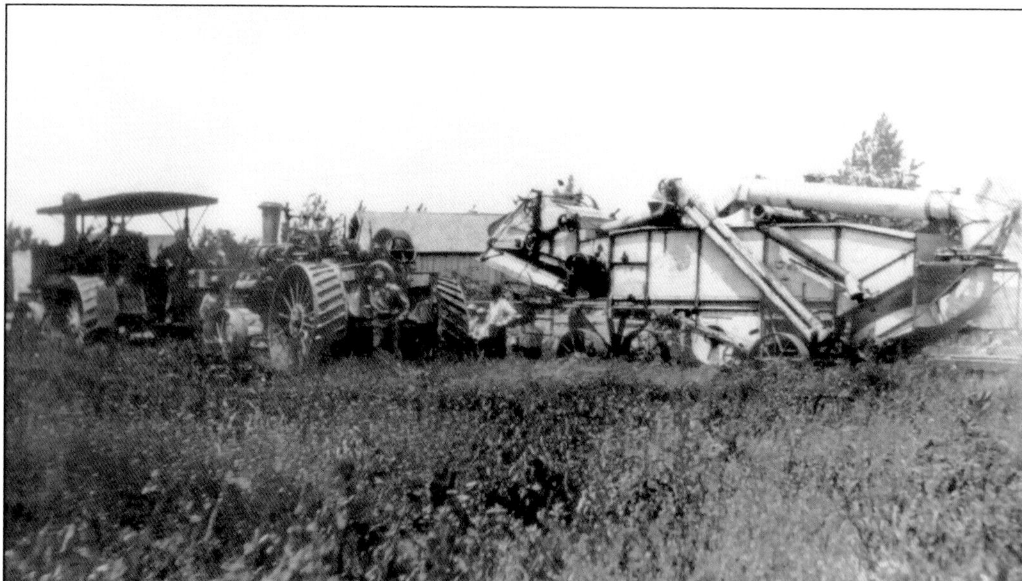

Robert Blades and his threshing machine were always around Gladwin. He owned a threshing machine business that was in operation at harvest time. Blades moved to Gladwin County in 1900 and lived the rest of his life on the farm located on Blades Road, which is just south of Beaverton. His threshing skills were well known, as he was a chief gleaner of the Dale Grange Arbor of Gleaners. (Courtesy of John Blades.)

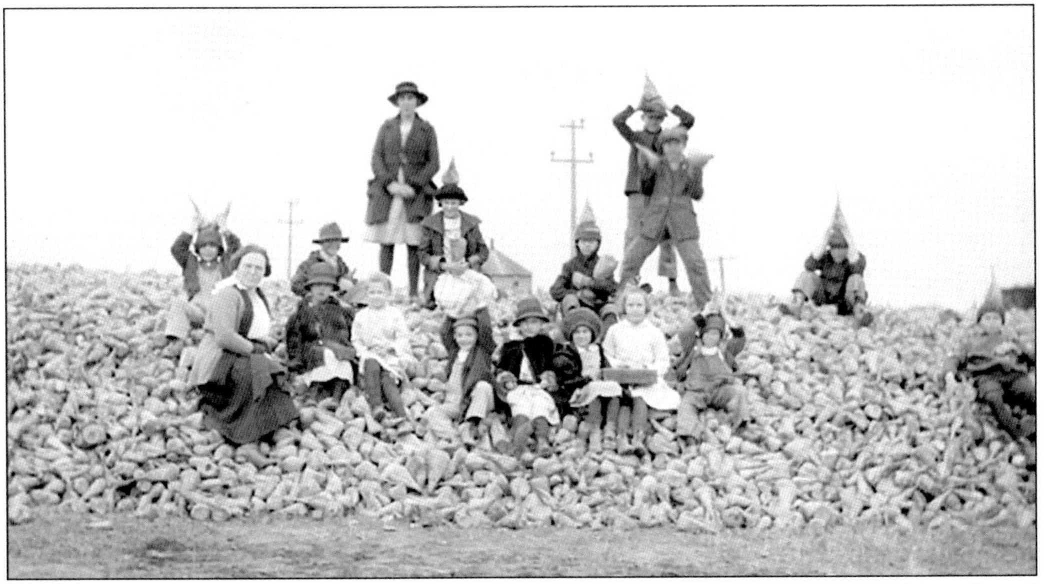

Many of the early farmers in Lyle started growing sugar beets as soon as enough land was cleared of tree stumps. A. C. P. Evans owned the sugar beet weighing station near the railroad tracks. His daughter Virginia remembered a German man from Bay City going around much of Grout and Beaverton Townships getting farmers to contract growing sugar beets for the sugar factories in Bay City and Saginaw. The sugar beet piles became the playground for local children on their way to and from school, as this photograph indicates. (Courtesy of Virginia Evans McCulloch.)

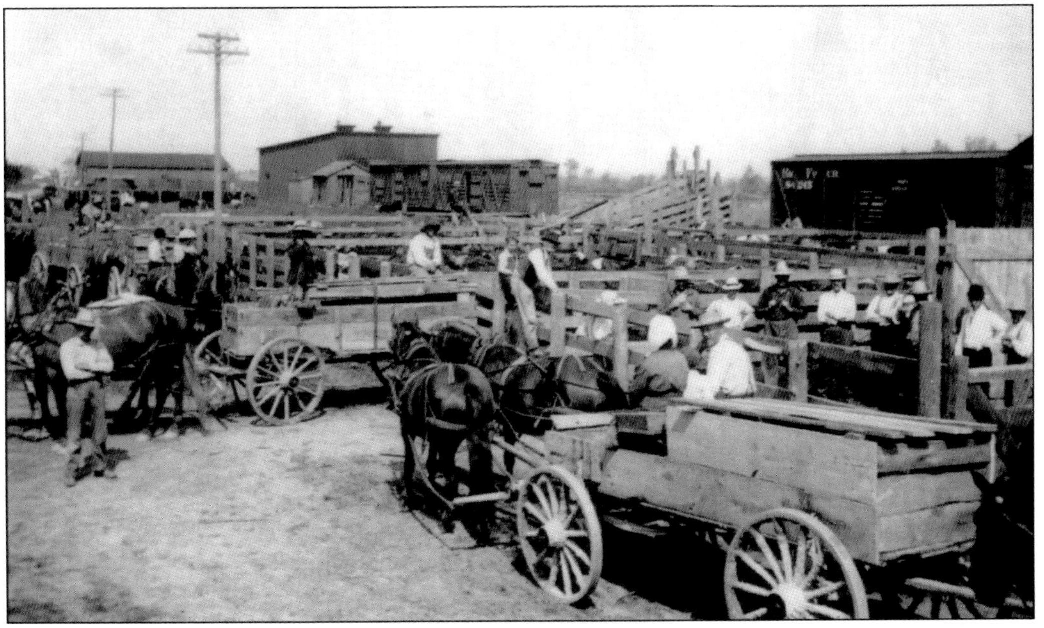

This is a photograph of the Gladwin stockyards around 1910. They were located on the east end of the town north of Cedar Avenue between State Street and the railroad tracks. It is an excellent example of three major entities of the Gladwin economy merging together at the dawn of the 20th century. Farmers are bringing their product (in this case livestock) to the railroad, and in the background is the sawmill.

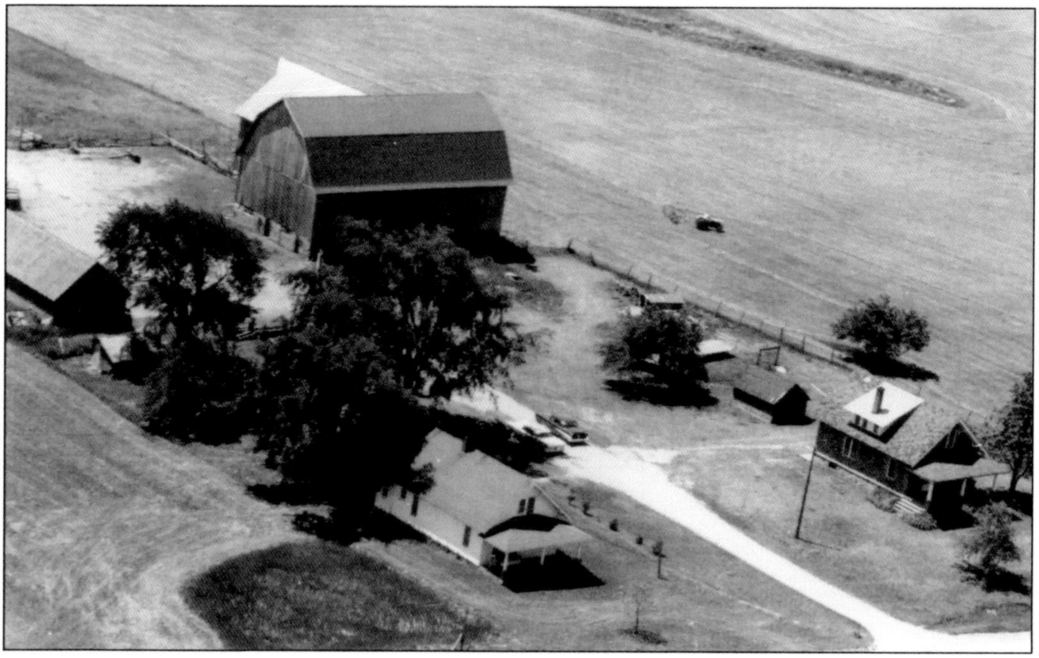

Located in section 18 of Grout Township, this is the original Walter Walker farm as it looked in 1957 on the southwest corner of Kerswill and Clarwin Roads. Walker came to Gladwin in 1887 and bought 40 acres just west of his grandmother Josephine Chatterton's farm. Now a centennial farm, it is part of the Bernard Walker farm. (Courtesy of Ben Ball.)

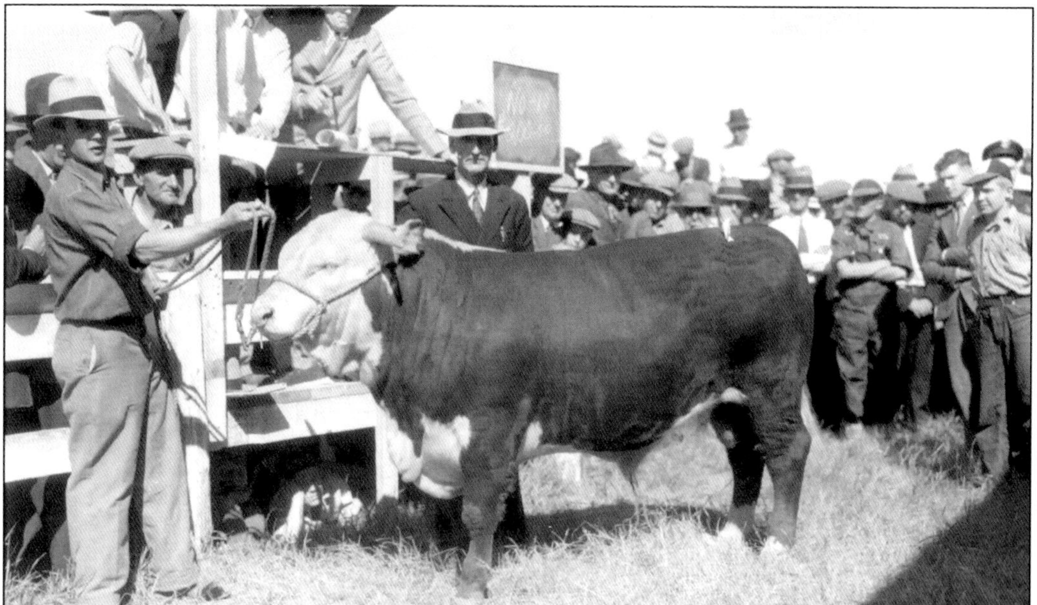

This prize Hereford bull is one of many that went through the 1935 Gladwin Annual Cattle Auction. With the large tracts of timberless land and the abundance of artesian wells, cattle are a natural fit in Gladwin. In April 1931, local breeders and farmers met to plan the first cattle auction at the fairgrounds in June. That first sale featured 17 bulls and six heifers from breeders all across Michigan.

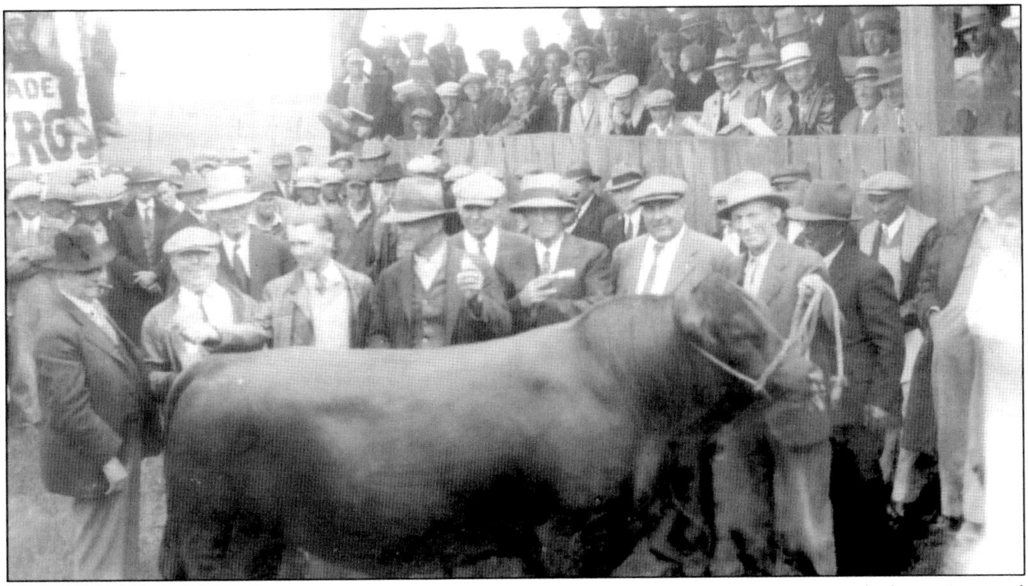

This Black Angus bull was sold to Frank Sheehan of Gladwin Township at the Gladwin Annual Cattle Auction in June 1938 for $710. Five local businessmen, including G. E. Lee, Archie Graham, Guy Ridley, Dave Hawkins, and Doc Myers donated cattle. Sidney Smith of Lake Orion consigned this Black Angus bull.

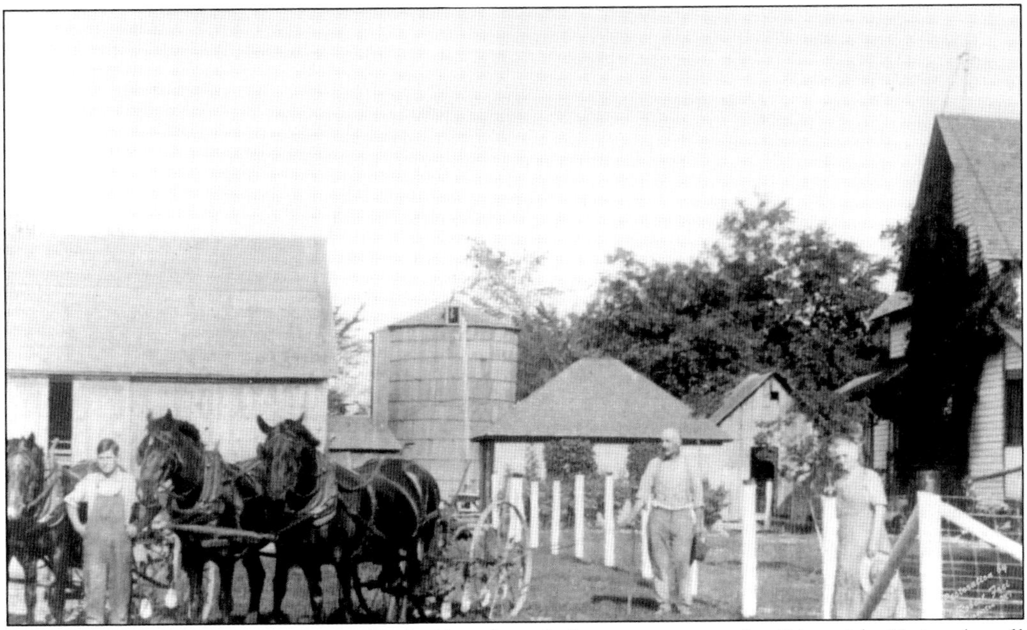

This picture shows Willis McCulloch (front) with his parents at the Riverside Dairy (small white concrete building). The dairy produced butter and buttermilk, which was sold to the local grocery stores. Enough butter was taken each month to Mount Pleasant to put two McCulloch daughters through Central Michigan Teachers College. The dairy closed in 1940. (Courtesy of Virginia Evans McCulloch.)

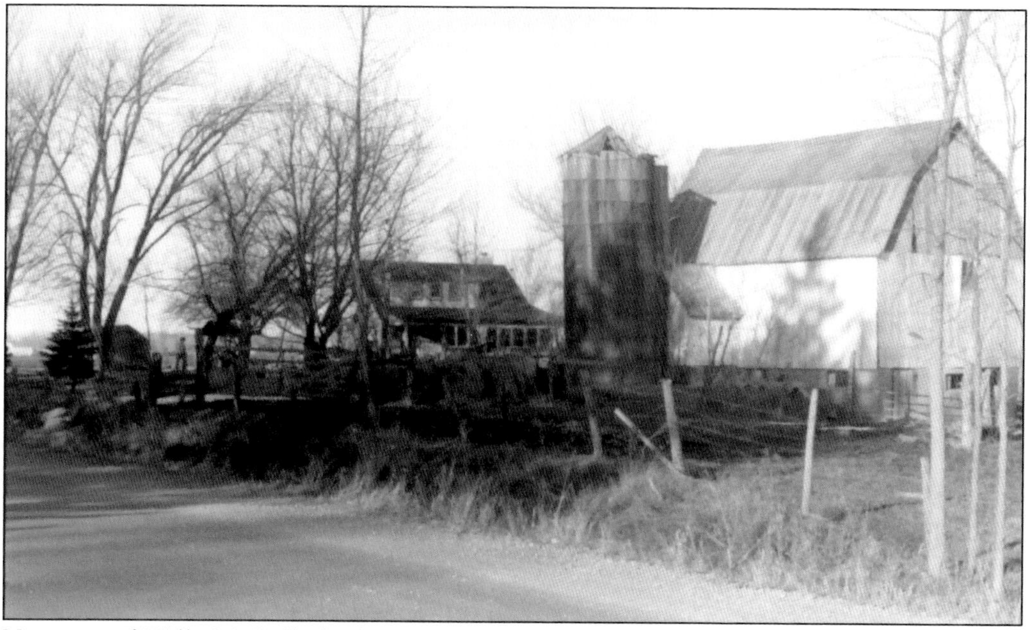

Virginia and Willis McCulloch's farm was directly across McCulloch Road from the McCulloch homestead and Riverside Dairy. Notice the silo on the side of the barn. It came from a 1930s Montgomery Ward catalog and is made from grooved cedar planks, approximately 30 feet in length. They raised six boys and one girl on the farm. Willis died in 2001, and Virginia still lives there today. (Courtesy of Virginia Evans McCulloch.)

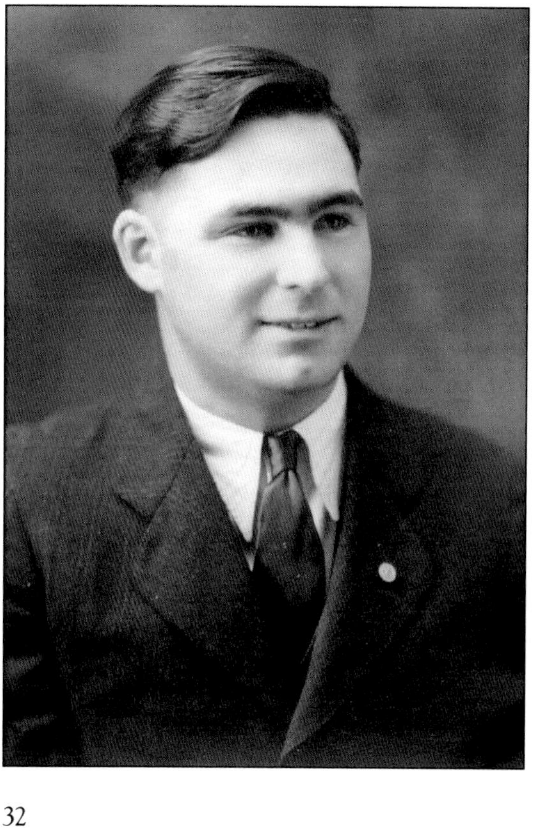

Willis quit school in the eighth grade to run the family farm. The Beaverton High School agriculture teacher started a new program called the Future Farmers of America (FFA) and talked him into returning to high school. He graduated in 1932 and was chosen as State Farmer of Michigan and the National Future Farmer of America the next year. Willis went to St. Louis, Missouri, to receive his certificate, which was the first time he ever left the state of Michigan. (Courtesy of Virginia Evans McCulloch.)

Four

Black Gold in Gladwin

In 1858, a 13 foot, hand-dug well in Oil Spring, Ontario, Canada, produced free-flowing oil in the Michigan Basin Dundee Formation. One year later, Col. Edwin Drake drilled a commercial well at a depth of 70 feet in Titusville, Pennsylvania, and the search for "black gold" was on. It was not until 1886 in St. Clair County that oil was discovered in Michigan. At that time, oil's primary use was for a by-product called kerosene, which was used as fuel for lamps. The first commercially successful oil field was found in the Deindorfer Woods located in the city of Saginaw in 1925. By this time in Gladwin County, the lumber era was over. Agriculture had already seen its best years and the county needed a boost. It came with the discovery of oil near Beaverton in 1934. Immediately after, Gladwin County's population showed a 30 percent increase. By 1937, the Buckeye oil fields were producing more oil than any other field east of the Mississippi River. Gladwin County was producing 40 percent of Michigan's oil. Although the Michigan Oil and Gas Association crowned Gladwin "king of the eastern United States," the crown was worn for only a brief time. With the discovery of oil in other counties, by the end of 1938, Gladwin had only 20 percent of Michigan's total oil output. By the mid-1940s the boom was over. With the surges in the price of a barrel of oil and the development of new recovery processes, the fields still garner interest today, but oil will never be king in Gladwin County again.

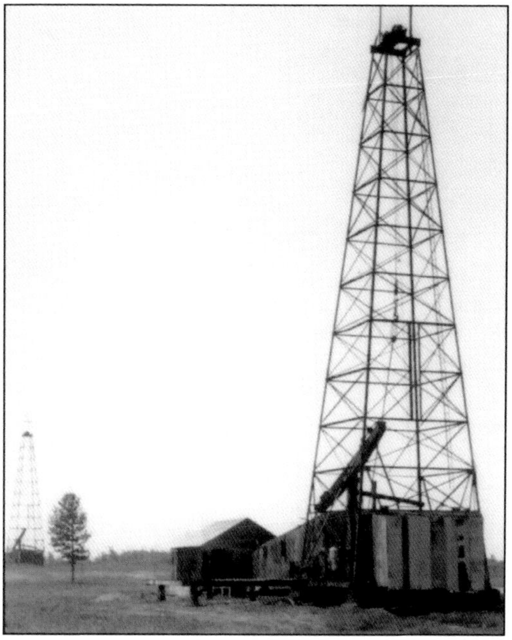

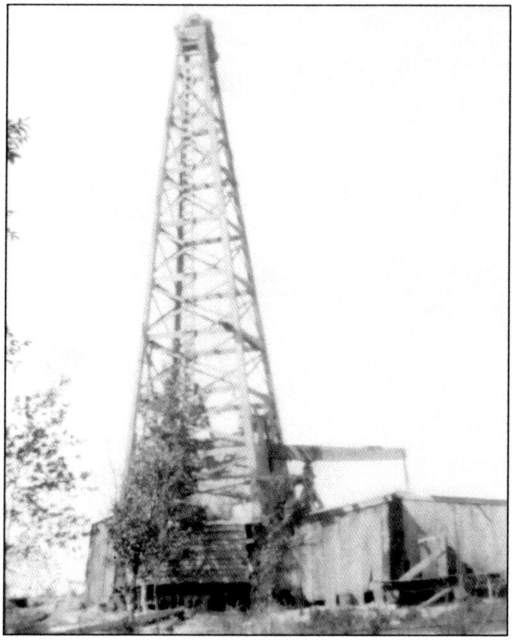

Michigan is ranked 17th in oil production and 11th in natural gas production among the 34 oil- and gas-producing states. Prior to developing a commercial use for oil, many people drilling for good water considered it a nuisance to discover oil. In 1934, oil was discovered in the first well (right), and in 1935, it was developed near Beaverton in the South Buckeye oil field. This made Gladwin County the 12th county in Michigan out of 83 to discover oil.

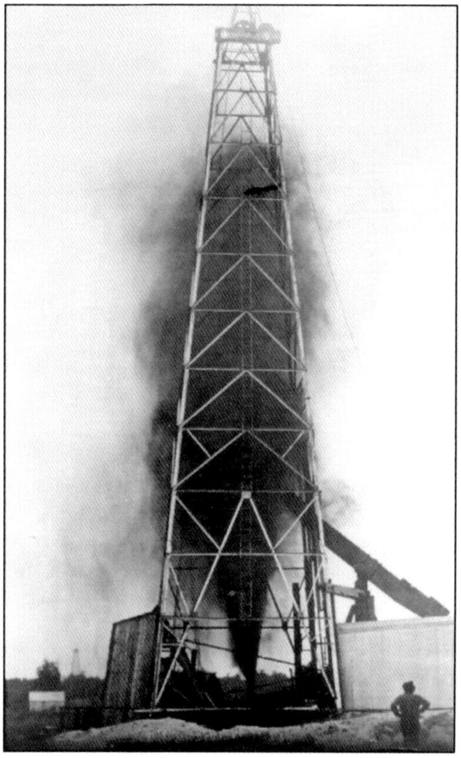

The gusher was a common method to bring in a well. The practice made the event a spectacle and promoted a carnival-like atmosphere. This practice was not only wasteful and environmentally disastrous, but extremely dangerous and unnecessary. On July 31, 1931, a blowout killed 10 people in Greendale Township in Midland County. Most of the workers in the field were glad to see this practice abandoned.

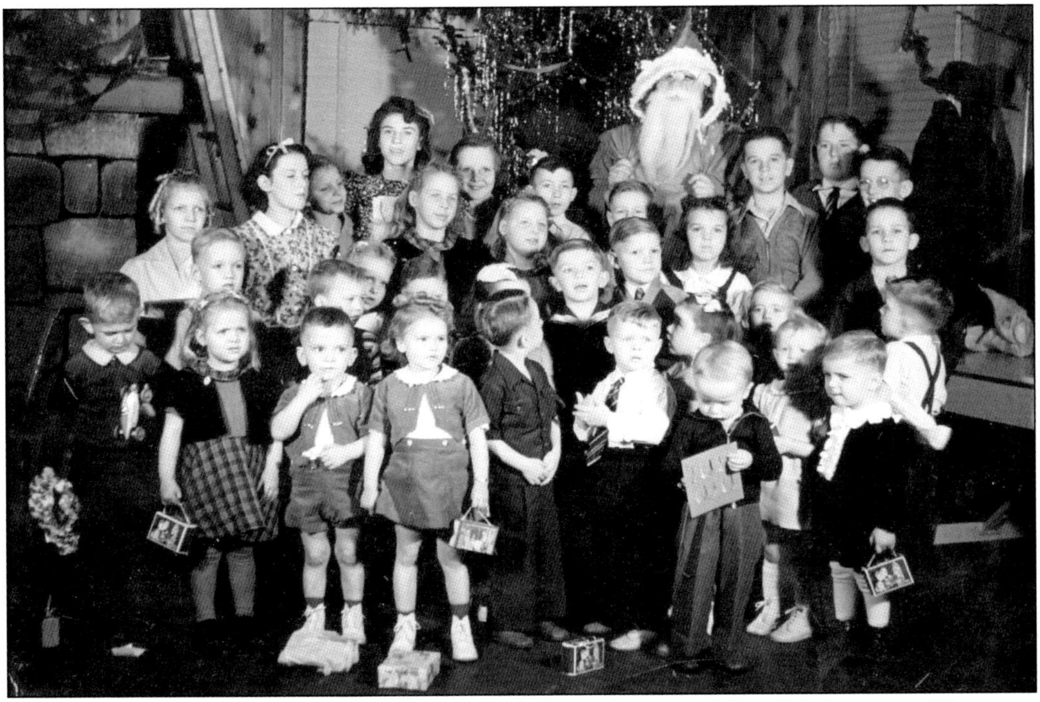

One of the events many children looked forward to was the annual Sun Oil Company Christmas party. This is a picture from the 1941 gathering. The economic impact the company had on the city and county of Gladwin is immeasurable. Many of the civic improvements made to the area would not have happened without its financial support.

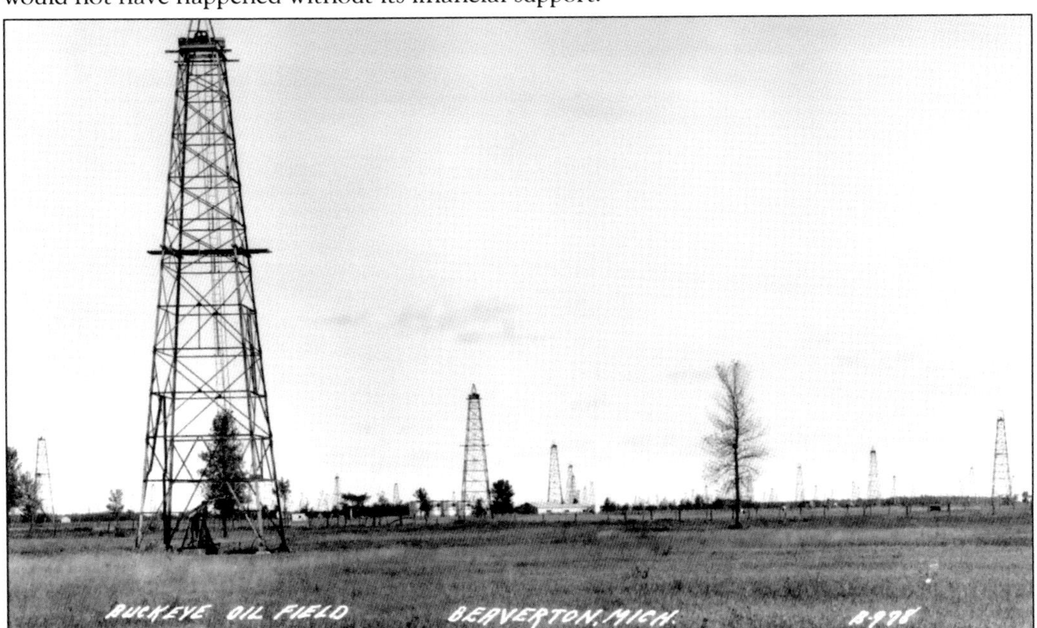

This picture taken of the Buckeye oil field shows how closely the derricks were situated. There are at least 36 derricks shown. The oil field was developed in 1935, and by April 1937, there were 63 wells that pumped 17,000 barrels of oil. By 1946, 129 wells had pumped over a half million barrels.

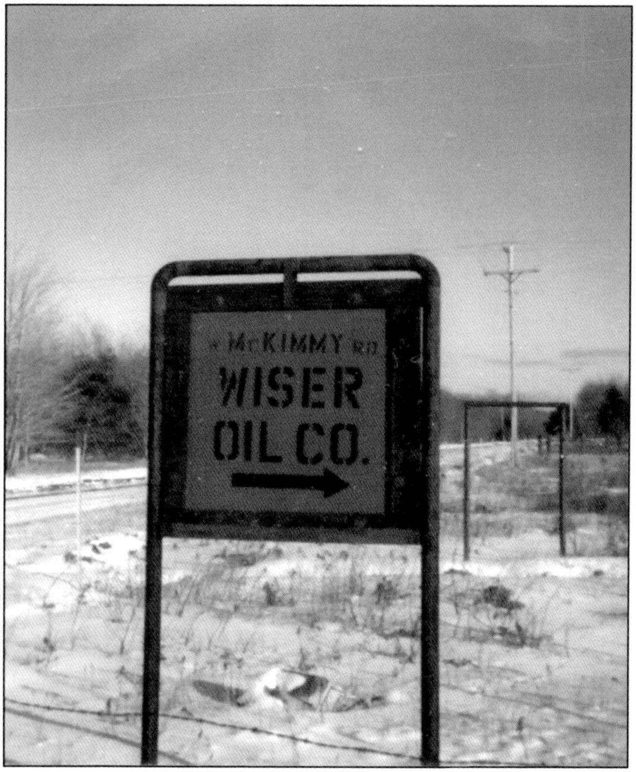

Wiser Oil Company began using enhanced oil recovery methods by water injection, bringing the oil up the wellhead. Technology using the cable tool drilling method was very inefficient in the initial boom years of the 1930s and 1940s. It is estimated that less than 30 percent of the original oil in place was recovered. (Courtesy of Marie Plude.)

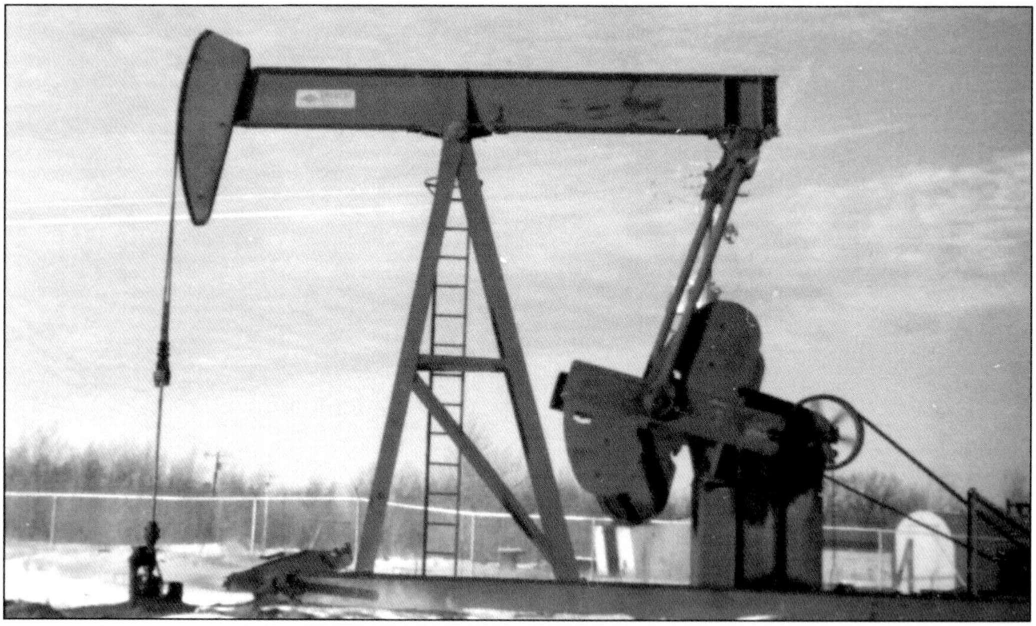

Improved equipment like the modern jack pump and improved recovery techniques have rejuvenated the oil fields in Gladwin. When oil prices in the 1960s were at $3 per barrel, the wells were not profitable, but when oil tripled in price by 1980, investors took another look. With the price of oil jumping up to $100 and gas prices hovering around $3 a gallon, the Gladwin oil fields may spark interest again. (Courtesy of Marie Plude.)

Five

Thermoforming Capital of the World

One of the by-products of petroleum is plastic. One of the largest developers and manufacturers of plastic is the Dow Chemical Company, with headquarters just 20 miles from Gladwin County. The thermoforming industry grew with the increase in demand for plastic products. The basic principle of thermoforming is heating a plastic sheet, forming the plastic with a mold under pressure, and finally trimming the formed part. Gaylord Brown took this simple concept and turned Gladwin County and specifically Beaverton into the thermoforming capital of the world. Many of his employees spun off related thermoforming businesses with his blessing. The combination of the close proximity of plastics experts at Dow Chemical and entrepreneurial businessmen helped spawn Robinson Industries, Lyle Industries, Modern Machinery, C. R. Equipment Corporation, and many others. Many of the plastic-formed containers seen in virtually every fast-food franchise in the world might have its origins in Gladwin County. Brown Machine alone has manufactured over 10,000 thermoform machines with related equipment. At one point, the businessmen of Beaverton financed their own billboard to indicate the proper exit from the expressway to Beaverton because clients from Europe and the rest of the world were getting lost. Eventually, the highway department put up an exit sign and the businessmen sold their billboard for a profit.

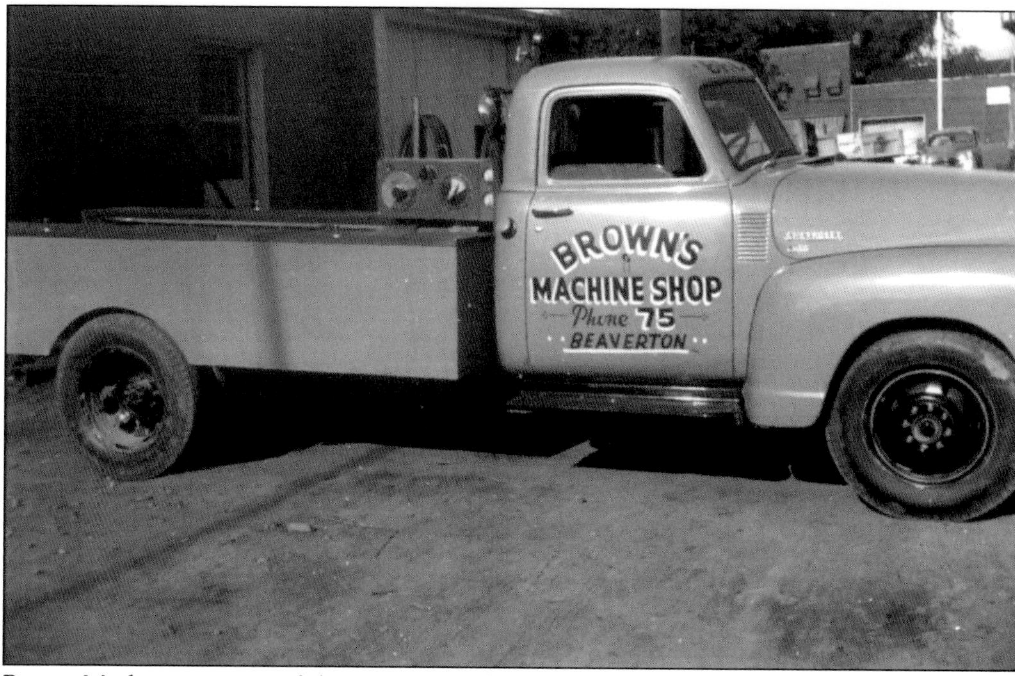

Brown Machine was one of the major manufacturers in Gladwin County, manufacturing over 10,000 thermoforming machines. (Courtesy of Brown Machine.)

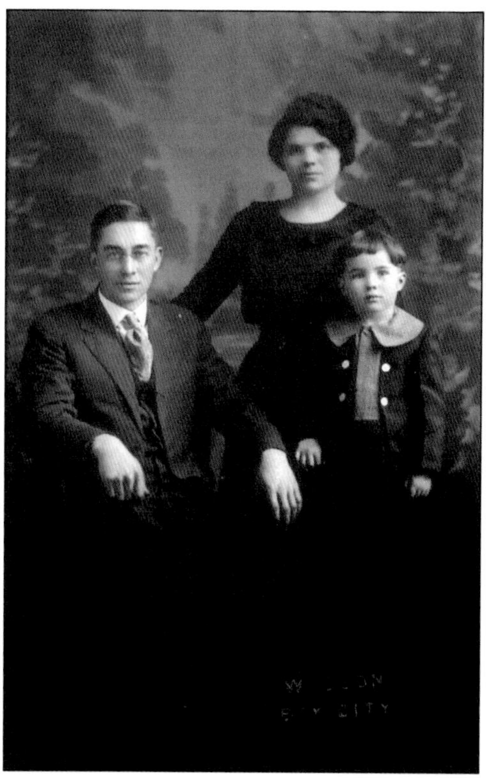
This 1921 picture shows Charles A. Brown, his wife, Lizetta, and their son Gaylord at age eight. Charles was a mechanic by trade. He and his son had a general repair garage in Beaverton. During the Depression when oil was discovered in Gladwin County, they began working in oil equipment repairs. In 1945, Charles made the decision to retire and sold his interest in the business to Gaylord. (Courtesy of Brown Machine.)

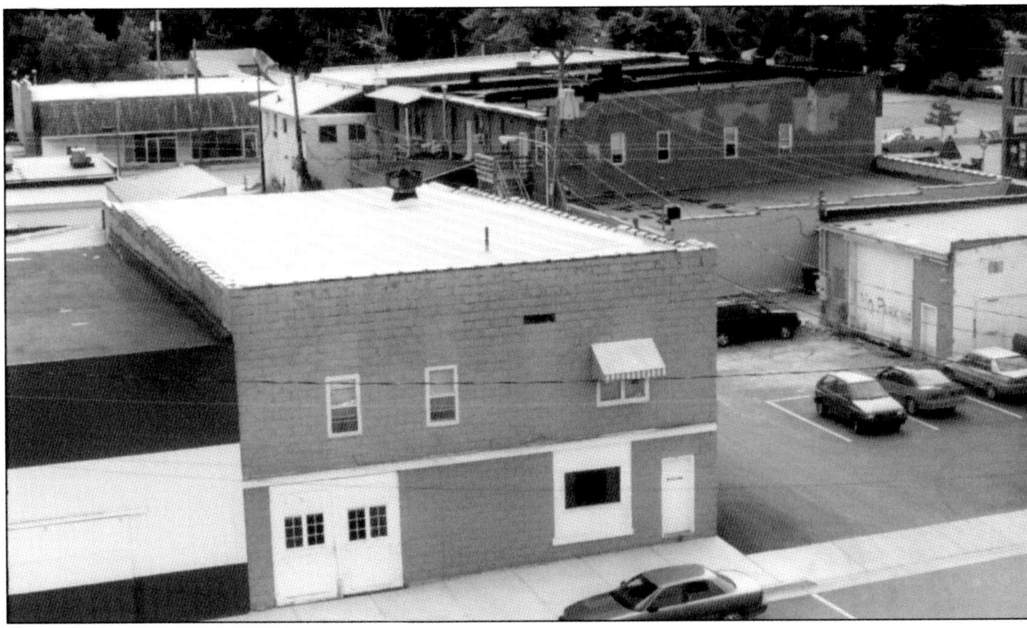

Charles's repair business started in this building, which was a blacksmith's shop originally and then a machine shop. As the business began to expand, an auxiliary building was added but was eventually torn down for parking. Most people in Beaverton remember this building as the Shepard building, named for the construction company that moved in when Brown Machine established its complex on the other side of Ross Lake. (Courtesy of Brown Machine.)

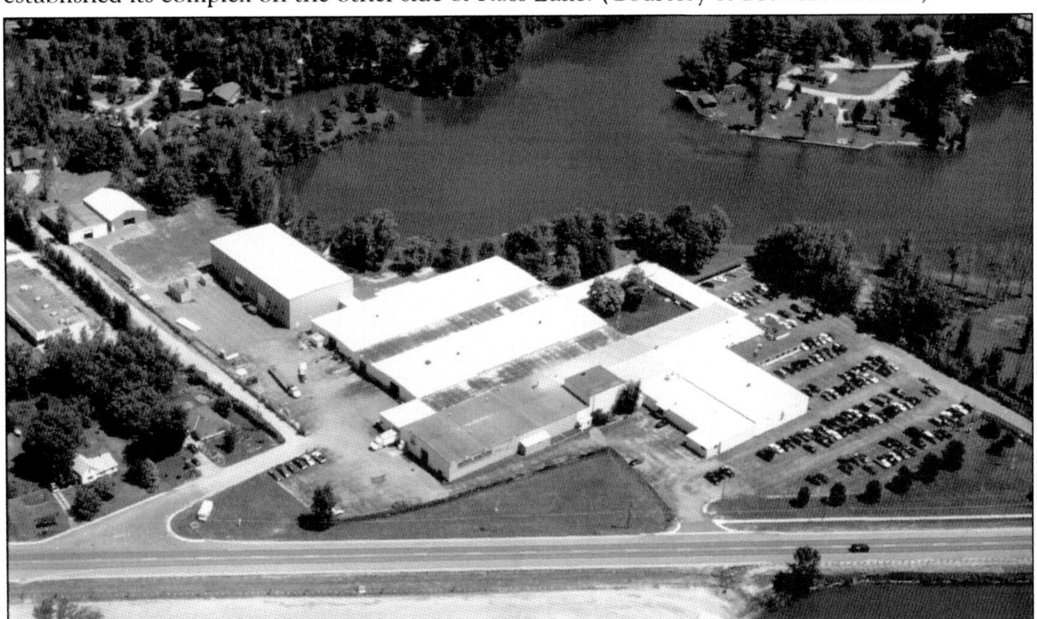

As this picture indicates, Brown Machine has grown into a large industrial complex on the north side of Ross Lake. Over the years, it has expanded to make thermoforming machines that manufacture entire door panels for automobiles, foam egg crates, and the first automatic cup transfer system. It constructed one building for a machine that stamped out plastic boat hulls for the recreational market and the U.S. Coast Guard. (Courtesy of Brown Machine.)

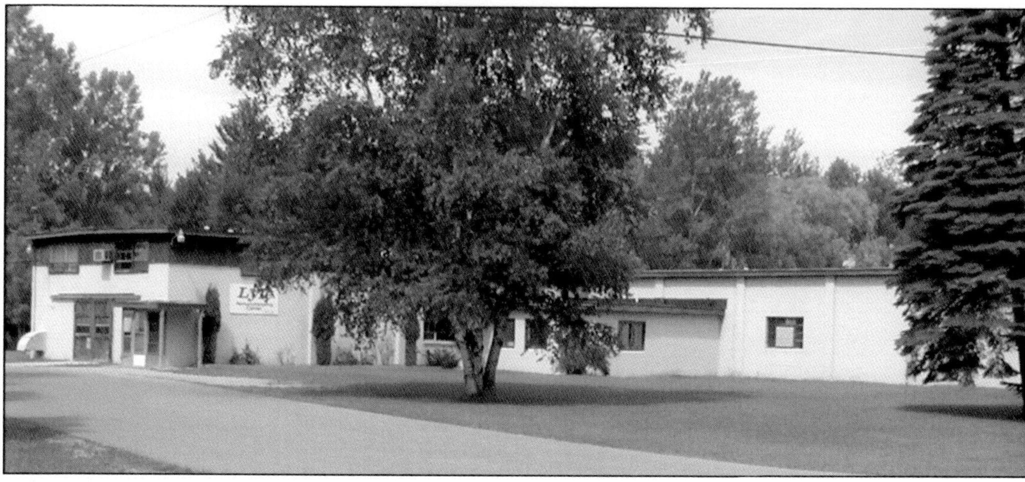

Lyle Industries was started by another creative genius named William Oberloier in 1965. His interest in plastics and thermoforming began while working in the aircraft industry in Chicago. Literally returning to his roots, Oberloier built Lyle Industries on the property he was born on in 1916, just down the road from the town of Lyle.

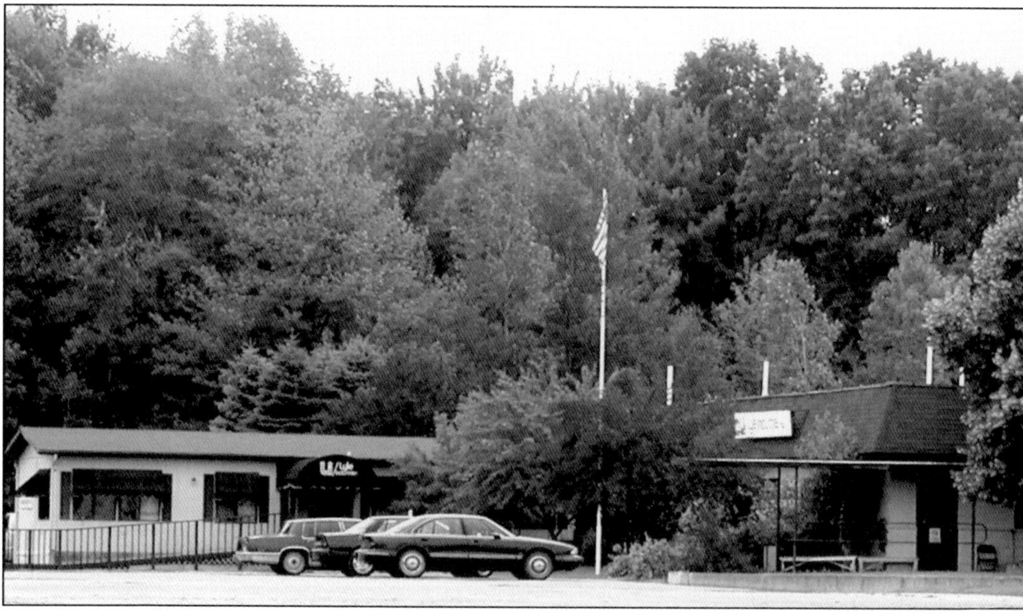

Lyle Industries began as a bottle trimmer manufacturer and rebuilder of thermoforming equipment. Oberloier sold the business in 1980, and the company has expanded to have over 60,000 square feet of production space. Now with more than 100 full-time employees, Oberloier looks back at age 90 and says, "My little business ended up paying for a lot of lunches around here!"

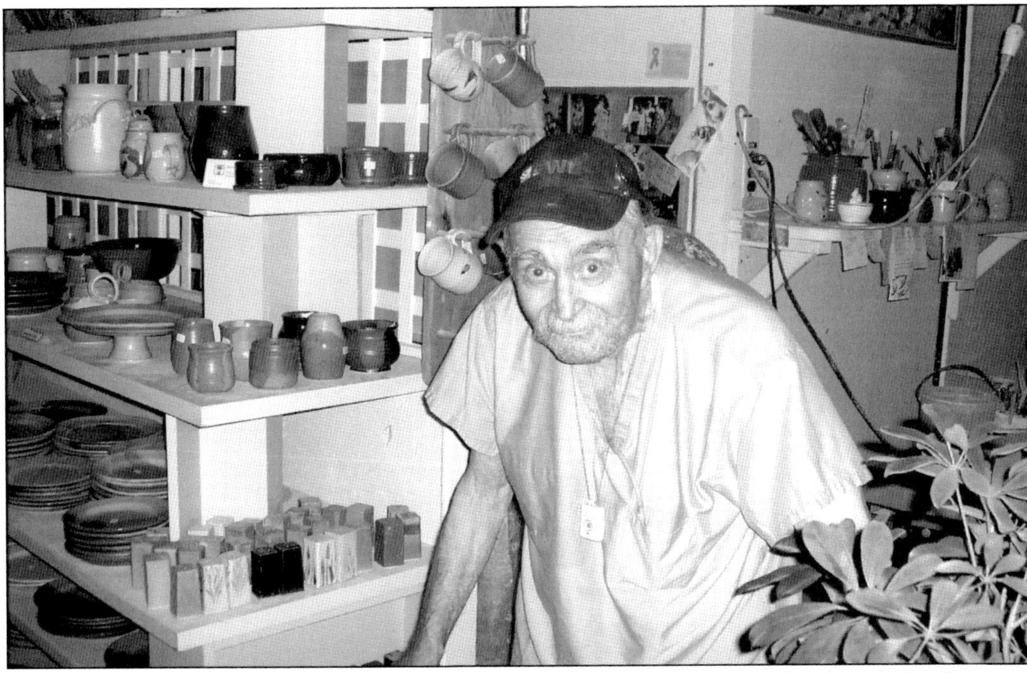

Oberloier's body is getting older, but his creative brain is still working. After he sold his business, Lyle Industries, in 1980, he and his wife, a former art teacher, opened Oberloier Studio. They specialized in pottery products, featuring dinnerware, bakeware, and home furnishings. But Oberloier is always looking for ways to make their products faster, easier, and more efficiently. He is constantly working on making things better. His home is a masterpiece of efficiency, an energy saving but still artistically attractive structure. The property is sprinkled with ponds, bridges, sculptures, and a variety of plants, flowers, and trees to rival many botanical gardens. In September 1981, he dedicated his masterpiece sculpture of a dragon at a festival that he and his wife started to raise funds for the Gladwin City Council of the Arts. Made from scraps that he says were "just lying around," the dragon is 18 feet high, 14 feet wide, 60 feet long, and weighs approximately four tons. These are all significant accomplishments for a man who spoke no English until he started going to the Lyle School at age five.

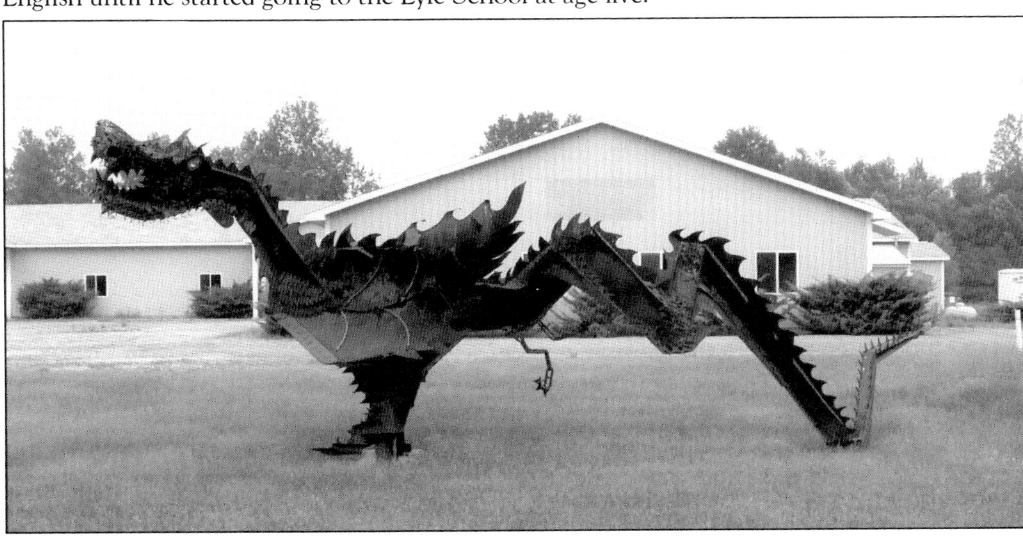

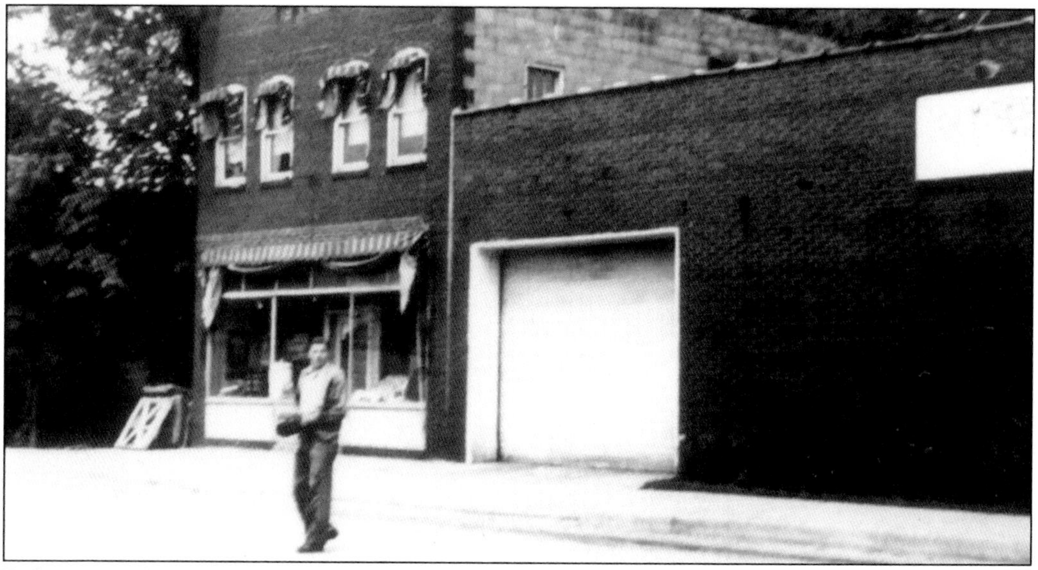

Robinson Industries started in the garage of the company founder, Fred Robinson, and is still a family-owned business. This picture shows the state garage in Beaverton where Robinson Industries moved to when it began to expand. With a new contract to make refrigerator door liners, it soon outgrew the garage and moved to a new complex built on the family farm where it remains today. Robinson and his wife, Ardis, worked side by side until he passed away in 1975. Utilizing Gaylord Brown's thermoforming process, Robinson Industries serves a variety of industry markets, including the automotive, medical, electronics, and furniture businesses.

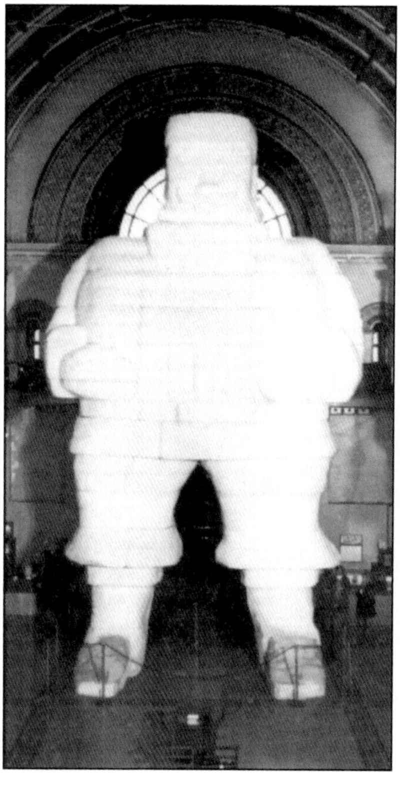

Robinson Industries built the Santa Colossal in 1949. He stands over 50 feet tall, weighs about four tons, and is carved out of Styrofoam. This giant Santa was the creation of Walter Dowell, the art director of the Indianapolis Industrial Exposition. Over 100 people worked on him at various times. After completion, he was shipped to Indianapolis by train on four boxcars. Upon arrival, Santa Colossal was reassembled to stand and greet visitors at Union Station.

Six

THE GRAND FORKS OF BEAVERTON

In the late 1880s, large stands of timber near the confluence of the Tobacco and Cedar Rivers attracted the attention of the Ross brothers. The patriarch of the family, Donald Gunn Ross, made the decision to take advantage of these natural resources and set up a logging operation in 1890. After building the Sapless Paving Blocks Mill on the peninsula now covered by Ross Lake, the new home of the Ross family needed a name. Having riverbanks lined with cedar trees made Cedarville a good choice. By May 1890, the Flint and Pere Marquette Railroad had already built tracks to Cedarville, and the mill had 30 employees, but two other locations already had that name. So by September, the railroad had approved a new name, Grand Forks, which lasted for four months. Then the postal service decided Michigan already had too many locations beginning with "grand," including Grand Rapids, Grand Ledge, and Grandville. The name Meran lasted just over a month. After the postal service chose Donald Ross to be postmaster, he picked the name Beaverton to honor his hometown of Beaverton, Ontario, in Canada. The name stuck, and in 1894, Beaverton became a village. Then in 1903, it officially became the city of Beaverton.

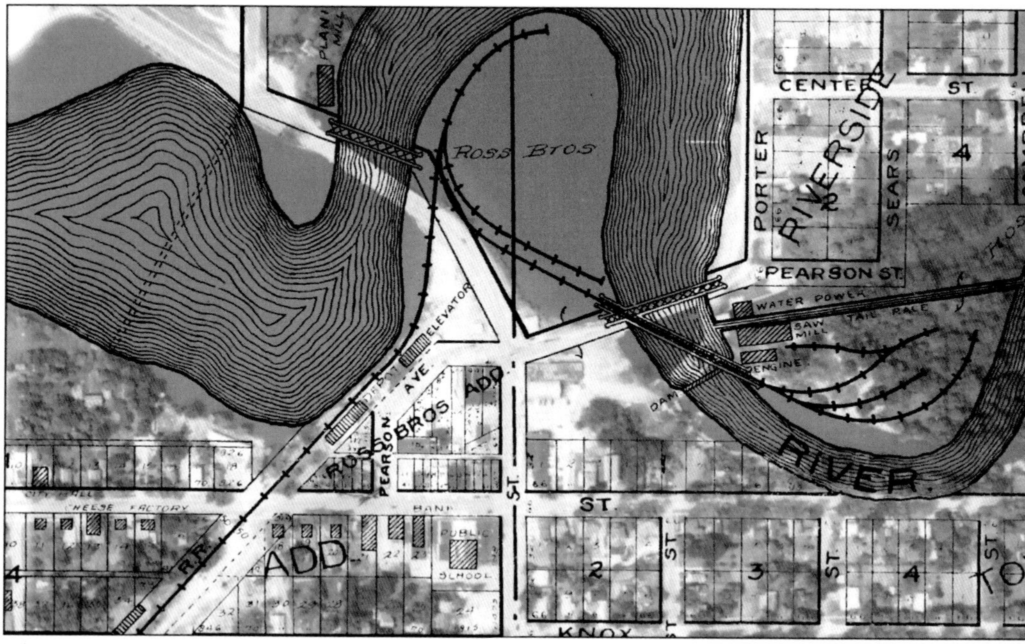

This is a 1906 plat map of Beaverton superimposed over a 1964 aerial photograph of the same place. (Courtesy of Robert Frei.)

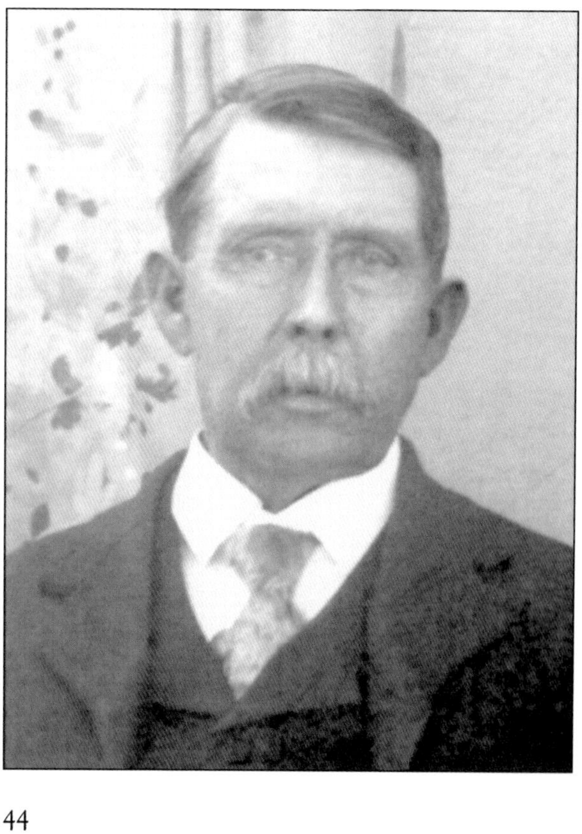

Donald Gunn Ross grew up in Beaverton, Ontario, in Canada. In 1890, Ross moved from Clare to Beaverton and established several businesses relating to the logging industry. These included many lumber camps, a shingle mill, and the band sawmill known as "the Big Mill." Sons Ronald and William Ross stayed in Beaverton to form the Ross Brothers Company. They had camps and portable mills as far north as the Meredith area.

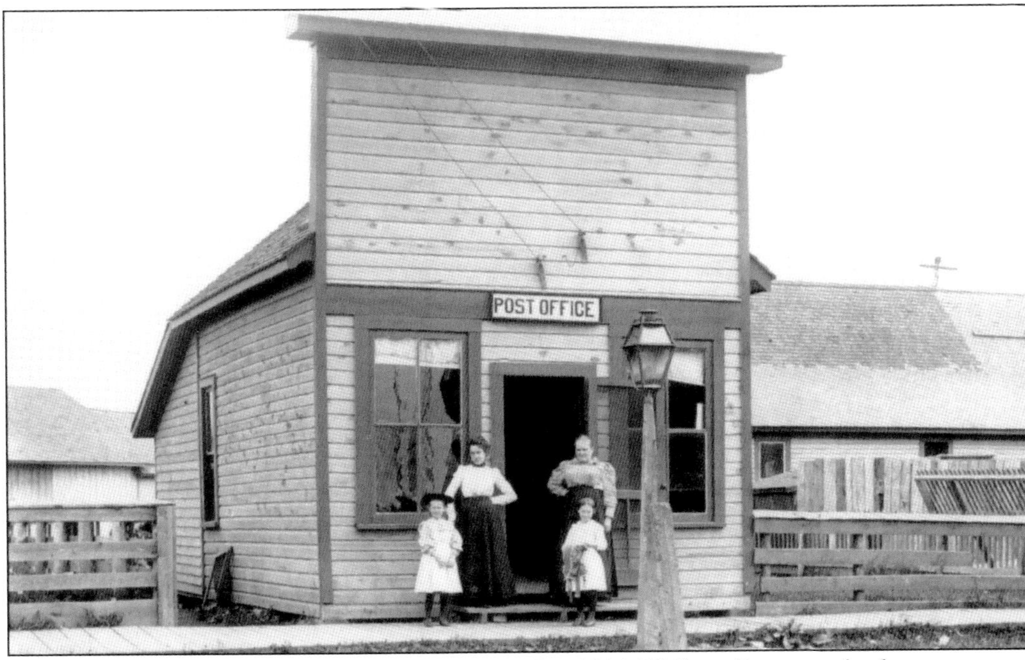

The city of Beaverton's first post office was opened in 1904. William Ross was the first postmaster with Ronald Ross's mother-in-law as assistant postmaster. Cyrus McKibben, the first mail carrier, took a route through Dale, across the Tobacco River up through Billings Township, and on to the Knox school and back. A second carrier, David Mode, was added a few years later to cover Buckeye Township. Then George Taylor came aboard to cover west of Beaverton to Bard.

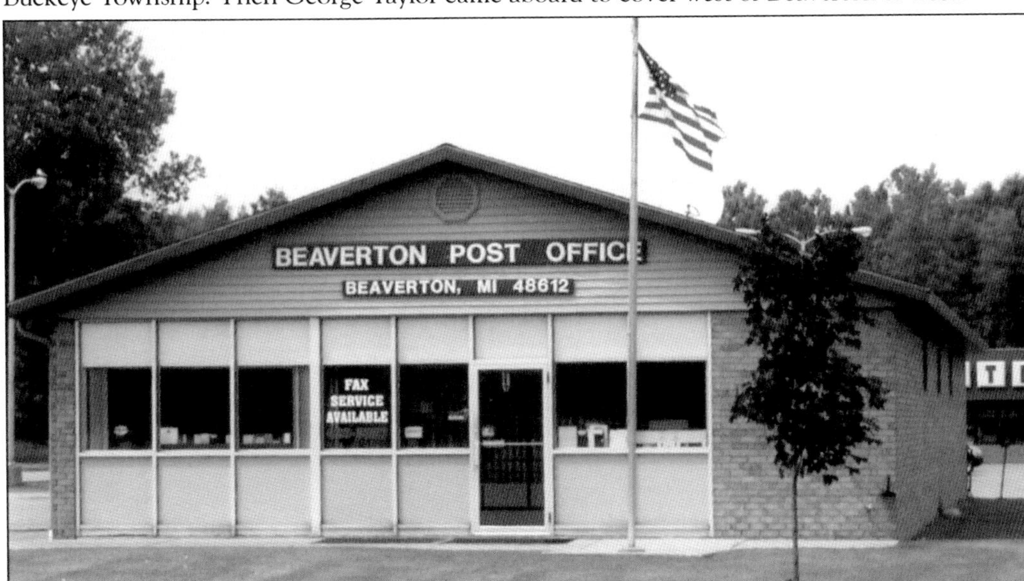

A new post office was built across the lake near the new small business district that was being developed. This sparked a minor controversy among the residents of Beaverton. Many people and merchants were very upset about the post office no longer being located in the downtown area. This prompted the passage of the "Beaverton Law," which said all small town post offices would be located in the primary commercial district.

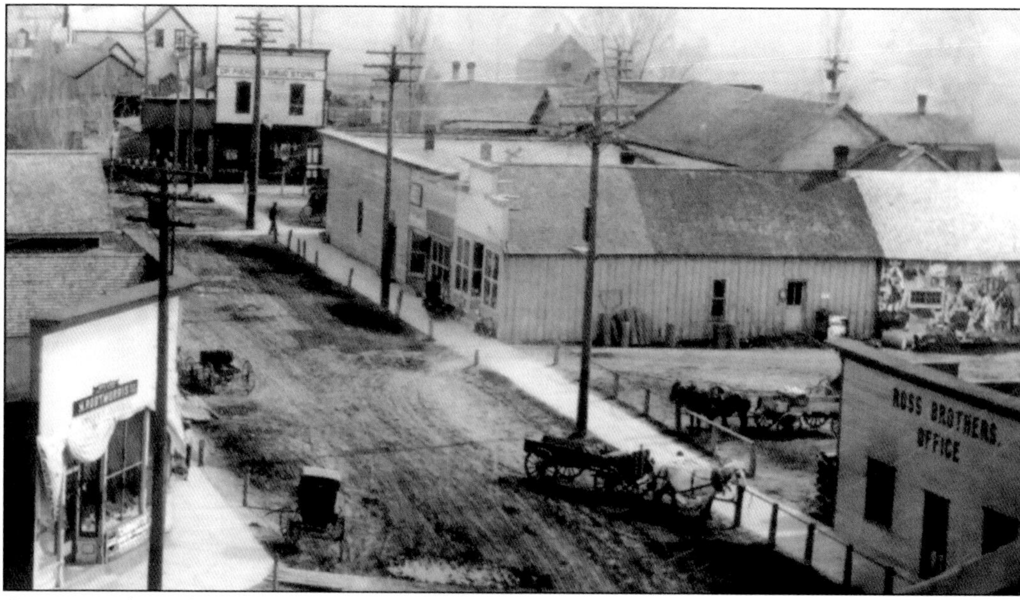

On one night in late September 1909, one of the greatest disasters in the history of Beaverton occurred. It started with a small fire in the back of Mann's saloon, quickly spread through a vacant store, and ignited dynamite that was stored in the back of Powell's hardware store. Pictured above is Pearson Street looking north around 1902. From left to right on the right side of the street are Mann's saloon on the corner, a vacant store, Powell's hardware, a vacant lot, and the Ross Brothers office.

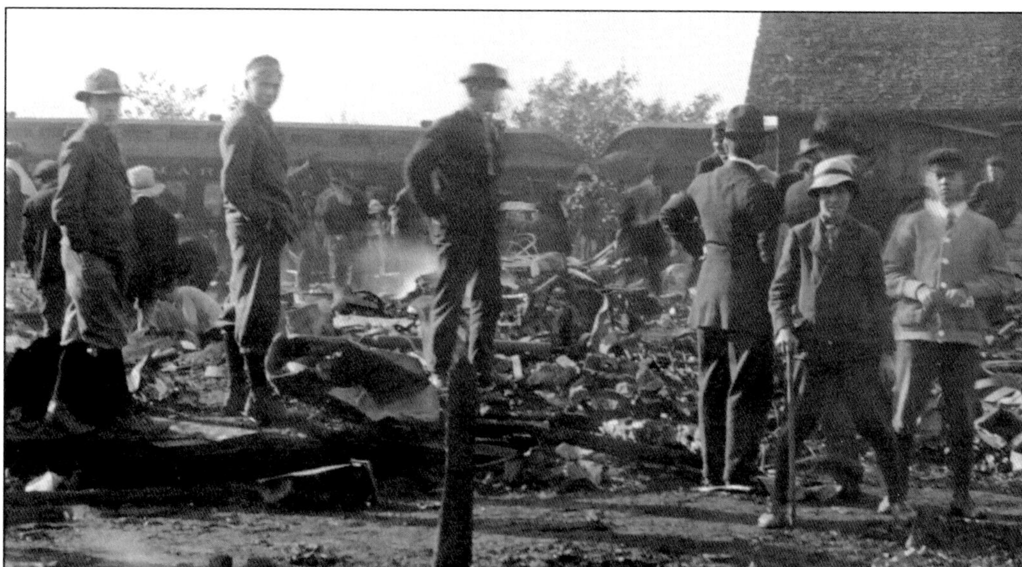

At about 11:00 p.m., a fire was spotted, and when the people on the scene realized the impending danger, everyone was evacuated to a safe distance. The ensuing explosion and fire from the dynamite (reported to be between 300 and 600 pounds) totally destroyed six buildings and badly damaged at least a dozen others.

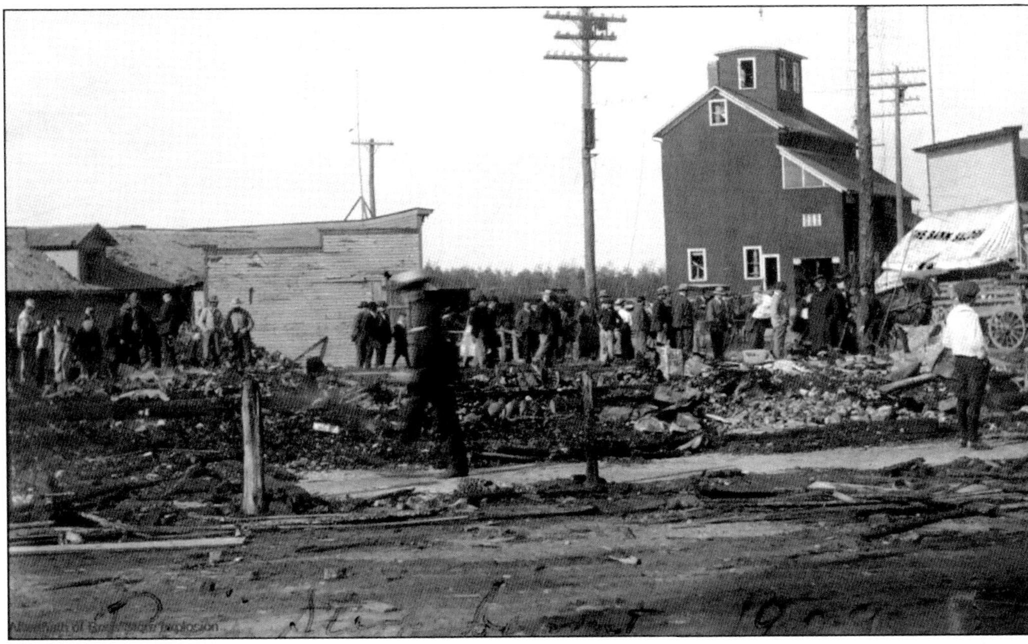

This photograph shows the people gathered to examine the damage. Notice the railroad cars in the background. In the midst of the chaos and confusion, prior to the explosion and fire, several men remained calm enough to realize just how serious the situation was. Someone remembered that more dynamite was stored in a railroad car on the tracks in the danger zone. Putting themselves in harms way, the men pushed the rail cars far enough away to prevent an even larger disaster.

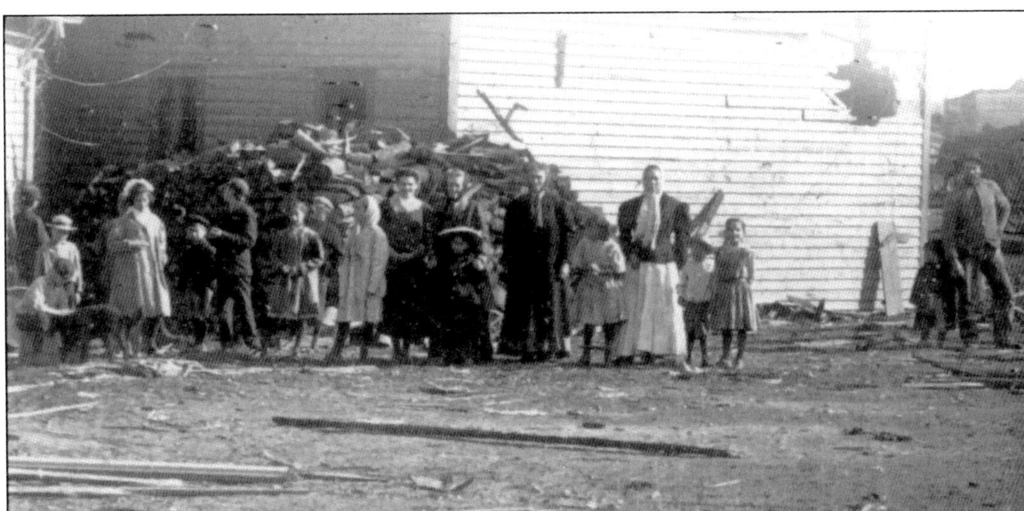

People put on their Sunday best to have their pictures taken in front of the damaged buildings left by the explosion in September 1909. This picture also shows the power and destructive force of the dynamite. The hole in the building is from a bale of barbed wire stored in Powell's hardware store. The heavy bale was sent like a missile through the wall from half a block away.

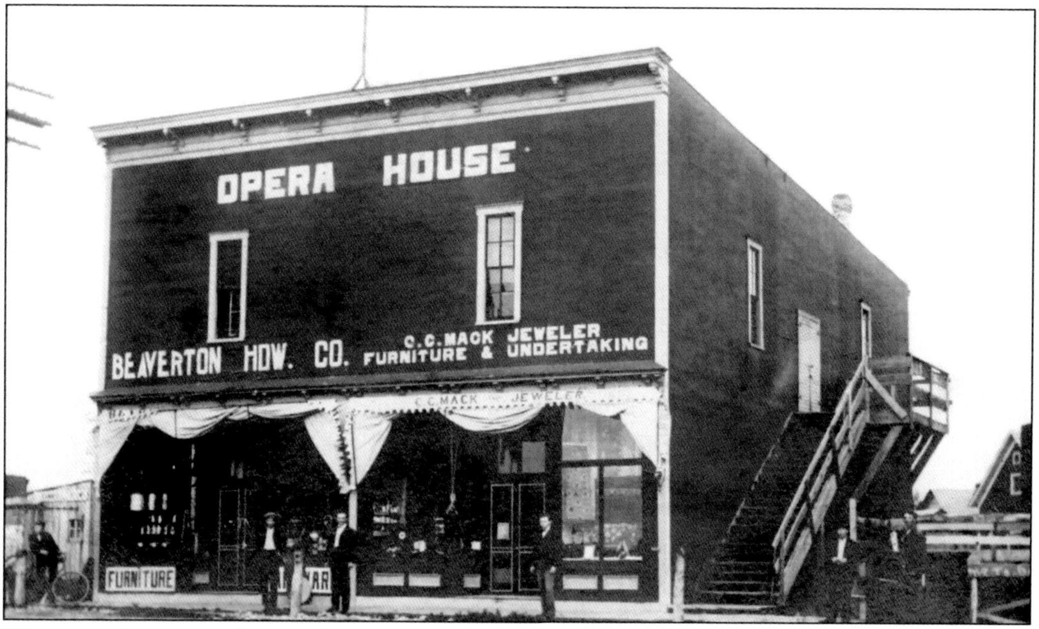

The opera house, as shown above, was a common sight in many towns across Michigan. This one in Beaverton was located on Pearson Street across from the train depot. Most opera houses, including this one, had an open second floor that served as a banquet hall and meeting area for local organizations. Many churches got their start with Sunday services there until they could afford to build a church. This building burned in a 1938 fire.

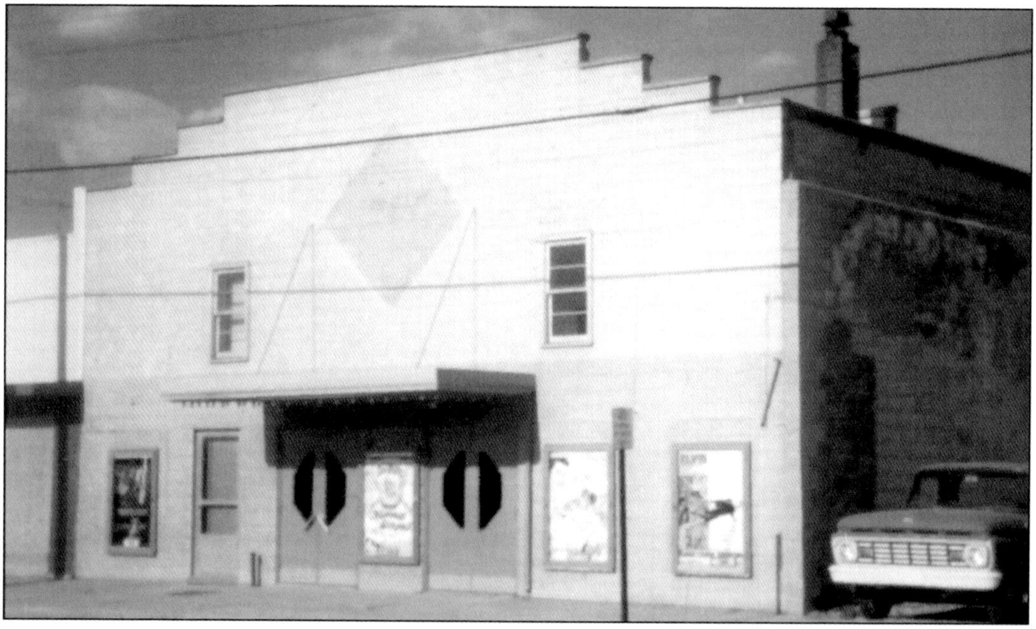

Construction for the Gem Theater in Beaverton started in 1939 and was completed over a year later in the fall of 1940. The doors opened at 7:00 p.m. on October 1 with the feature *No Time for Lonely*, starring James Stewart and Rosalind Russell. The building was air-conditioned, had a 400-seat capacity, and had something new called a "crying room" in the balcony. It is still in operation today on a limited basis.

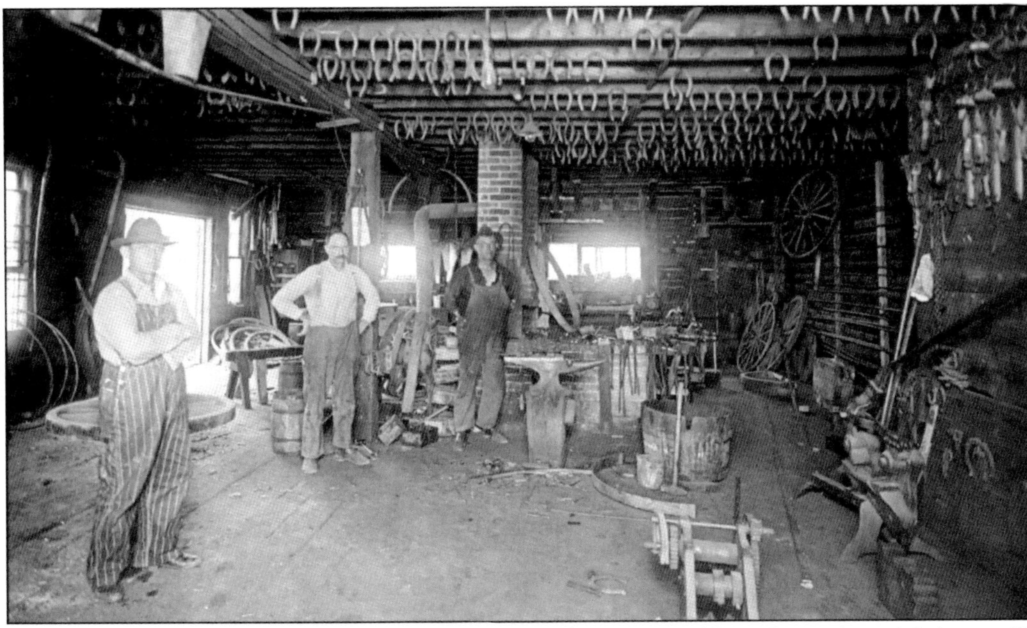

Cash Carey had his blacksmith shop on the corner of Pearson and Ross Street (now Michigan 18) from 1924 until 1964. An essential trade in the early years, many blacksmiths continued to thrive on their skill to make things from metal; Carey did the same. On an interesting note, Carey and his wife, Mildred, had five daughters who delivered the *Bay City Times* from 1926 to 1938. (Courtesy of Leo Asch.)

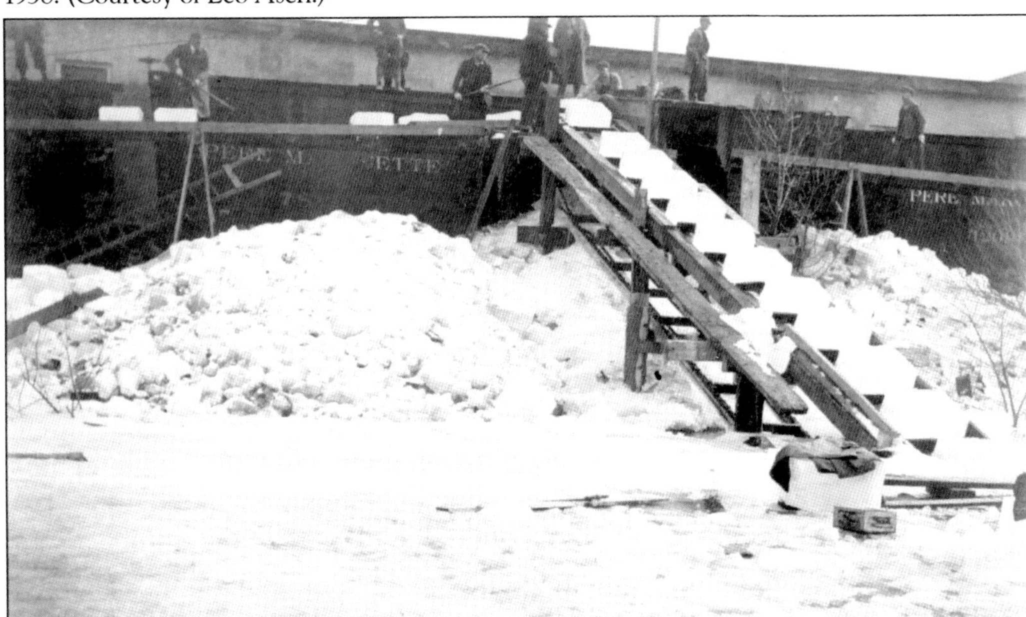

There are still many people who do not take ice for granted. Even with the invention of refrigeration, a refrigerator for the home was very expensive and the icebox was still used by many homes in Beaverton well into the 1950s. Ice from Ross Lake was a popular way for many farmers to make a wintertime living. Blocks of nature's coolant were loaded on train cars and shipped to ice houses in Bay City and Saginaw.

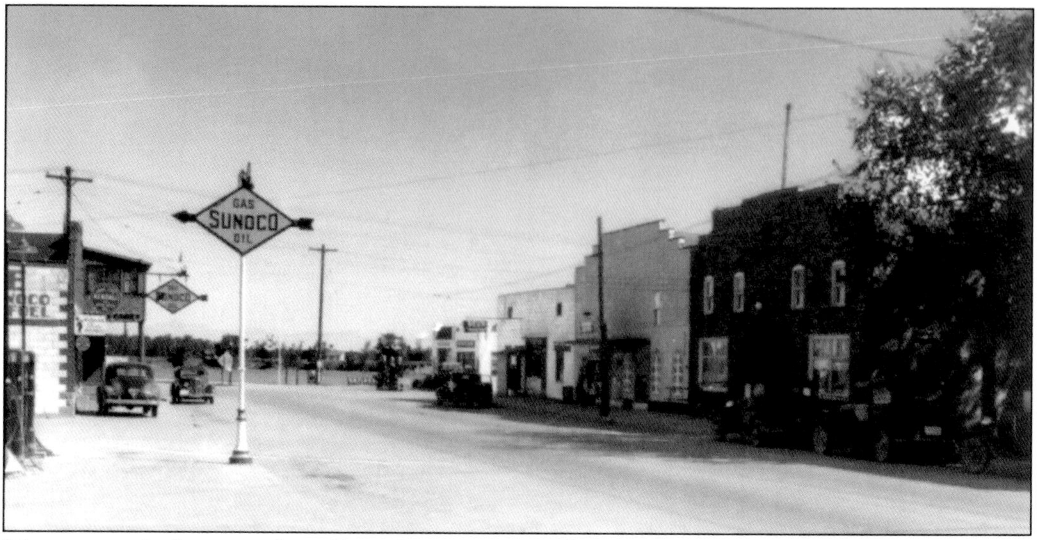

This view is looking north on Ross Street, now Michigan 18, in Beaverton from the northeast corner of the Beaverton Tavern. On the right is the Beaverton Community Building and the Gem Theater. The Sinclair gas station is on the corner. The Sunoco station is now a Shell gas station. The overhanging porch is part of the apartment where Cash Carey and his family lived above his blacksmith shop.

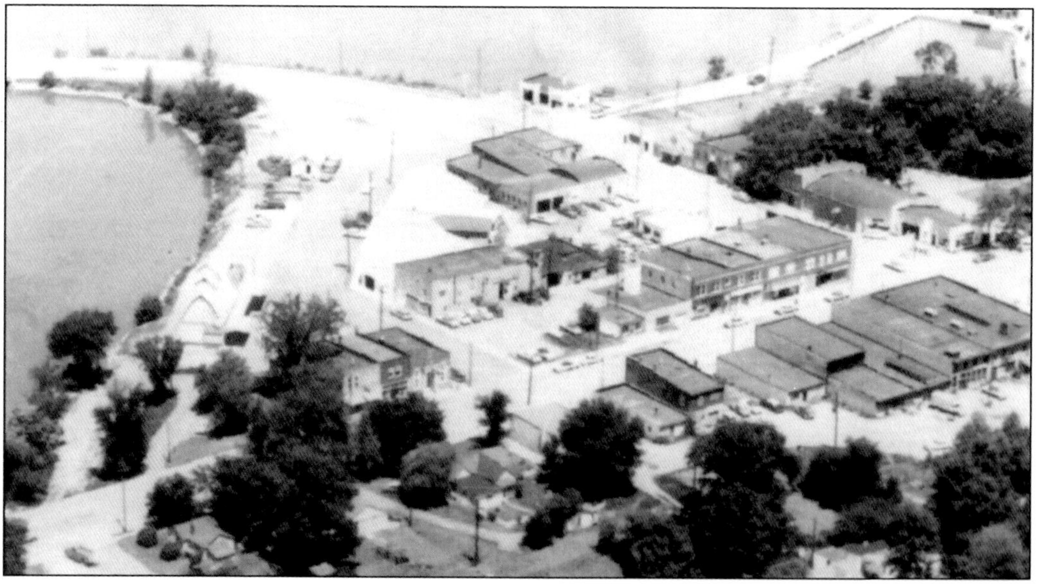

This 1950s aerial view of Beaverton clearly shows the second elevator along Ross Lake. The large building on the far right is the Muscle Shoals Hotel. Next going north on Ross Street is the Beaverton Tavern and Colbuck's Chevrolet. Cash Carey's building was on the corner where the Shell gas station sign is today.

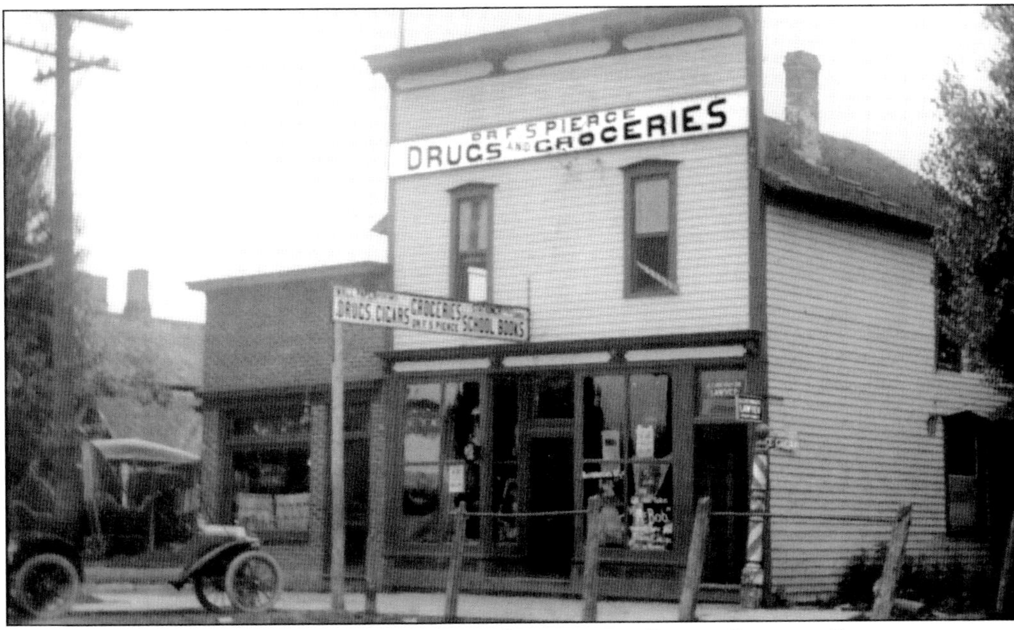

This is a photograph of Dr. Franklin Pierce's drug store on Brown Street in Beaverton around 1911. By then, the store had added groceries, a barbershop, and S. C. Reynolds' law office on the second floor. Pierce went to school at Albion College and got his medical degree from the University of Michigan and Chicago's Rush Medical College. (Courtesy of Bev Kitner.)

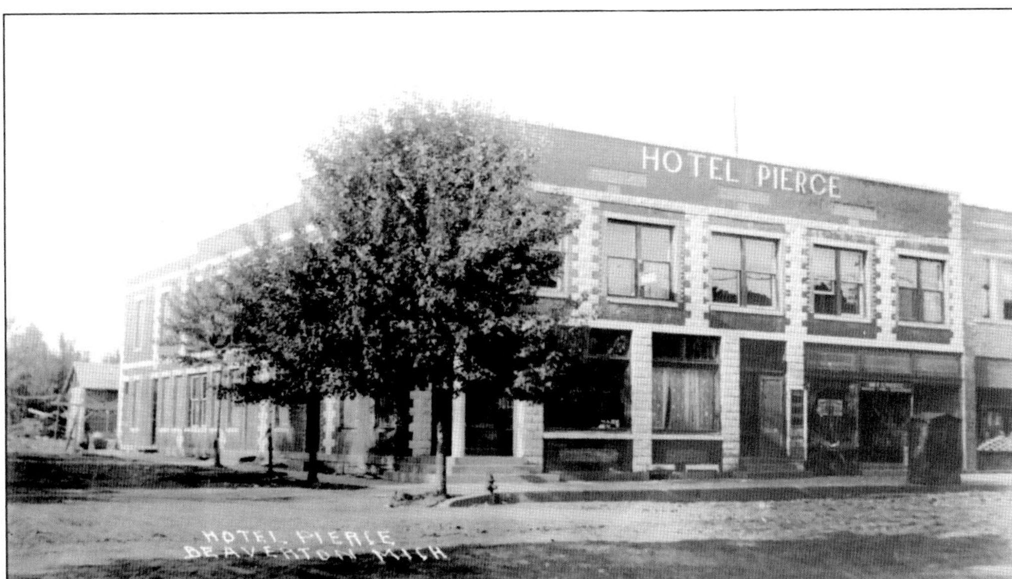

Pierce built the Pierce Hotel on the southwest corner of Ross and Brown Streets in 1912. The construction was completed and the hotel opened for business in 1912. The hotel was sold and renamed the Muscle Shoals Hotel. It remained open until a fire destroyed the building in April 1975. At the time of the fire, the hotel housed the Gladwin County Branch Library, a salon, barbershop, the Ragle Plumbing and Heating business, and apartments on the second floor. Today the space is a parking lot.

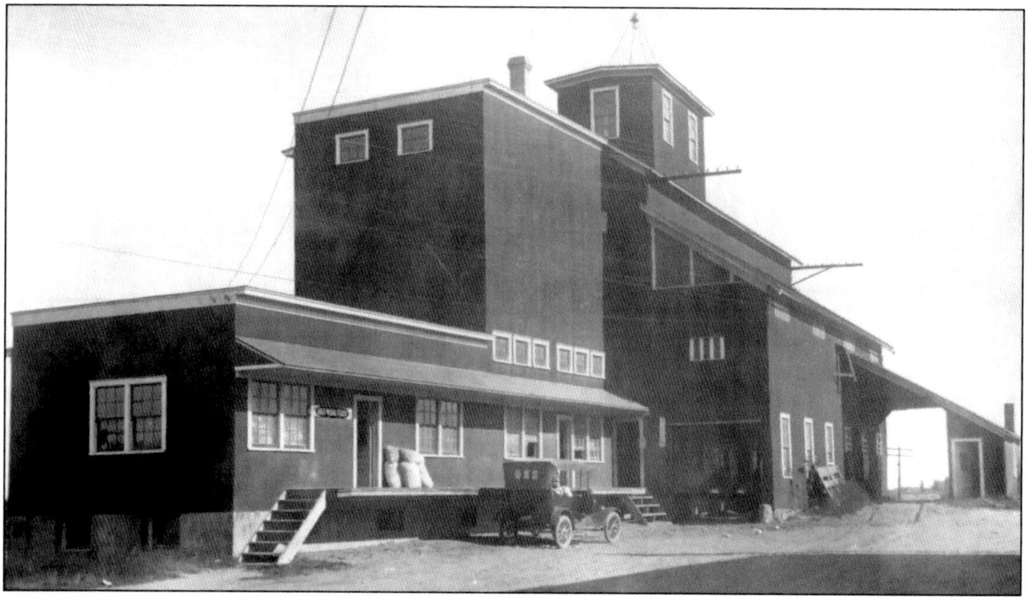

The Ross Brothers Company elevator was completed in January 1903 at a cost of $9,000. Powered by a 30-horsepower motor, it was the very latest in design, which made it the only elevator in the state with that technology. It was located next to the water and was destroyed by fire in 1935.

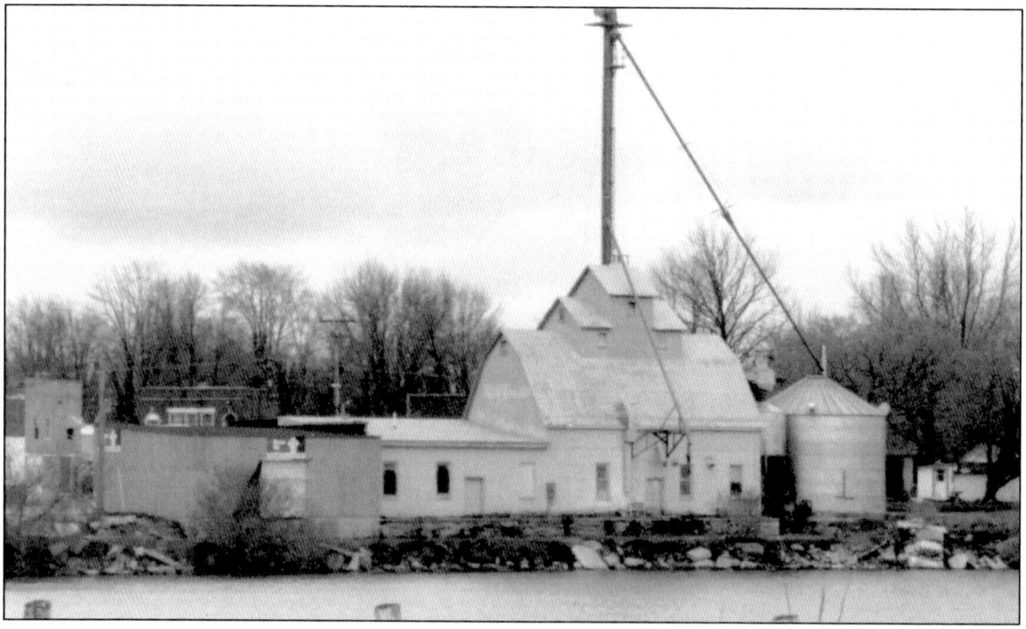

When the Ross elevator went up in flames in 1935, the entire facility was destroyed except for an addition that had been built on the west end. The decision was made to build a new elevator onto that addition. That elevator served local farmers for over 64 years until it was demolished in 2000. (Courtesy of Bev Kitner.)

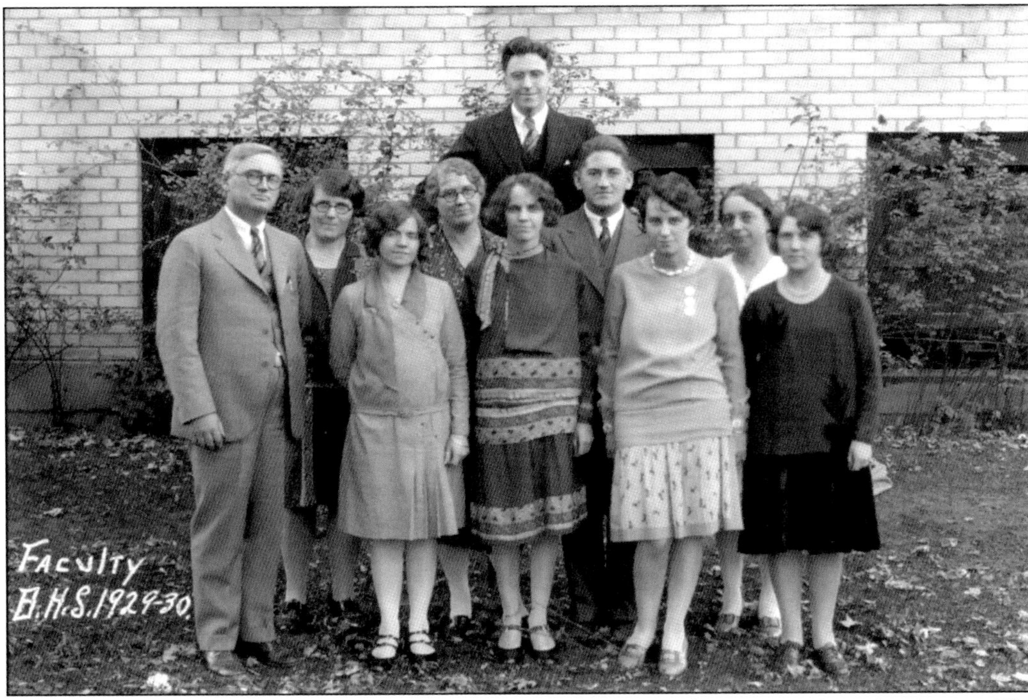

The Beaverton Area Rural Schools began consolidation in the 1929–1930 school year. The picture above shows the first faculty. From left to right are (first row) Superintendent G. Sheppard, Margaret Fisher, Lucille Fisher, Evelyn Clark, and unidentified; (second row) Emma Soldan, Mac Shell, Ralph VanValconberg, and Ethel Whitman. James MacConnell is in the back.

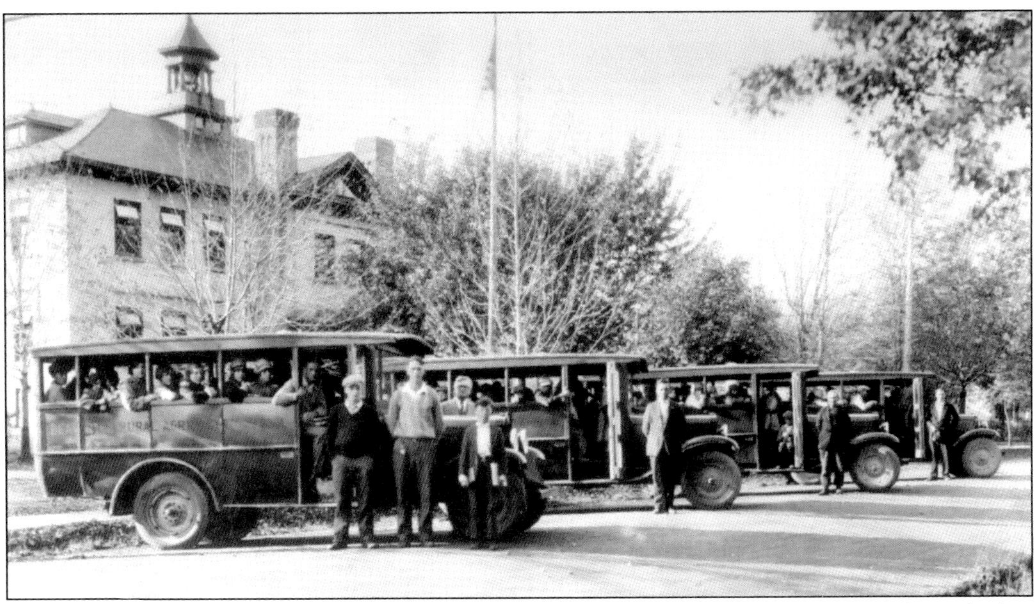

Beaverton needed school buses after the consolidation in 1929. Here is the 1929 Chevrolet bus fleet in 1930. The first driver, Lester Burr, is with Sheppard behind the hood of the first bus. The second driver is Gira Crockett, the third driver is Ernest Hodges, and the fourth driver is Ollie Kitchen. The Beaverton school in the background was built in 1908.

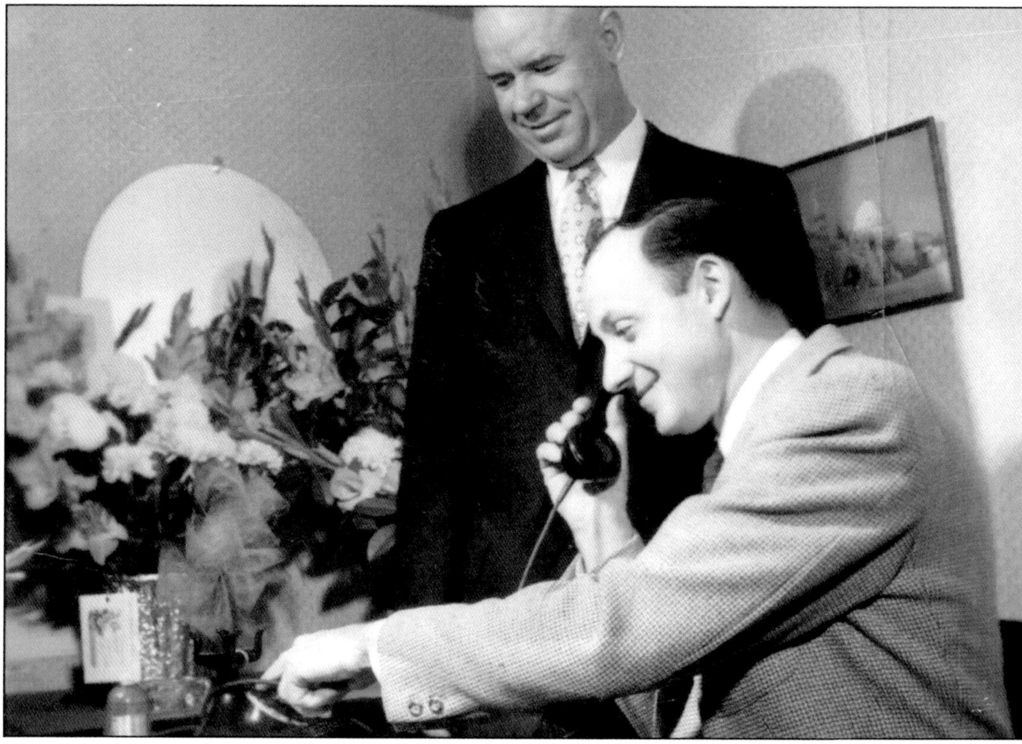

The first frame building in Beaverton was the telephone office just west of the current city hall block. It survived the 1909 explosion and was managed by Mattie and Margaret Bolin, who served as operators for the telephone company for over 50 years. The picture shows Mayor Adolph Presidio making the first direct connect telephone call with a dial telephone.

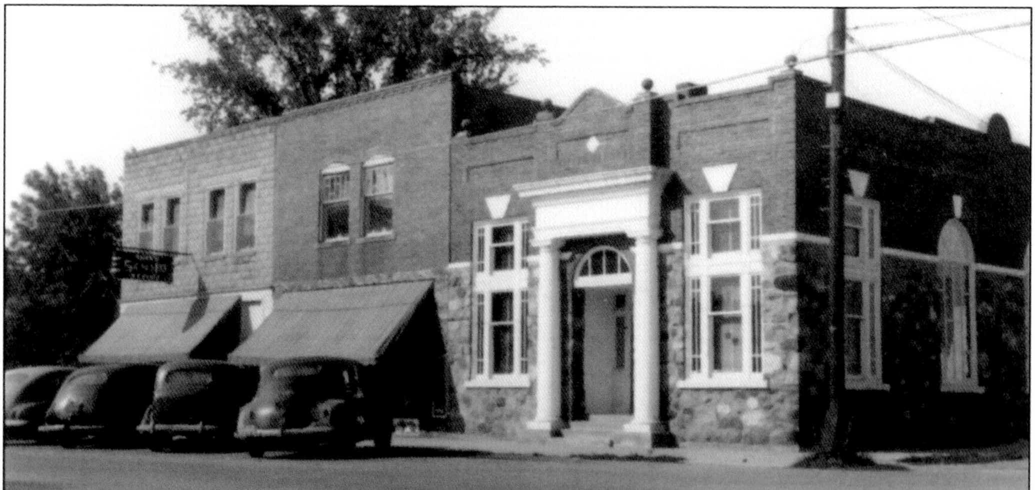

The People's State Bank building, shown above, was completed and opened its doors in 1917. Later the bank building on the corner once occupied by Mann's saloon became the Beaverton State Bank after merging with the State Bank of Beaverton. It became the Gladwin County Bank after World War II. When the bank built a new facility, the old bank building became Beaverton City Hall. The building next to the bank is Mitchell's Grocery Store and next to that is Agin's Variety Store. (Courtesy of Robert Frei.)

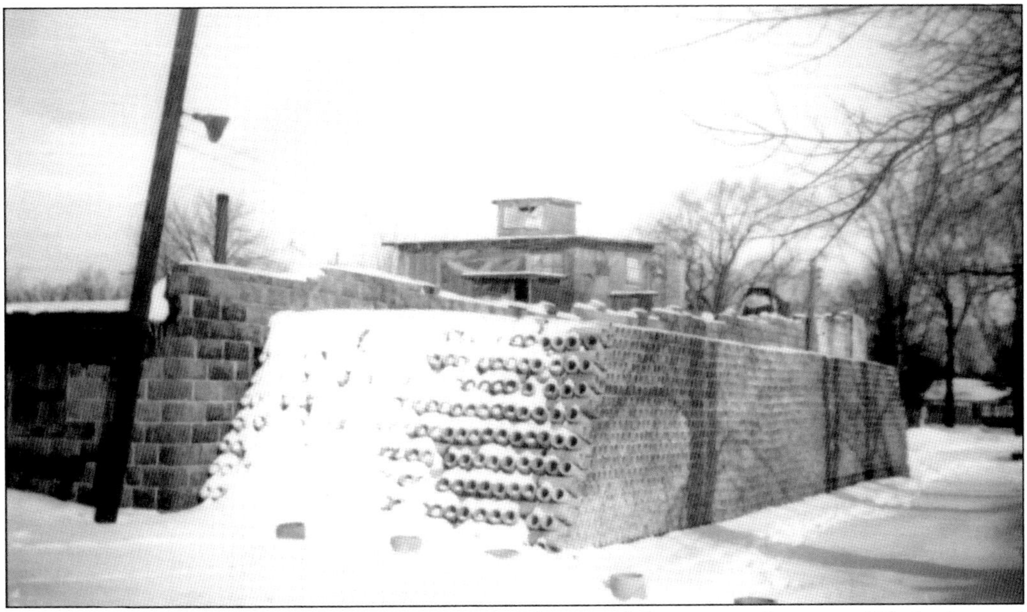

A fixture for over 50 years, the McKimmey family owned Beaverton Concrete Works located southwest of Glidden Road and Michigan 18. J. L. McKimmey owned and operated the tile and brick plant from 1900 to 1928. His son Ellis McKimmey took over and ran the company until 1958. It was eventually torn down in 1963. (Courtesy of Tom Ledner.)

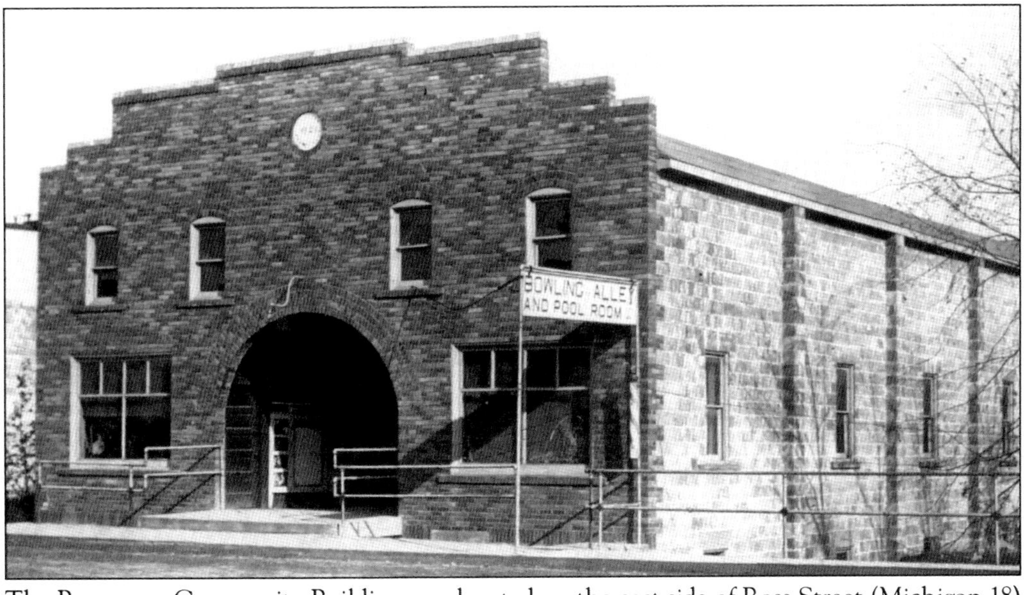

The Beaverton Community Building was located on the east side of Ross Street (Michigan 18) and built in 1922. It served as a theater, party hall, and meeting place. There was a bowling alley with locker rooms in the basement, and it was used as the school system's gymnasium for over 20 years. During World War II, the basement was used as the canning center where people could can produce from their gardens without charge.

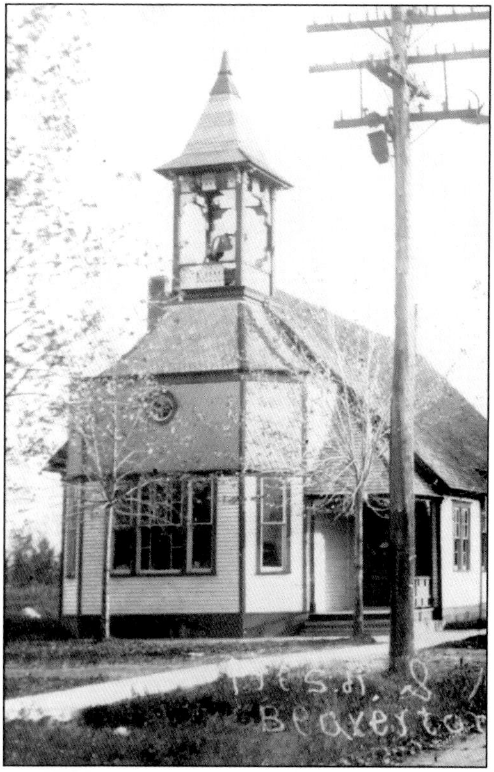

The First Presbyterian Church on Ross Street was the first organized church in Beaverton and predates most of the commercial buildings and homes. The land for the church was deeded to the board of trustees in December 1895. The first minister of the church was Rev. E. H. Bradfield, who served in the pulpit in the Gladwin church as well. Donald and Les Ross's daughter Velma was the first person baptized in the newly formed church in Beaverton. The building was dedicated in December 1896.

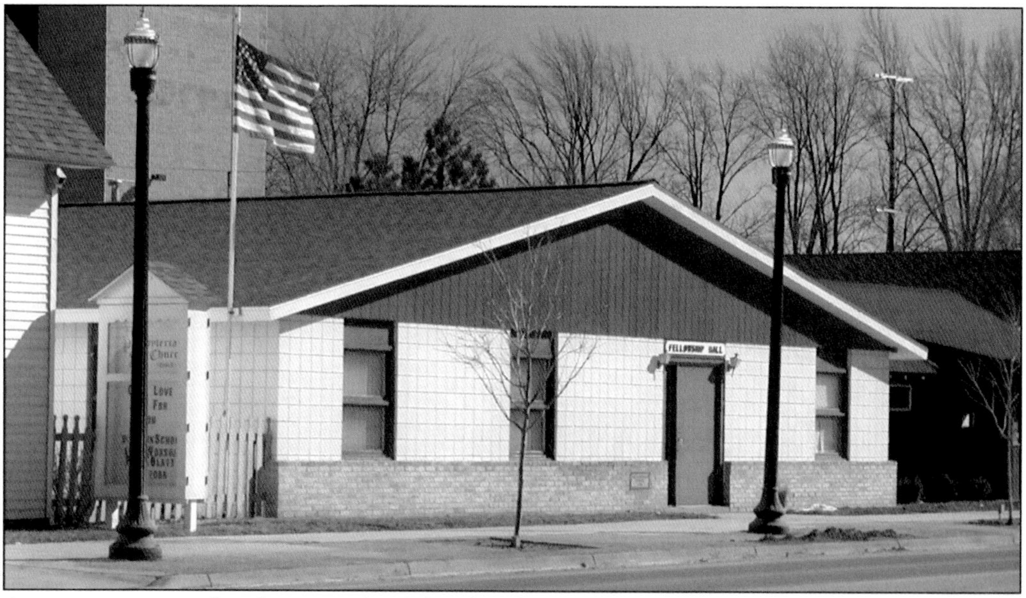

A manse was completed just south of the church in September 1903 with the Reverend A. C. Austin as its first occupant. The structure was destroyed by fire in September 1913 along with the early records of the church. A new Presbyterian Fellowship Hall was built and dedicated in January 1968. The Reverend Karen Blatt got her call to the church in March 2000. The first church in Beaverton still stands today just a few blocks from the corner of Ross and Brown Streets.

Seven

A City on the Cedar

The *Cedar Register* was part of C. C. Foutch's store in 1877. The printing office was built in 1878 and the newspaper became the *Gladwin County Record*. Cedar consisted of Foutch's general store, the newspaper office, and next to it a store owned by Minnie Foutch (his sister and the first businesswoman in the area). There was a move in 1875 to make the Chappell Dam area known as Gladwin City the county seat. After some rather intense politicking, the resolution was voted down. With the rush of lumbermen to the area, by 1878, the village of Cedar had three hotels and 14 saloons, but it also had a post office, a school, and a brand new courthouse. The Michigan census of 1880 showed Cedar's population at 40. Problems with the name Cedar came up at the post office due to the fact that a Cedar post office already existed. A name change was recommended and Gladwin was approved as a village in 1885.

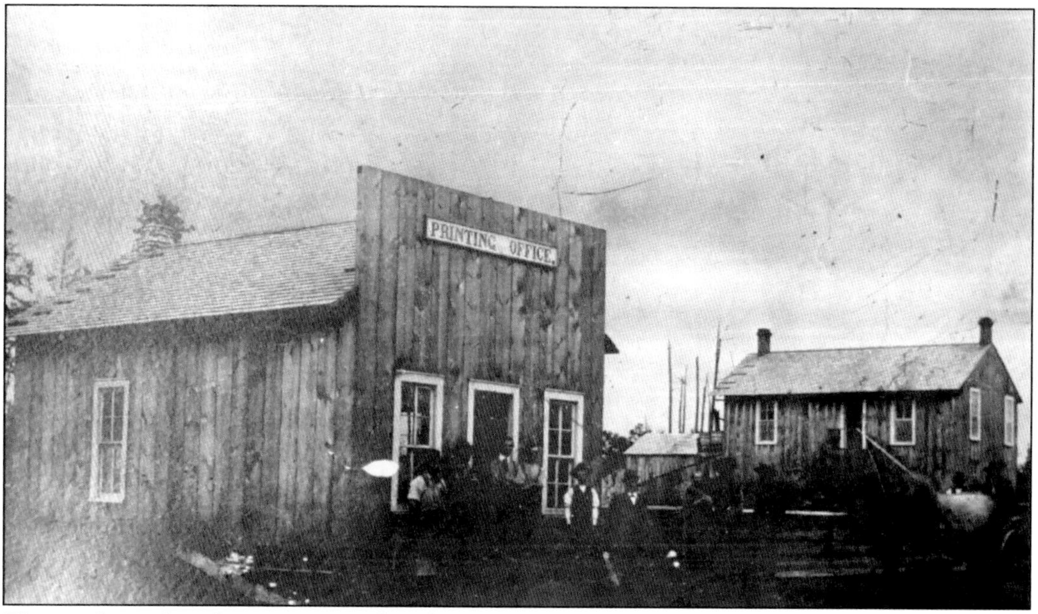

This is the earliest known print of Cedar (Gladwin) from about 1878. On the left is the new printing office and Minnie Foutch's store on the right.

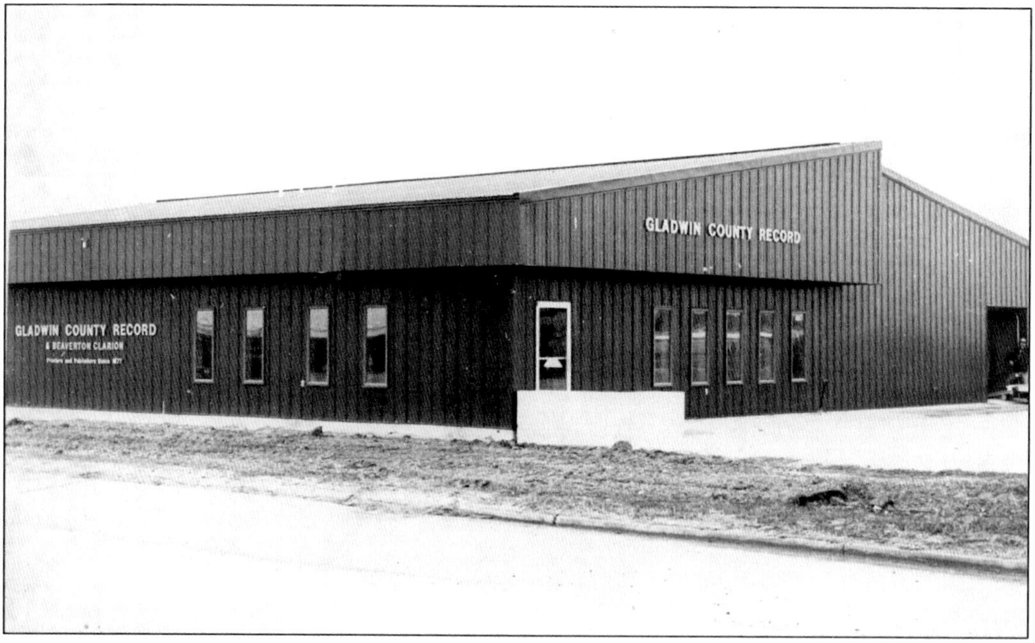

After Ink White, Paul Moon took over as editor/publisher of the *Gladwin County Record and Beaverton Clarion* and operated the newspaper until his son Roger took over duties in the 1960s. Roger oversaw the move to the new location at 700 East Cedar Avenue, shown above. The current publisher, Mike Drey, came to Gladwin in 1995 and remains in that position today.

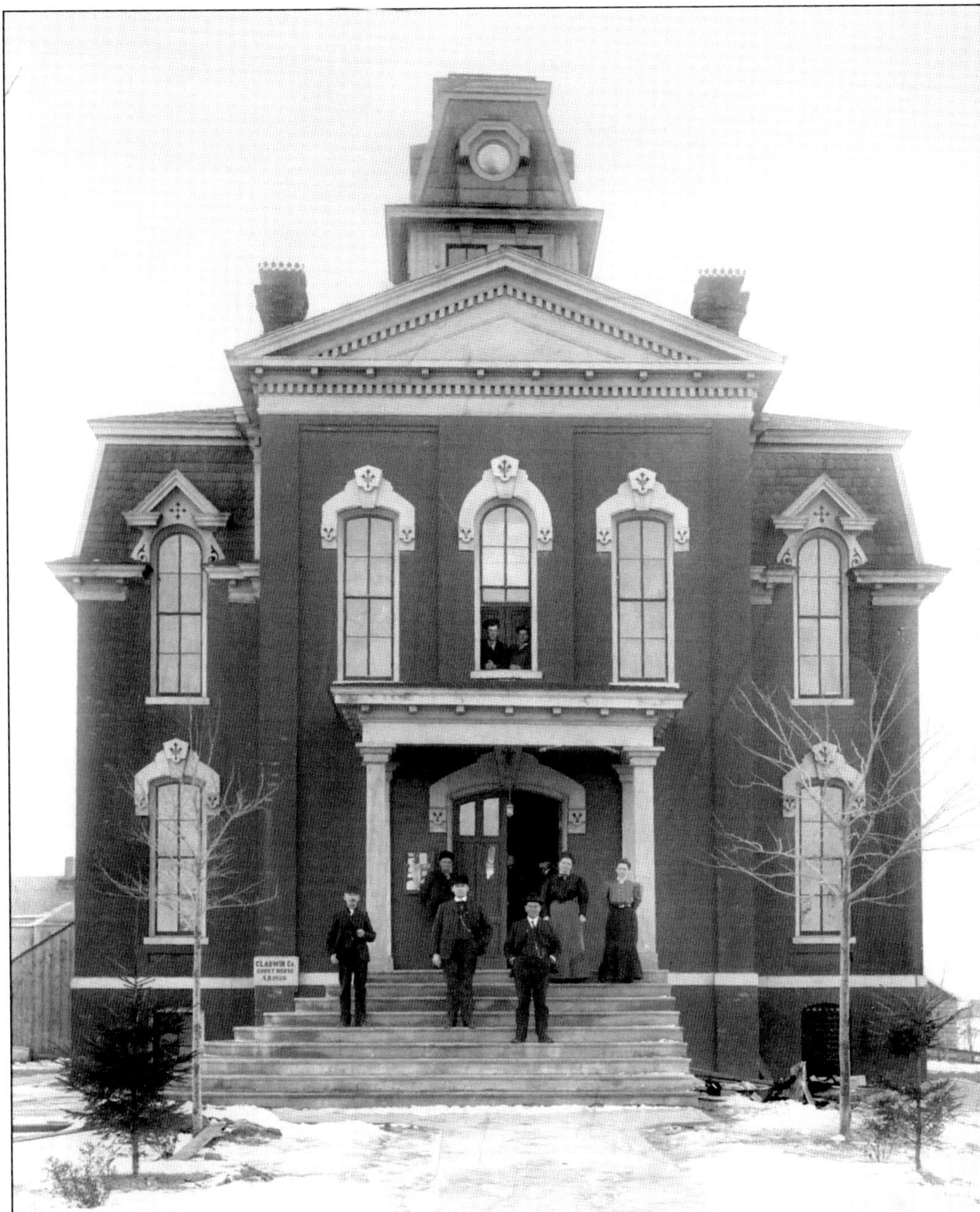

The courthouse shown above was constructed at a cost of $17,000 in 1877. Local citizens considered it a much better place to hold court than Elias Steele's barn. It was demolished in 1939 to make way for a new courthouse. The tin box in the cornerstone held a treasure of souvenirs, including copies of the *Midland Sun* and the *New York Illustrated Times*, one 1863 penny, a piece of rock, and a horse chestnut.

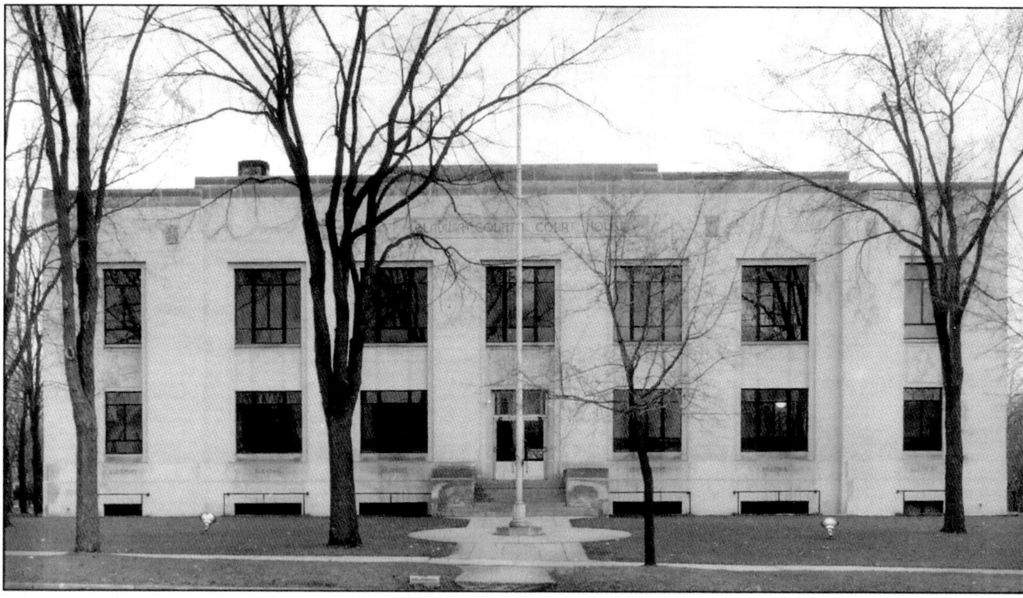

The courthouse was razed in 1939 after the construction of a new one. In 1938, the county board of supervisors earmarked money from the oil severance tax fund to finance the building. With declining revenues from the tax, it became apparent near completion of the project that there was not enough money collected to pay the contractors. A bond issue for $30,000 was put to a vote of the people. It won convincingly and construction continued. The building was finished and open for business in the spring of 1941.

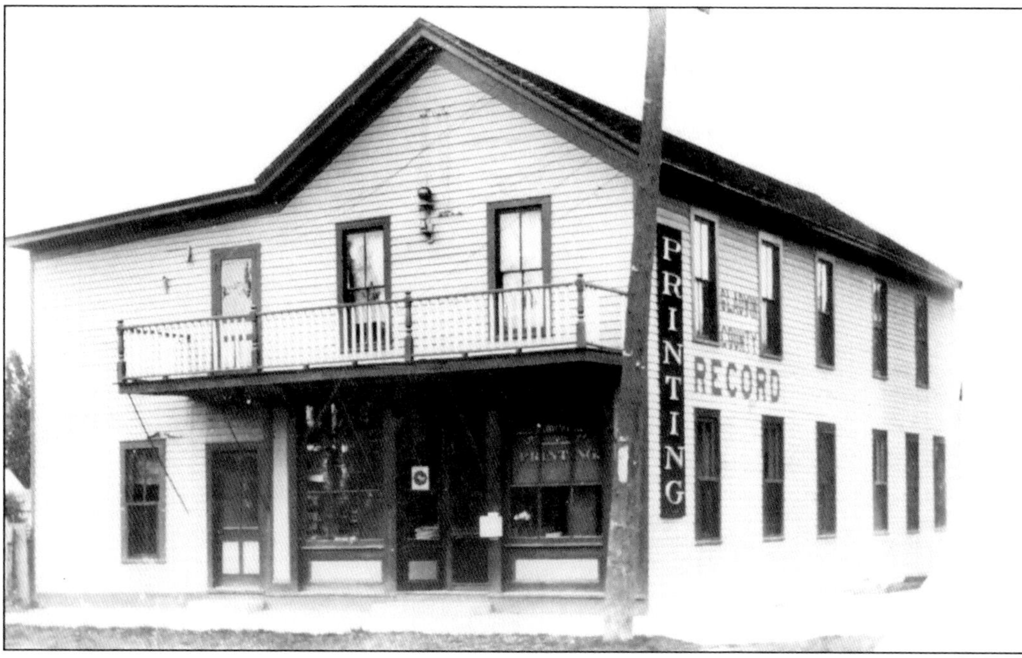

Eugene Foster purchased the *Gladwin County Record* in the early 1880s. He moved the newspaper's office to the northwest corner of Bowery Street and Cedar Avenue and served as editor until his death in 1928. The *Beaverton Clarion* was bought and combined with the Gladwin newspaper in 1932. Appropriately, Ink White was the publisher from 1935 to 1945.

In 1902, the Presbyterian church on Silverleaf Avenue was purchased and the Masons moved their lodge meetings to the new location. The church was moved 90 degrees in 1908 so the worshipful master could sit in the east, which is a part of Masonic tradition and ritual. However, the worshipful master at the time, Manville T. Peek, was killed during the turning of the Temple building. He remains the only Gladwin Masonic leader to die on the job.

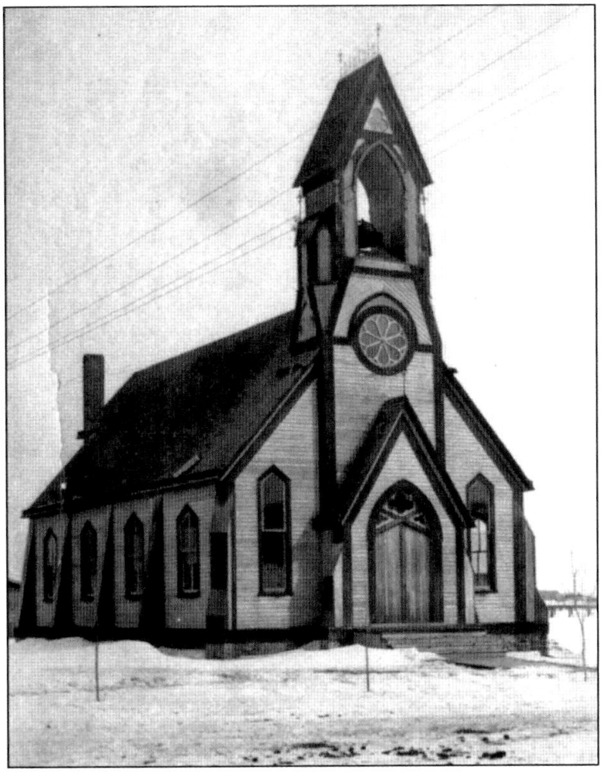

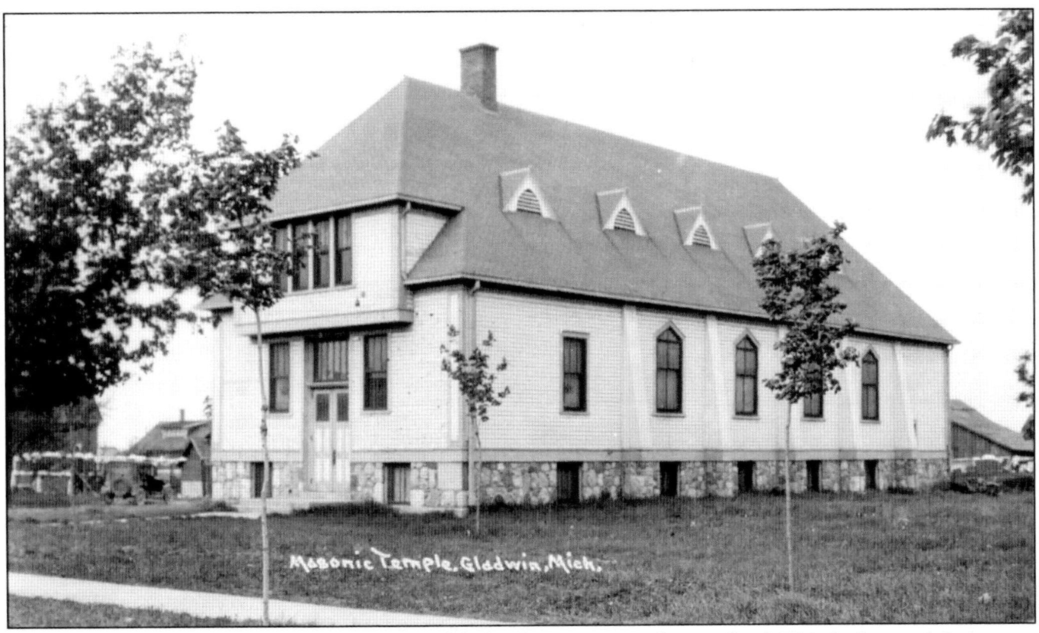

The Masonic lodge in Gladwin was established in 1890 and was the 397th lodge in Michigan. They first met on the second floor of the *Gladwin County Record* building. Familiar phrases such as "giving someone the third degree," "being square with a person," or "being on the level," are derived from Masonic symbols.

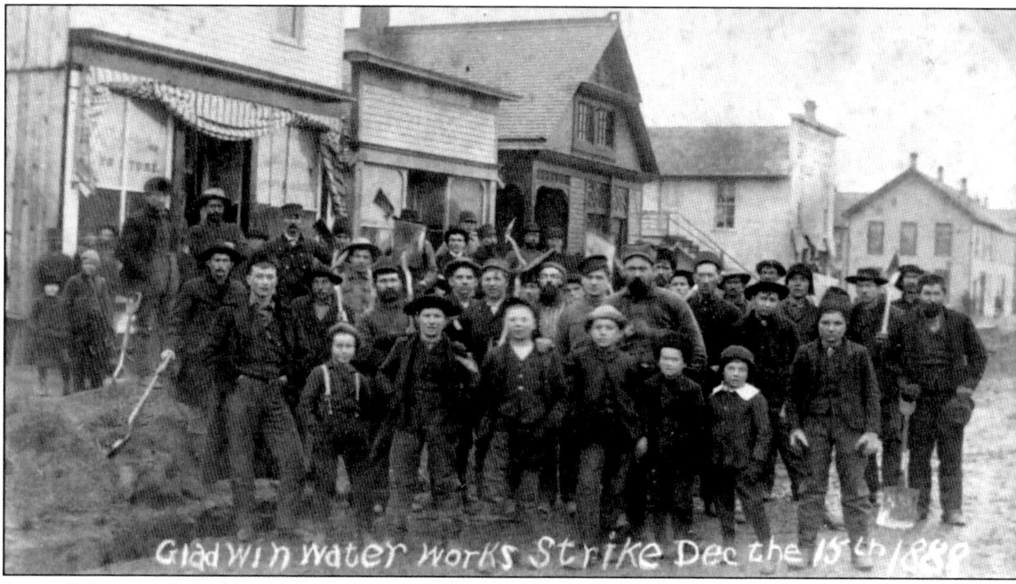

From left to right, the picture above shows a store, the post office, and the abstract building in 1888, which housed the Gladwin Abstract Company until 2007. The men in front of these buildings are the trench diggers for Gladwin's first waterworks. They went on strike to increase their wages to $1.50 per day for 10 hours of work.

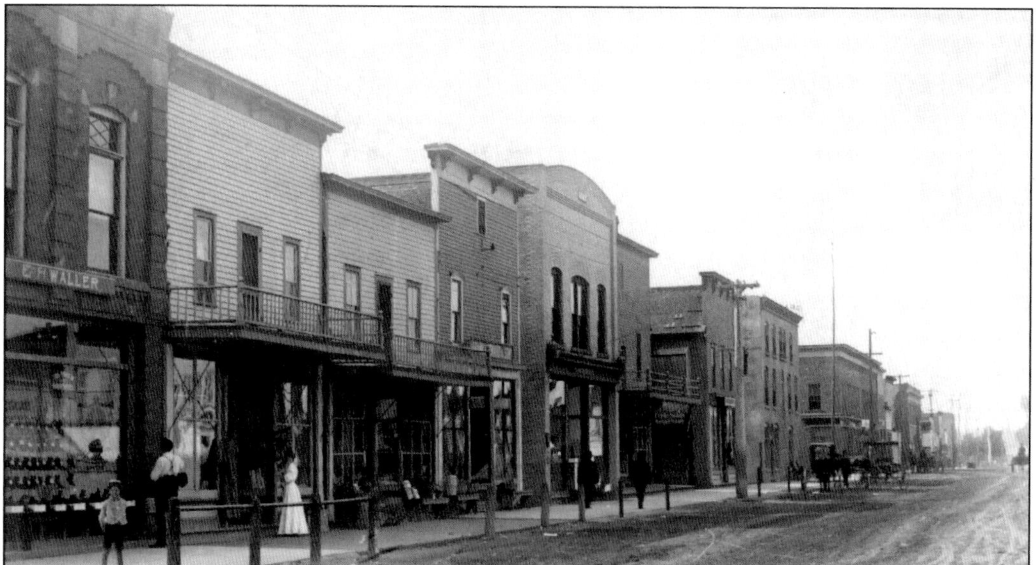

This is a view of downtown Gladwin around 1903. It shows the south end of Cedar Avenue from Silverleaf Street. The corner store was once the Foutch Restaurant. The next three stores burned in 1910 and were replaced in 1911. The Simply Charmed store and Mill End are there now. Sam Goldberg's store had the rounded top.

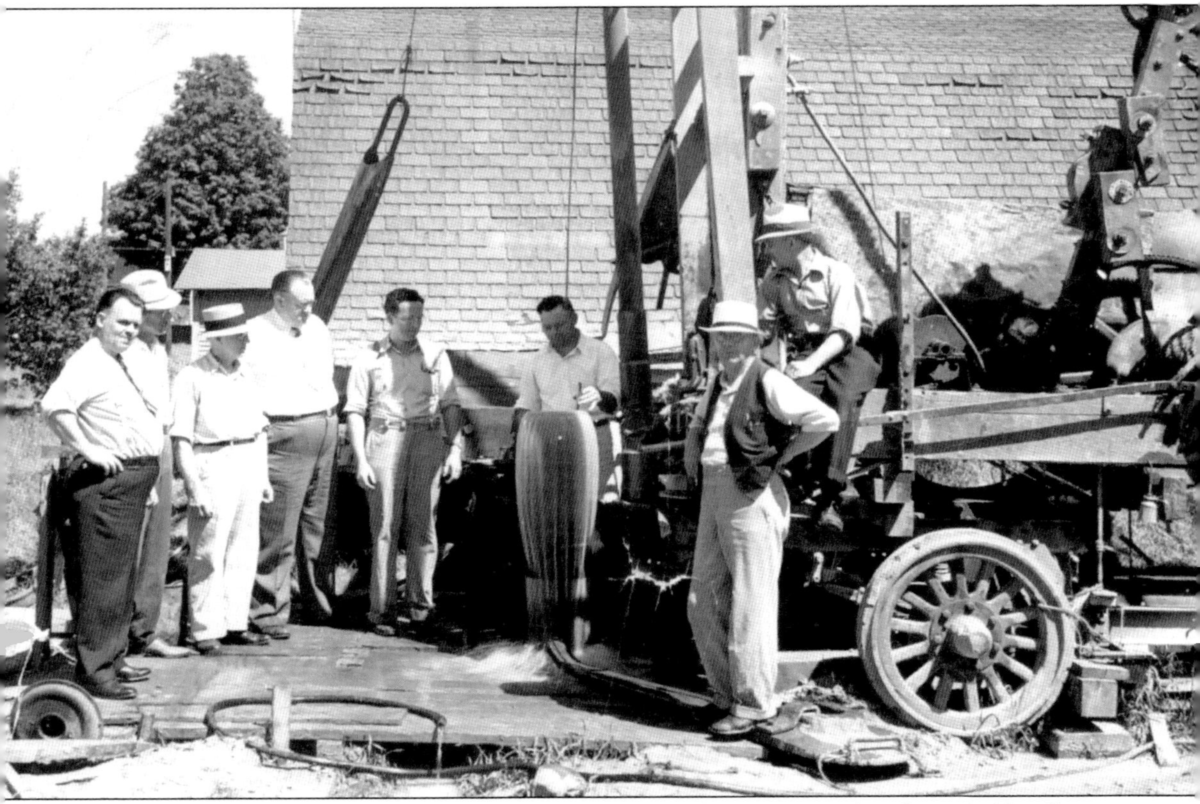

A new village well was drilled for the Gladwin Waterworks in 1889 with a flow of 125 gallons per minute. Getting water to the east end of town became an issue in the early 1900s, as one of many major fires in Gladwin's history broke out. Most townspeople watched as the east end burned; neither water nor enough fire hose reached that far. The picture above shows a new well being drilled for city water in 1937.

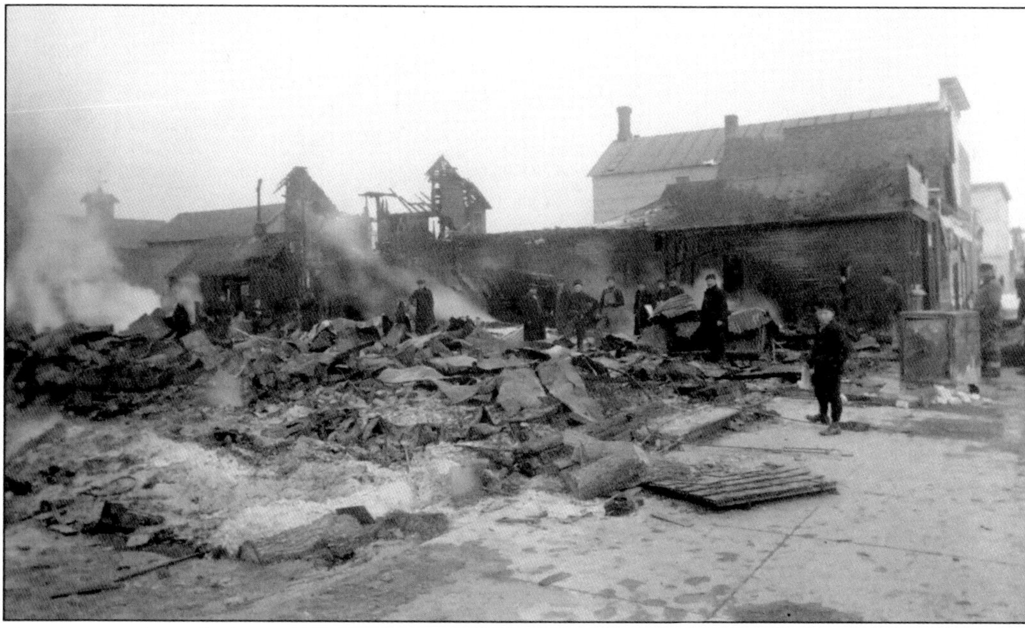

Fires have plagued the county and city of Gladwin throughout its existence. The first fire department in 1880 included a two-wheeled cart and a hose. In 1900, a fire took out one third of the city at a cost of $100,000 in damage. This fire in 1906 destroyed Isaac Hanna's store and one block of Cedar Avenue. The first building standing is the old Gladwin County Record office and the next building is the abstract building, which is still there today. (Courtesy of Clarke Historical Library.)

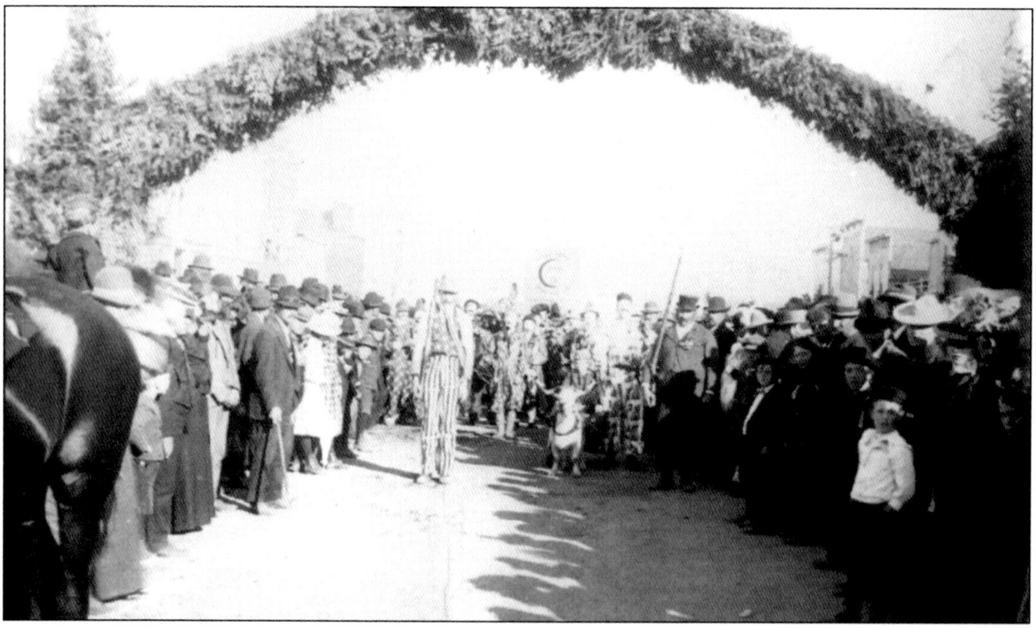

The first Gladwin Street Fair took place October 5 and 6 in 1899. At the corner of Cedar Avenue and Arcade Street, a 30-foot arch was erected to span the street with the word "Welcome" in big letters across the peak. This is a picture of the 1905 street fair with William Sainsbury dressed as Uncle Sam.

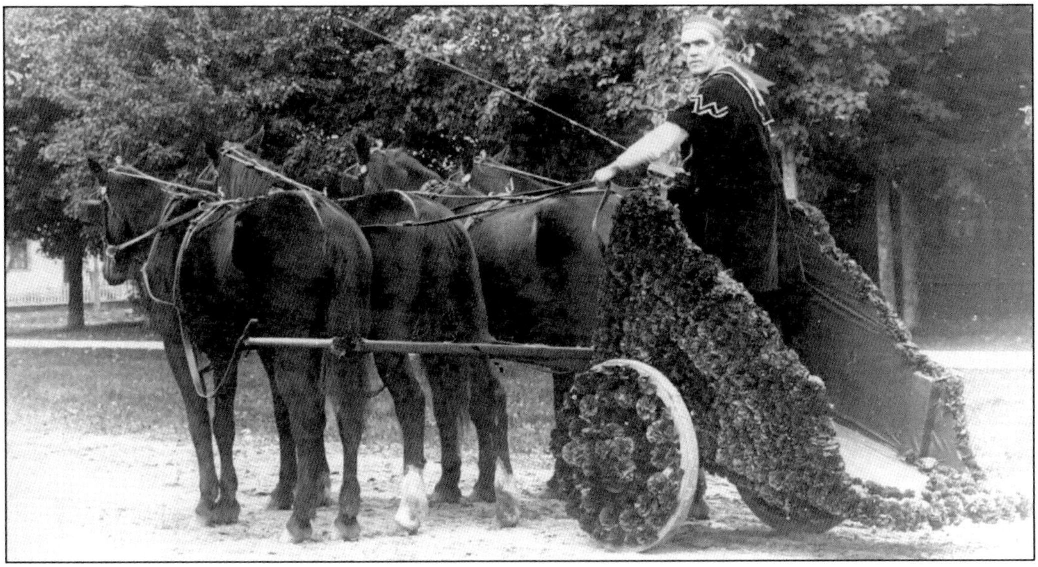

The man in the chariot is Earl Murdock, a participant in the 1906 Gladwin Street Fair. People came from all over central Michigan to watch the parades on both days during the first weekend in October. The floats were sponsored by local businesses and service clubs like Goldberg's Store and the Independent Order of Odd Fellows. Other activities included an art exhibit, a cake walk, and a bicycle decoration contest. The street fair probably lasted about 10 years, as the Gladwin County Fairgrounds was purchased in 1910.

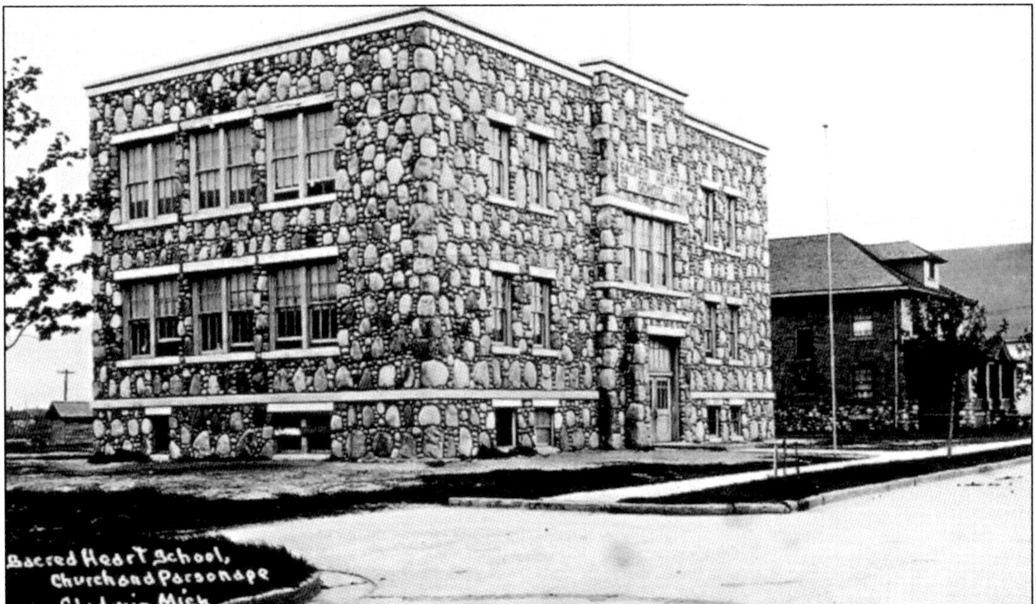

People of the parish, with their own lumber and fieldstone, built the Sacred Heart Catholic School in 1917 and 1918. It was said that Fr. Wendell Miller selected each stone. The two-story school opened in the fall of 1918 with five Sisters of Mercy teaching eight grades. Almost one year after the opening of the school, Miller died suddenly at the age of 42. The entire community mourned the loss.

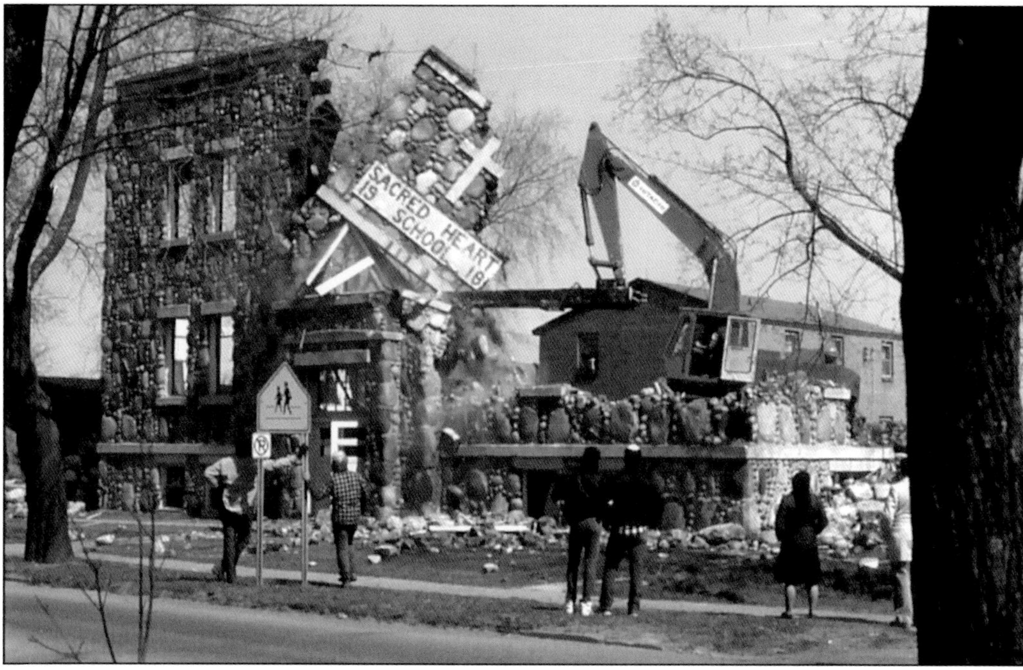

The Sacred Heart Parish School, built with fieldstone brought to the church, survived until 1986. Although many parishioners wanted to preserve the historic building, the repairs necessary to bring it up to code were cost prohibitive. Efforts to save the cross over the entrance crumbled, as it too was made from individual stones. (Courtesy of Ben Ball.)

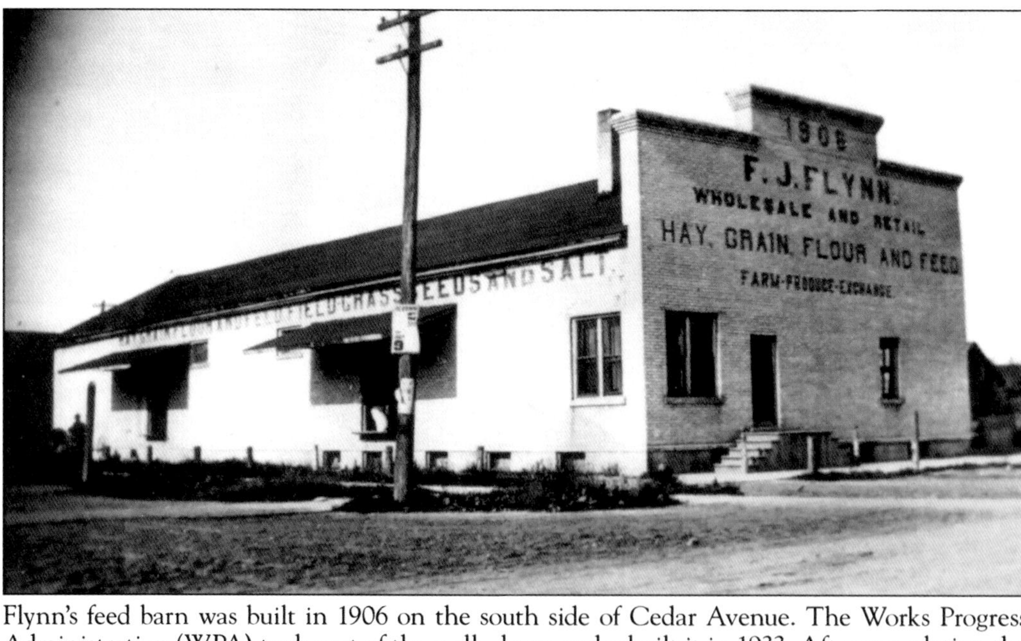

Flynn's feed barn was built in 1906 on the south side of Cedar Avenue. The Works Progress Administration (WPA) took part of the walls down and rebuilt it in 1933. After completing the project, it was renamed the Gladwin Community Building. (Courtesy of John Rhode.)

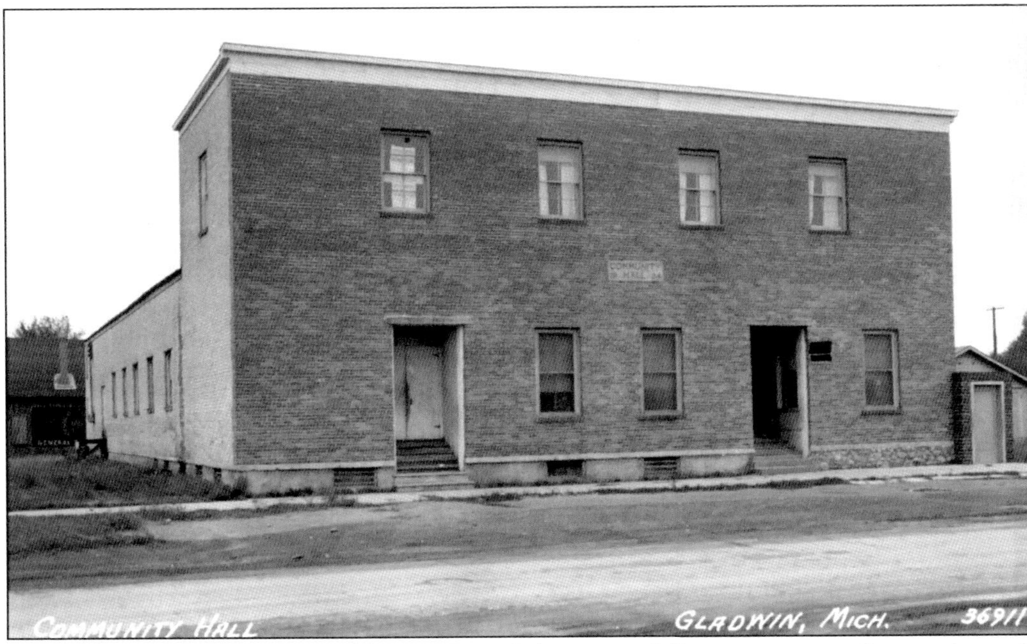

The Gladwin Community Building was used for many different purposes. It was the only gymnasium in town, and it had locker rooms in the basement. It had a stage for plays, served as city hall for a time, and housed the Gladwin Library for many years. It is now empty.

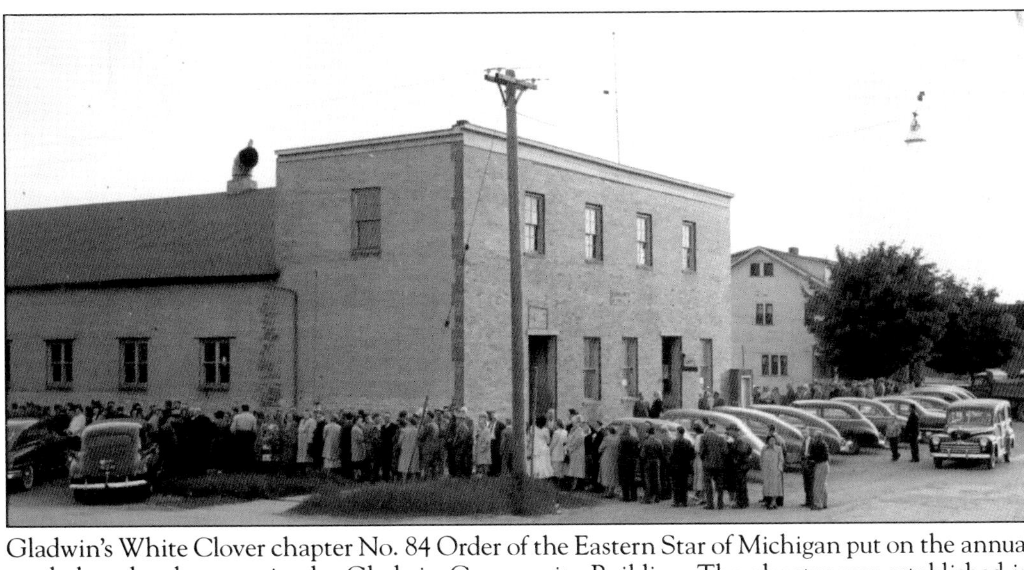

Gladwin's White Clover chapter No. 84 Order of the Eastern Star of Michigan put on the annual cattle breeders banquet in the Gladwin Community Building. The chapter was established in 1891 and is an affiliate organization of the Masons. Most Eastern Star chapters are noted for having excellent cooks, and the White Clover members have maintained that reputation. From the number of people lined up to eat in this 1949 photograph, one can assume the meal was good Gladwin beef and reasonably priced.

Here is a picture of the Gladwin County Library's new Bookmobile, which was purchased and began operating in 1962. Pictured from left to right inspecting the new vehicle are Lena Cronin, Etta Wilson, Else Kelly (the Gladwin librarian) on the step, and her husband, Wayne Kelly, in the truck. The Bookmobile only ran for five years and was discontinued for lack of funding. (Courtesy of Gladwin District Library.)

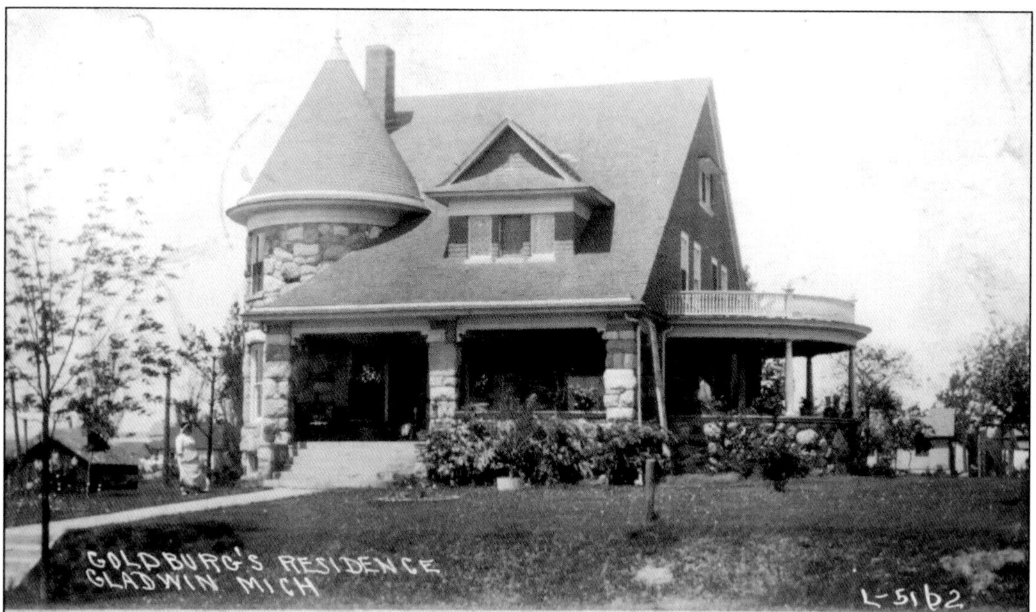

A young lawyer named Fern Smith started construction on his home on Cedar Avenue in 1898. Before its completion four years later, he died of typhoid fever at the age of 36. His funeral was held in the unfinished home. Charlotte Sutherland, Smith's granddaughter, still owns the home, and is now the Century 21 offices.

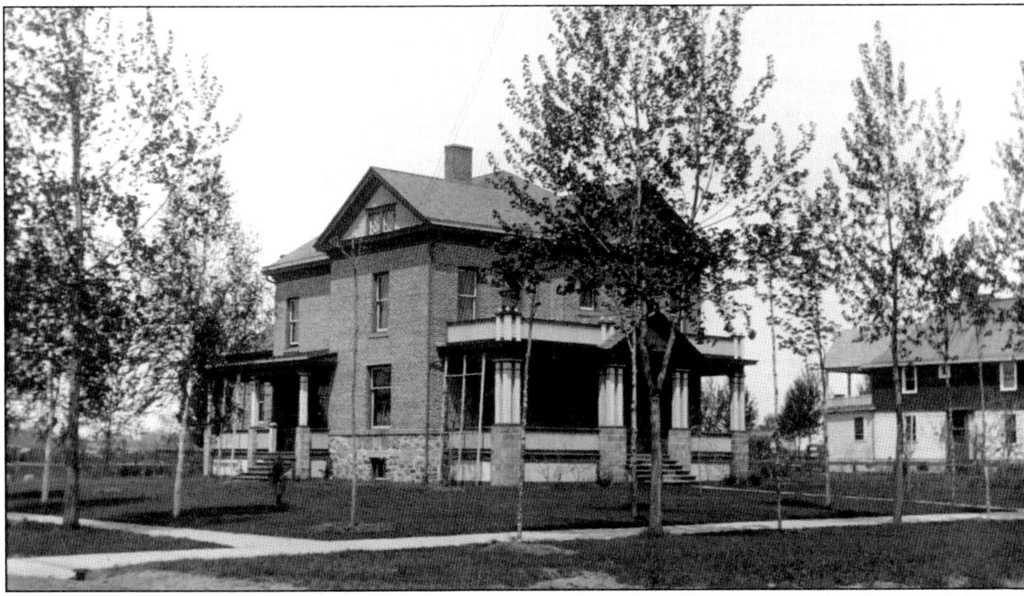

The Shaffer home on Bowery Street was constructed in 1904. It was one of the first brick homes built in Gladwin. John Shaffer, the owner and builder, owned a brick company and was also a contractor. He retired in 1903 a very wealthy man and continued to live in his home until his death in 1919.

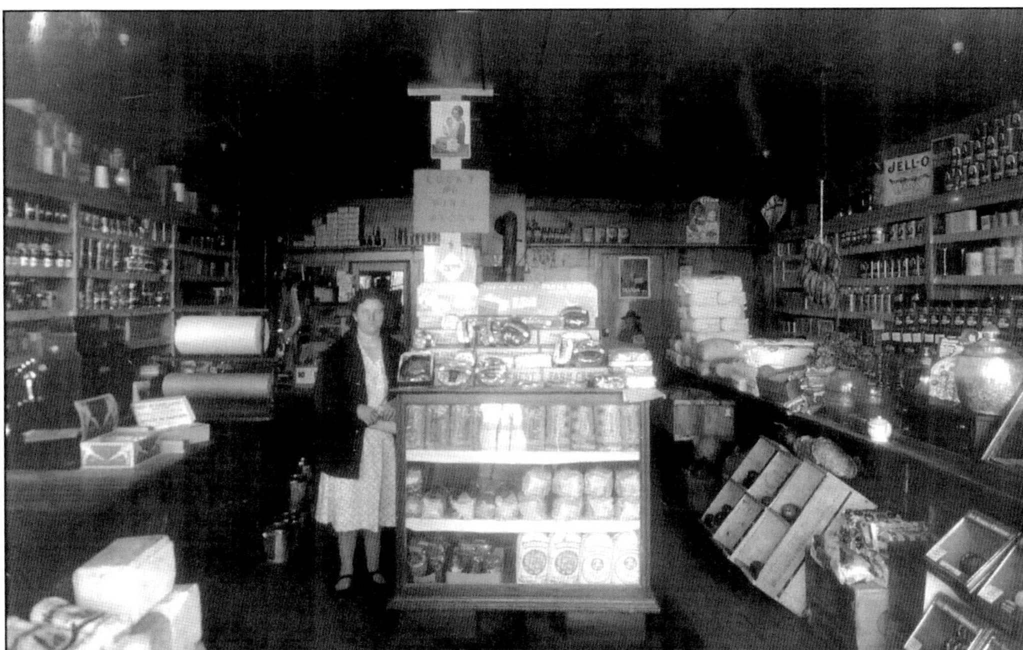

Martha Schindel Erdman was born in Ohio and moved to Gladwin in 1914 at the age of nine. The photograph above shows her in William Bollert's grocery store on Silverleaf Street. She and her husband, Albert, bought the business in October 1930. Prior to that, the Erdman's ran an ice cream station in part of the old Farmer's Home Hotel, which then became the Behnke Garage. (Courtesy of Nadine Erdman Saiki.)

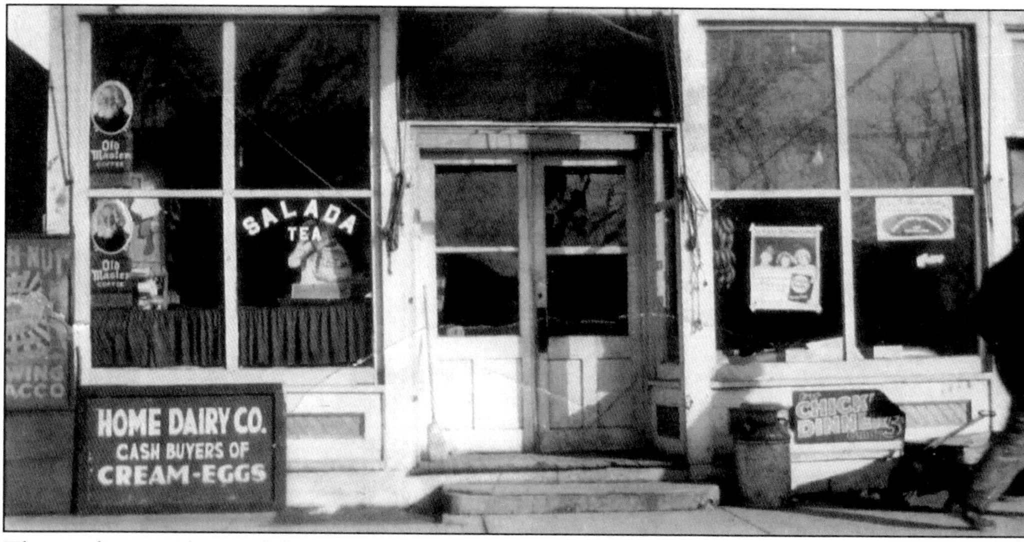

This is the storefront of the Home Dairy Company, which was owned by Albert and Martha Erdman. The site was formerly a grocery store. The Great Depression ended the business in 1932. They moved to Detroit where Albert worked in a factory until he earned enough money to return to Gladwin. He bought an 80-acre farm in Sage Township in 1933. (Courtesy of Nadine Erdman Saiki.)

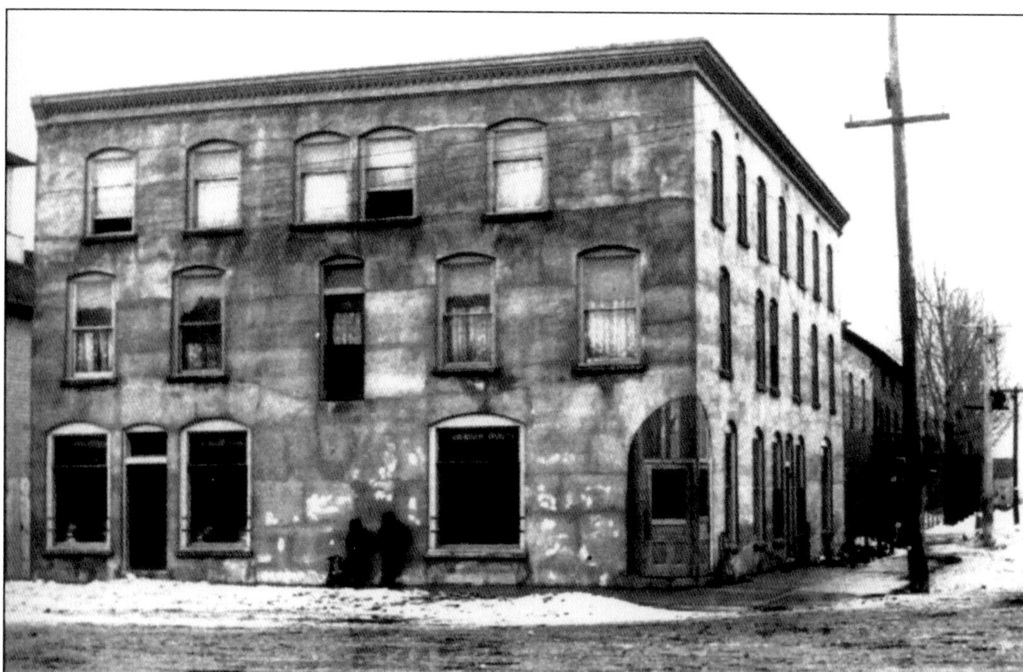

The Graham house on the corner of Antler Street and Cedar Avenue was built in 1893 and was originally called the New Commercial Hotel. The proprietor, Allen Whitman, advertised the hotel as a first-class house, and rates were $2 per day. The landlord, Alex Graham, added the three-story concrete portion in 1900. The Graham family operated the hotel until new owners changed the name to the Hotel Gladwin in 1936. (Courtesy of John Rhode.)

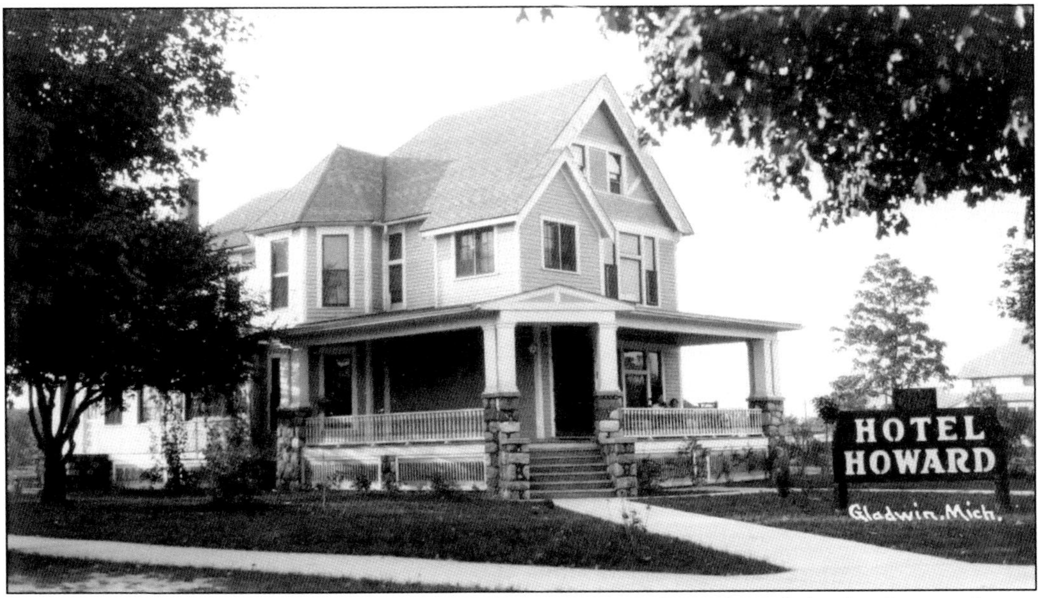

The Hotel Howard was located on the northwest corner of Maple and Antler Streets. It was originally the home of Hugh McClary. The hotel had a reputation for being a clean place to stay. That was not the case for the cabins out back. They had a somewhat more dubious reputation. The cabins disappeared first, which may have had something to do with the former mayor living nearby, and the hotel burned in 1973. Maple Manor is now on this corner.

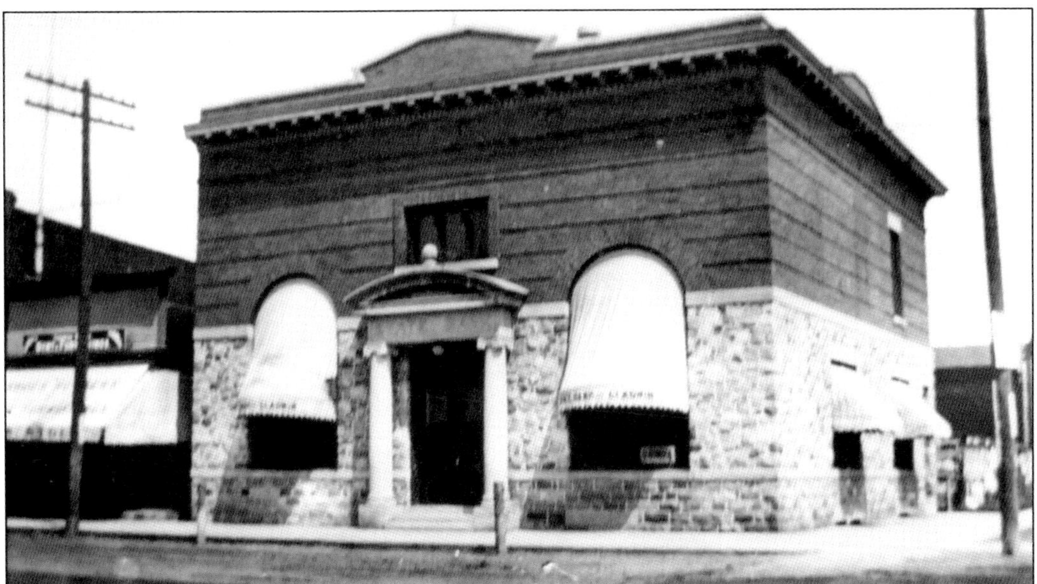

The first bank in Gladwin was a framed building on the corner of Antler Street and Cedar Avenue. In 1907, the brick building shown above was built across the street from the original bank and opened as the State Saving Bank. It was remodeled and enlarged in 1912, and then in 1927, the bank merged with the Gladwin State Bank. Another major remodeling took place in 1958, and the site is now occupied by a dentist's office.

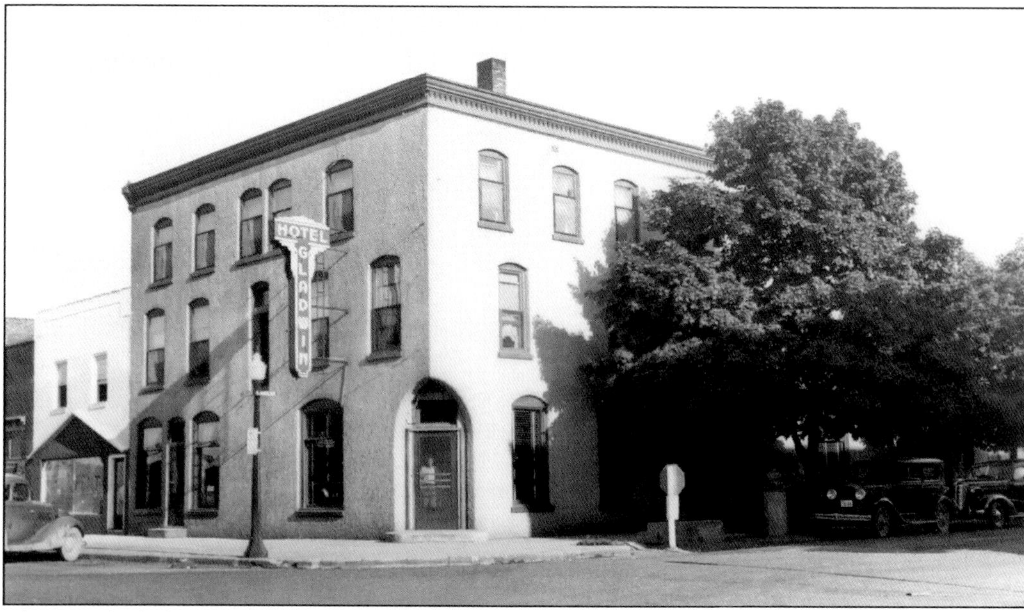

The Hotel Gladwin has gone through multiple owners. Frank and Walt Swartz took over in 1937 and operated the hotel until 1945. One interesting addition they made was a four-lane bowling alley. It was located on the back-west side of the first floor along Antler Street. Part of the dining room was taken out to make room. The next long-term owners were Pete and Louise Schultz, who ran the facility for 16 years. Louise sold out to the Heinbergs after her husband's death in 1971. The building was already starting to show its age when Bill Tuite bought the hotel. In 1978, the Gladwin area was hit with a huge snowstorm, dumping 18 inches onto an already snow-laden roof over the bowling alley. It could not hold the weight and collapsed. The entire building was condemned and the decision was made to demolish it. Tuite did save the bar from the lounge and it is still in use at the Hotel Bar on that familiar corner of downtown Gladwin.

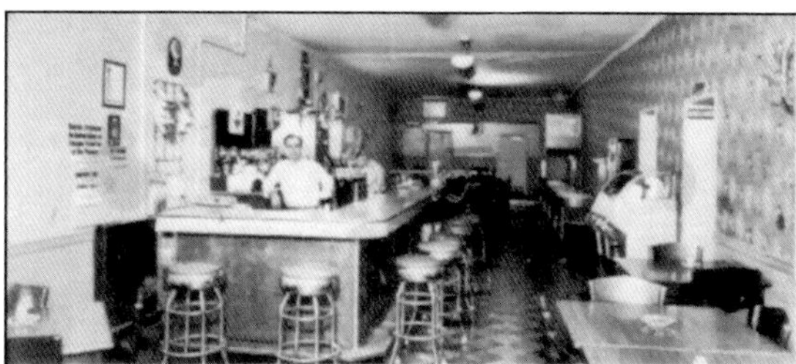

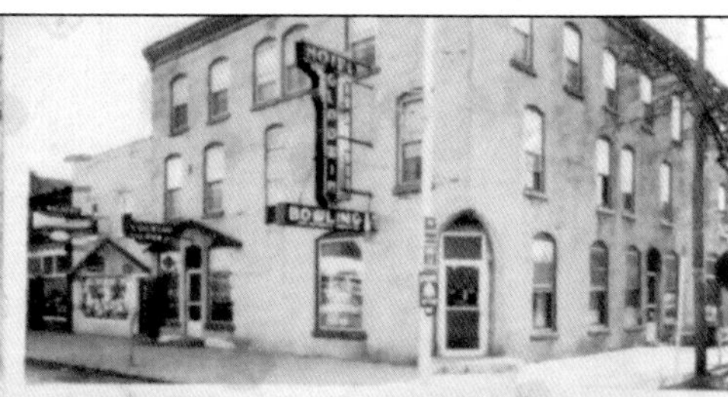

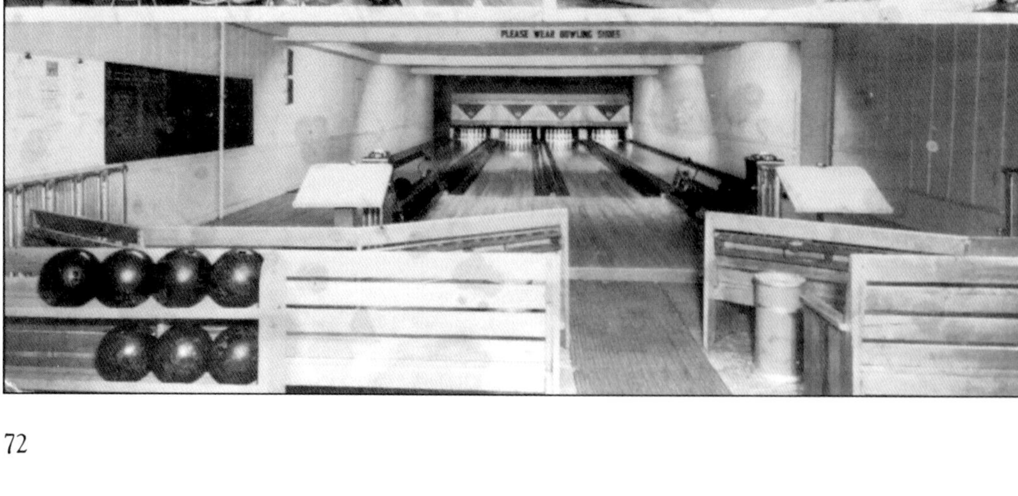

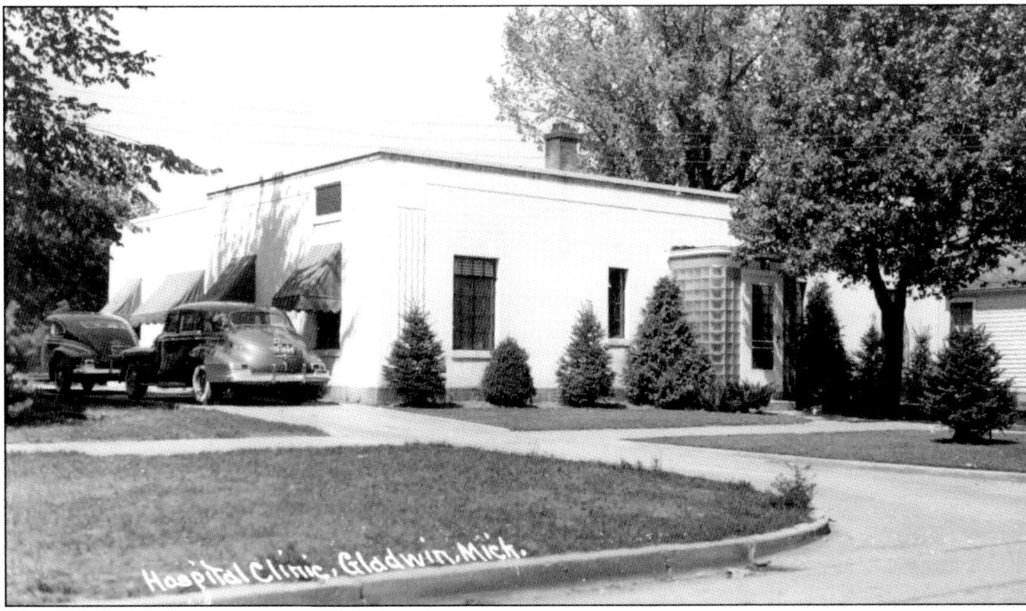

The first hospital in Gladwin was started in the Dutcher house in 1913, which is the one block north of Maple Manor on North Silverleaf Street. The picture above shows the private hospital built in 1938, which started as a 43 bed facility by Dr. Keith Coulter and Dr. Lawrence LaPorte. Gladwin is now served by a branch of the Mid-Michigan Health System.

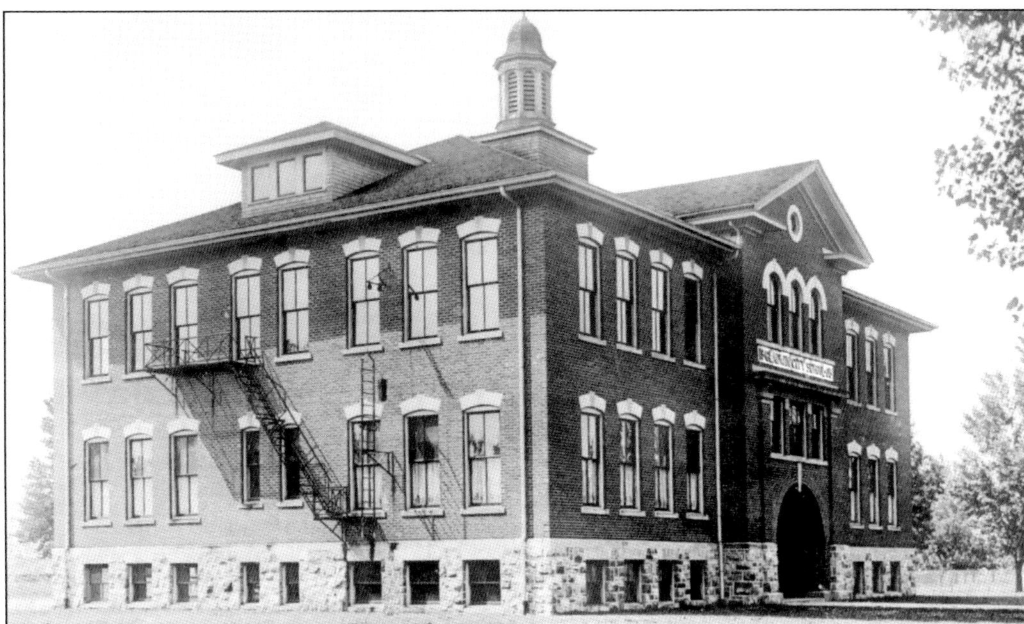

Gladwin's first school was built on land purchased from C. C. Foutch for $100. That land still has an educational building on it today. The high school shown here was the third school built, completed in 1905. Several additions later, it served the school district until it was torn down in 1967.

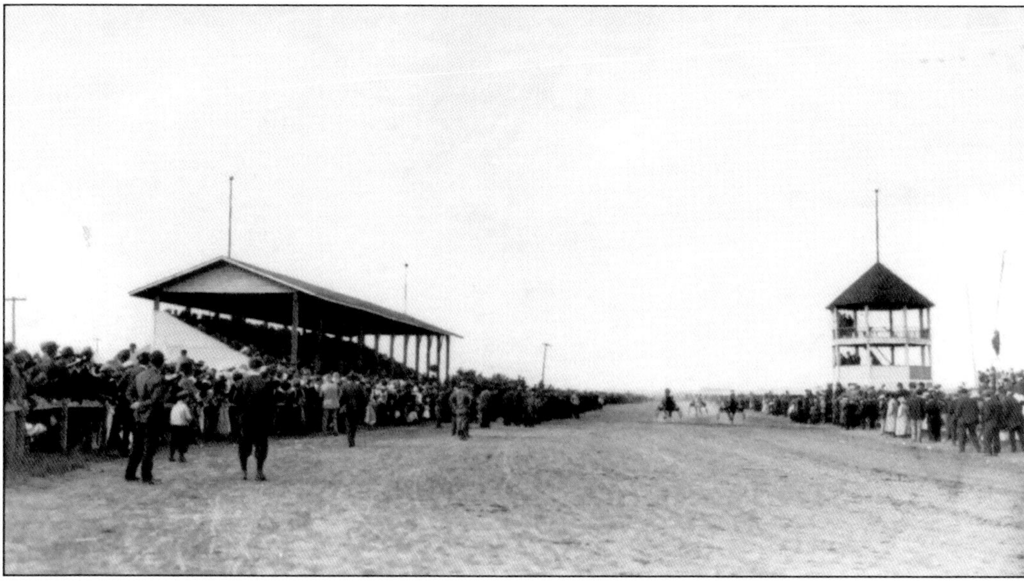

The Gladwin County fairgrounds was purchased in 1910 and is still operating today on south State Street. Horse racing was a popular event and the half-mile track has held many races for about a century. Each summer, the grounds are filled with agricultural products, livestock, and 4-H activities.

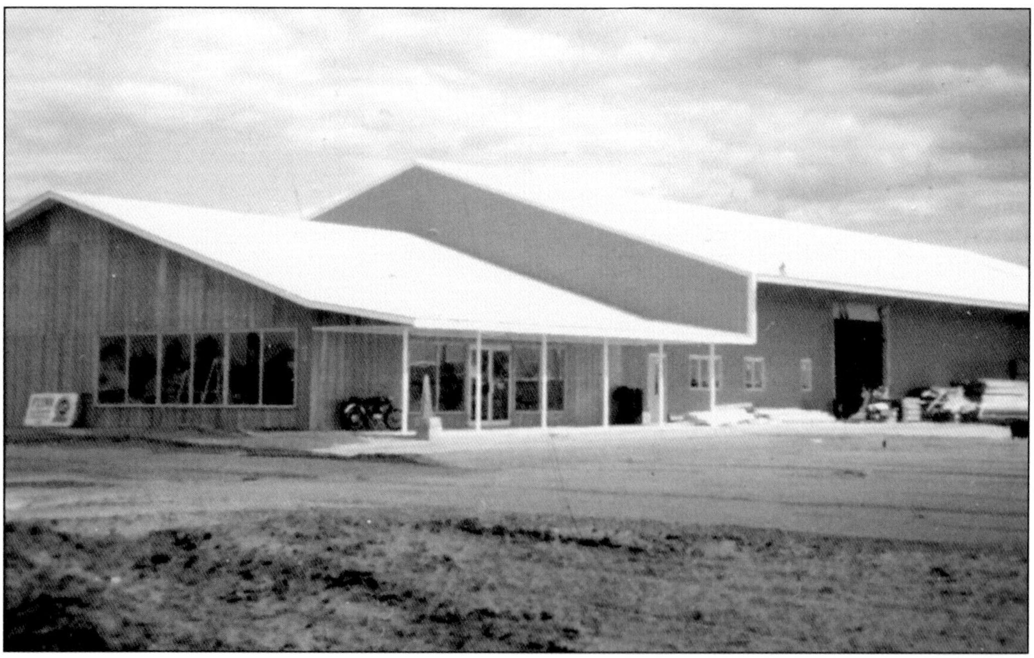

Flynn's Lumber operated on the corner of Antler and Maple Streets from 1947 to 1970. Ray Flynn's office was in Dr. Floyd Myers' animal clinic. In 1970, the company moved to the east end of town on Cedar Avenue, and the old property is now the parking area for National City Bank. On the left is the new Flynn's Lumber, and on the right is Flynn's old office and the after-hours animal clinic. (Courtesy of Margaret Flynn.)

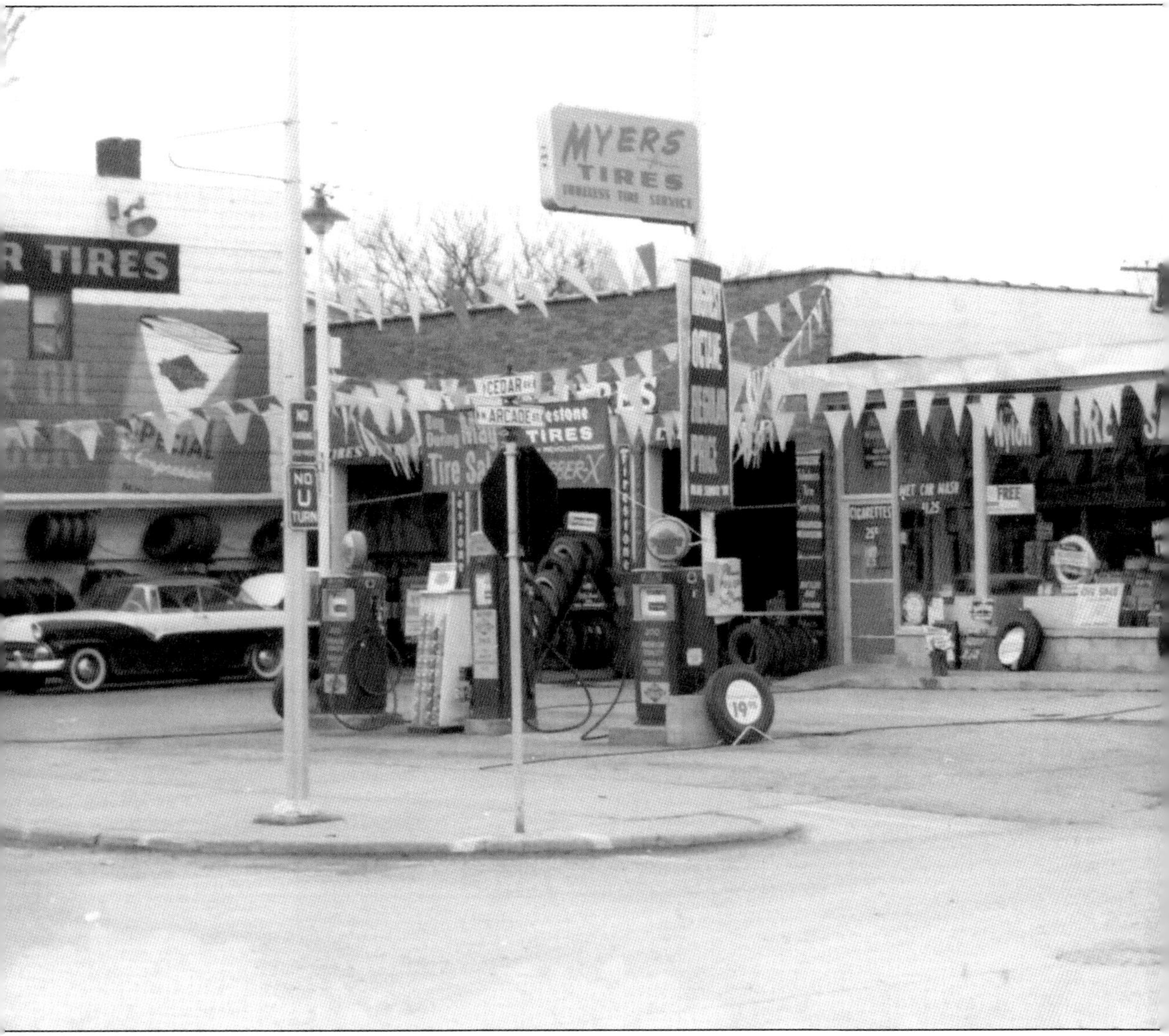

Needing something for his son Ralph to do, Floyd started the Myers Tire and Service Station on the corner of Arcade Street and Cedar Avenue in 1930. The business remained there until Ralph turned the business over to his son in 1983. At that time, the decision was made to move into the old Wolverine Camper building at the east side of town on Cedar Avenue. It remains there today as one of the oldest continually operating businesses in Gladwin. (Courtesy of Betty Myers.)

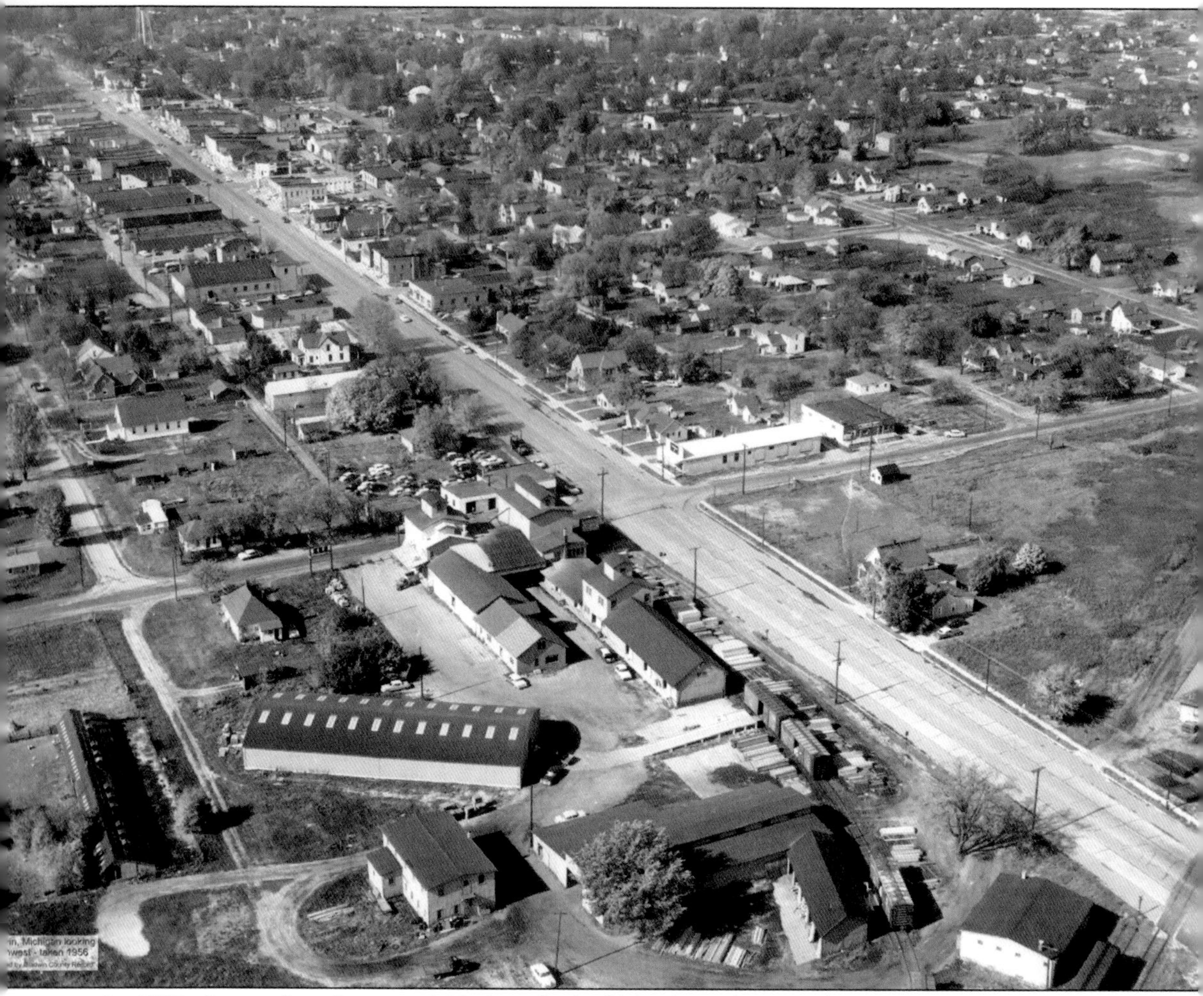

In 1956, this is what the city of Gladwin looked like from the air. This view is from the east end of town looking west. The big buildings in the foreground are primarily for Wolohan's lumber storage. The railroad tracks go to the elevator, which is now a Marathon gas station. Most of this space now has a strip mall and the newspaper office. Notice the railroad depot on the far right. It was moved to open space on the north corner of Cedar Avenue and State streets where the Gladwin Historical Society village is located. (Courtesy of Robert Frei.)

Eight

Crossroads around the County

In the 1860s, there were no roads in Gladwin County. Rivers were the highways and a few Native American trails took the early settlers from the northern edge of Midland County to the prime forests in the north. Two roads appeared on the 1873 map of the county, one from Loomis to Grout Township and the other from Edenville to the lumber camp known as Gladwin City. Logging trails and small gauge rails eventually became roads. Stops along the tracks eventually became towns. Farmers willing to carve out a road to pay their taxes got put on the map. In many cases, the road was not identified until someone got electricity and then needed a billing address. Some of the crossroads stuck, including Estey. But many have disappeared altogether. Places like Hard Luck, Wagarville, Winegars, Highwood, and Podunk are just locations on the map now. Other places like Albright Shores and Sugar Springs are large resort areas that are not even identified. Not all roads lead somewhere. In some cases, they just come to an end in the middle of nowhere.

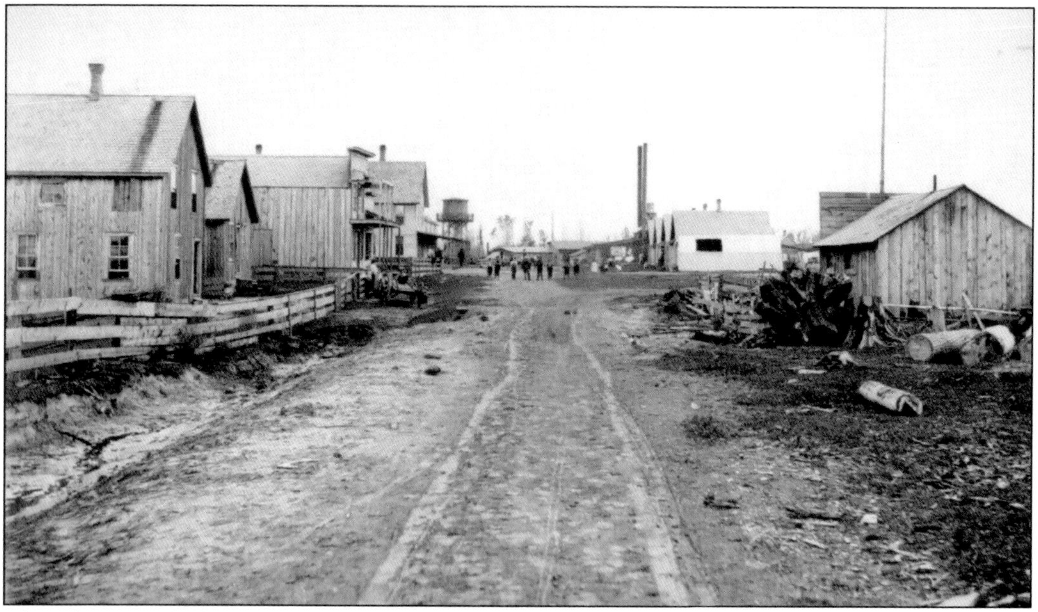

This photograph shows the Estey crossroads in the late 1890s.

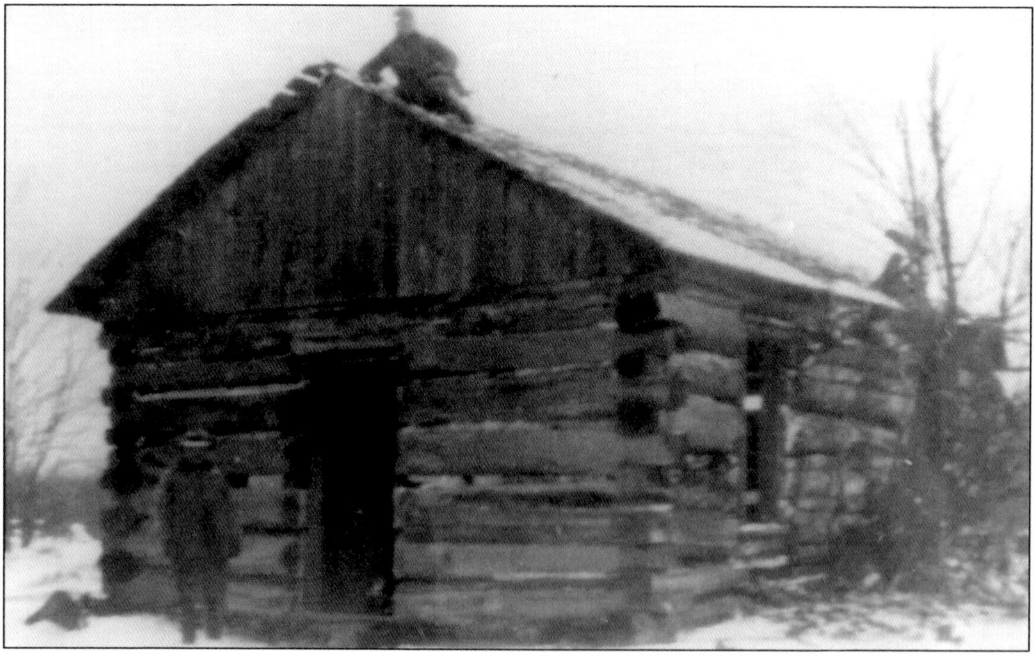

The first Estey school was built in 1891 one mile north of town. Here Paul Witte on the roof and Henry Mohrman are in the process of dismantling the school in 1926. A second, much bigger school had been built a half mile closer to Estey in 1905. When it burned, a third was built in 1911 and remained open until 1956.

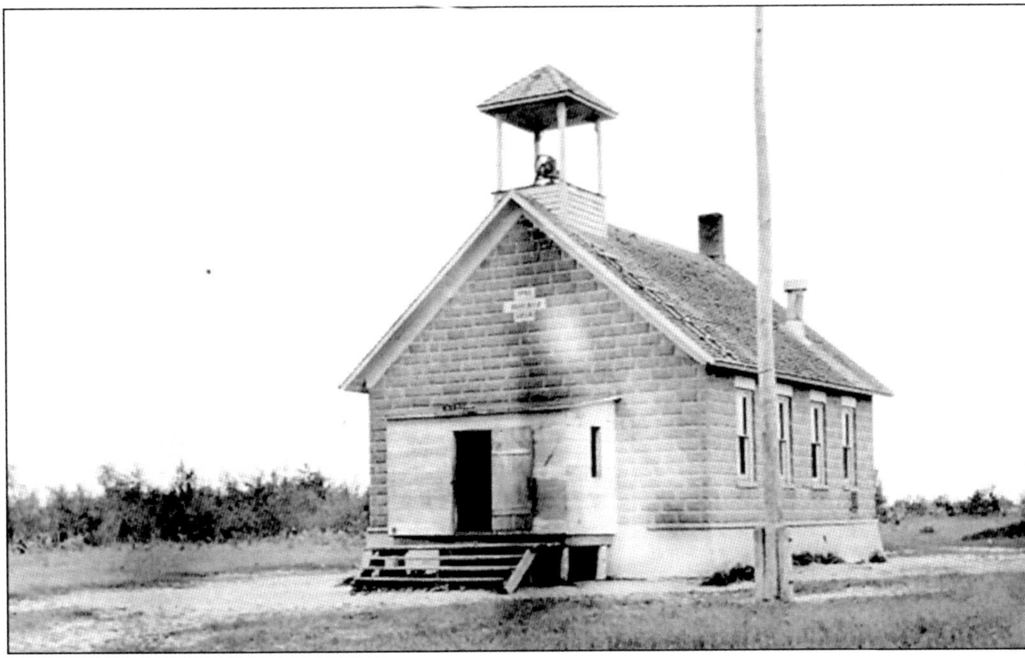

The first school built in Lyle was a small, wooden structure across the railroad tracks from the store. The picture above is the second school; a cement block one-room school building that was constructed on the corner of Lyle Road and Wade Road in 1910. It has since been remodeled many times and is part of a residential home today. (Courtesy of Virginia McCulloch.)

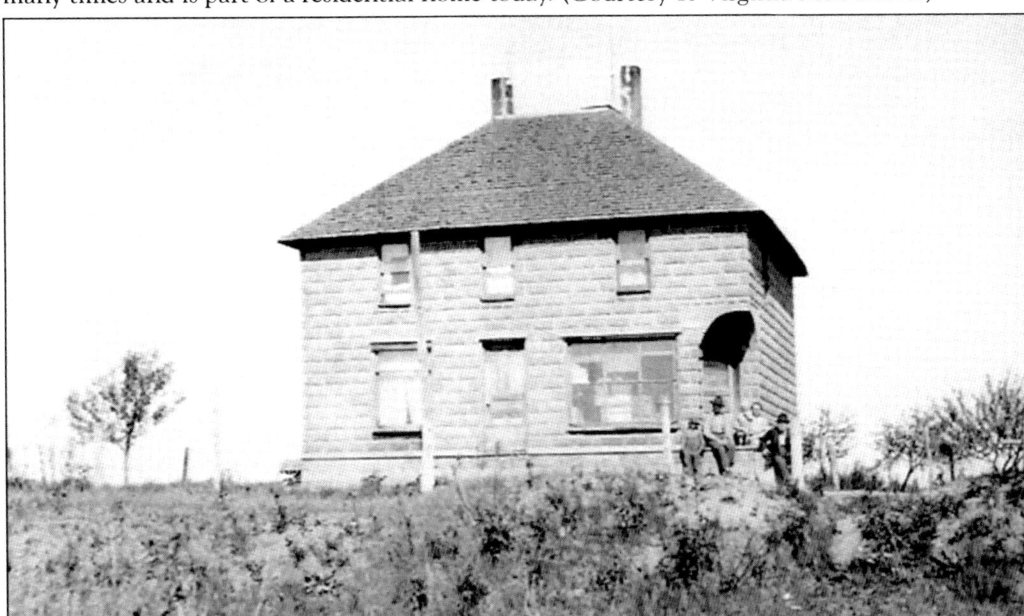

Fred Drake built the Lyle store in 1907. It was located in an area lumber camp originally known as Halfway because it was halfway between Beaverton and the railroad. Drake changed the name to Lyle after his daughter because there was a post office already named Halfway. The arched door in the corner was the portion of the house where the store and post office were located. (Courtesy of Inez Soldan.)

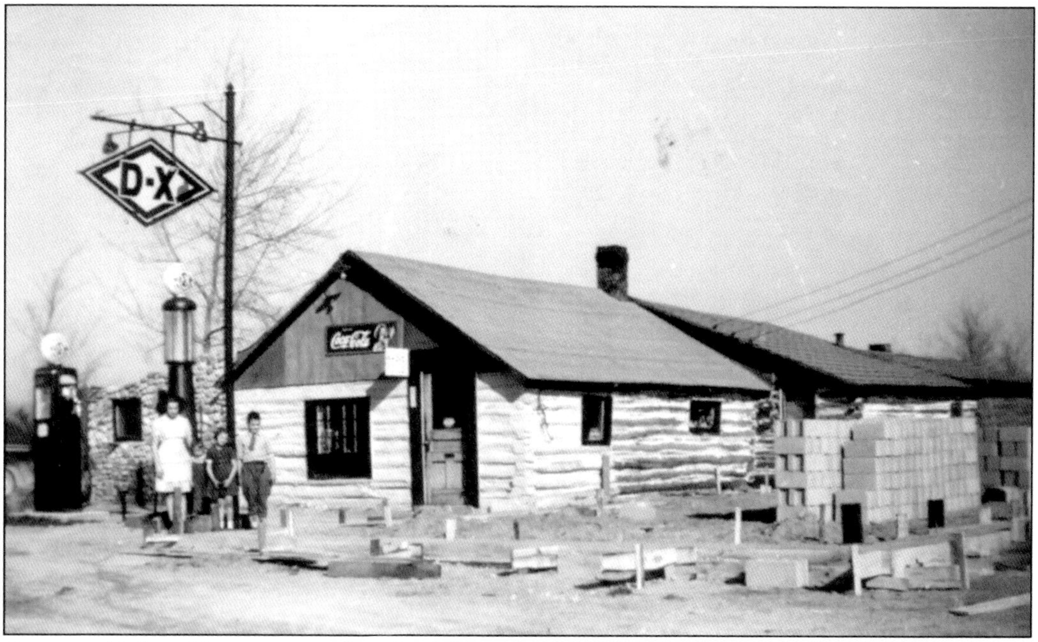

Oscar and Jelina Toutant moved to the Indian Lake area in 1945. They built the Toutant Store on Indian Lake Road and operated it for 40 years. It used to be located right on Michigan 30, and business was brisk. They added on to serve food and that is where everyone met for morning coffee. In 1960, the highway was straightened and the Toutant store became "off the beaten path." Despite this hardship, the store remains open still today. (Courtesy of Nancy Nakkula Prescott.)

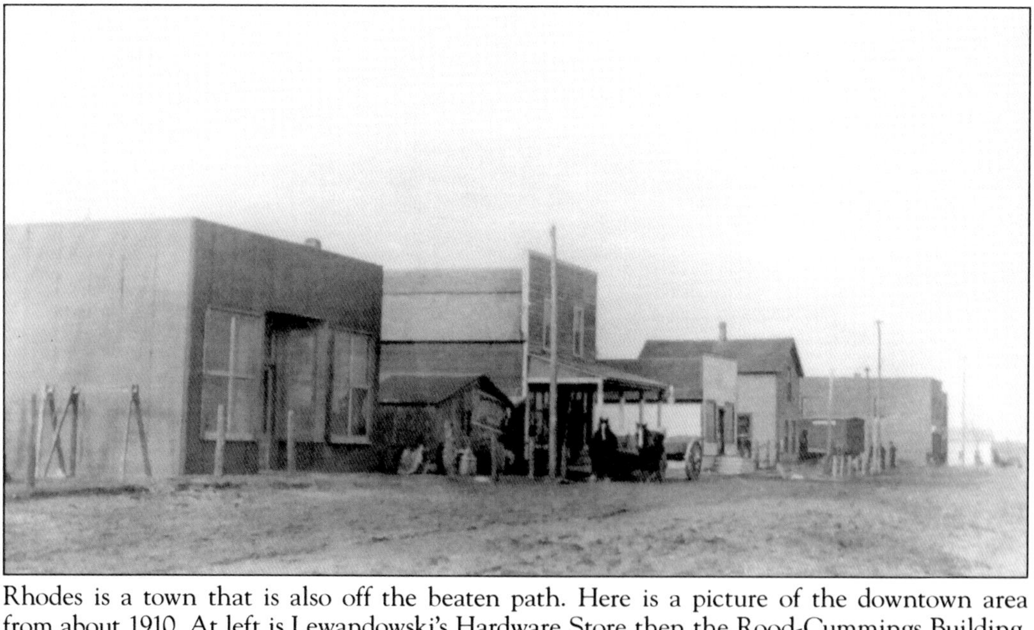

Rhodes is a town that is also off the beaten path. Here is a picture of the downtown area from about 1910. At left is Lewandowski's Hardware Store then the Rood-Cummings Building. Continuing left is the Varsity Bank, Conner's Dodge, and a railroad car. The large building at the far end is Hause Hardware and the post office. (Courtesy of Marilyn Freidle.)

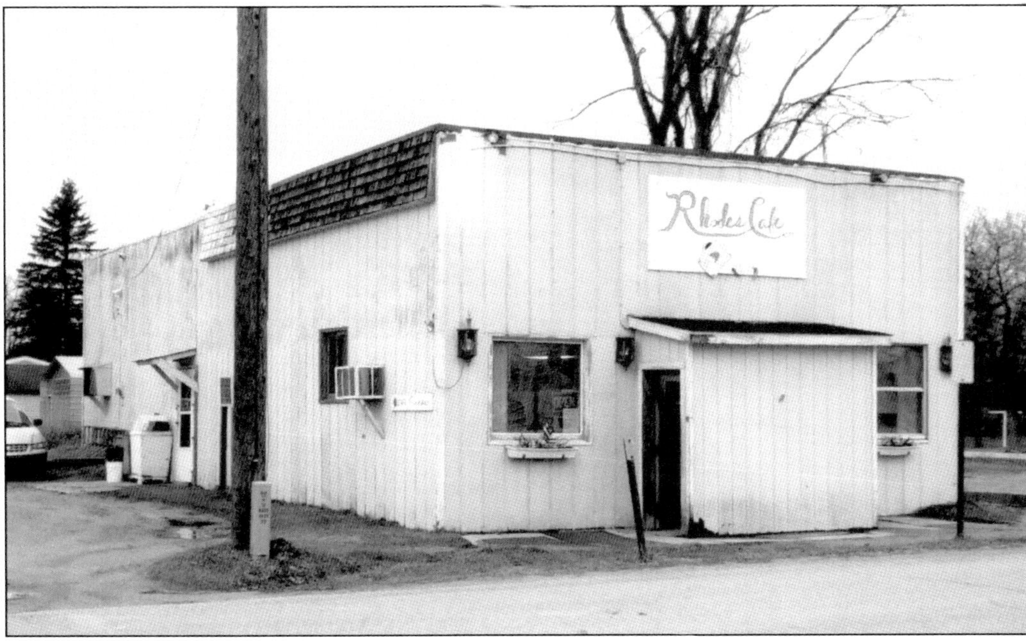

The Rhodes Café was originally Lewandowski's Hardware Store and is one of the few buildings left from the early days. Rhodes is located in Bentley Township, which started appearing on Gladwin County maps in 1891 after breaking from Buckeye and Billings Townships. Bentley split in half in 1919, and Grim Township was formed. (Courtesy of Bob Frei.)

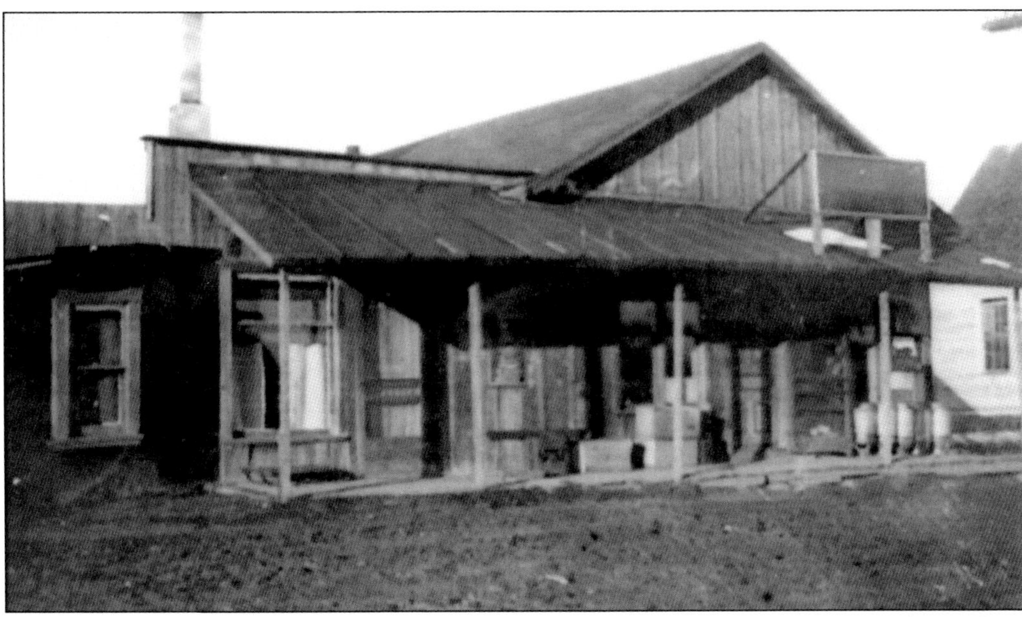

The Dale store started as a one-room log schoolhouse on the northwest corner of Dale Road and Freeman Road. Many lumber camps were located in the southern half of Tobacco Township, which separated from Billings Township in 1884. Later the building was expanded to accommodate a local store just west of the Tobacco River bridge and across from the township hall.

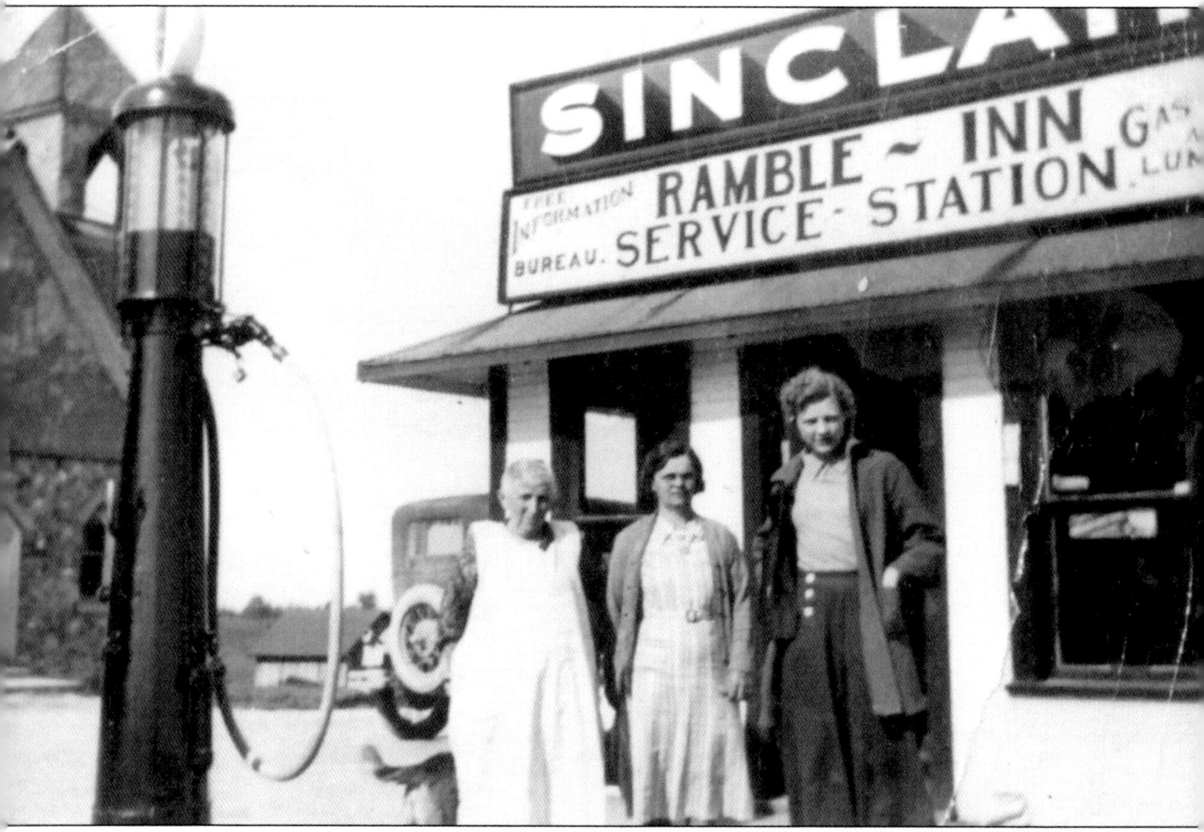

In 1923, the first settler on one of the four corners that became Skeels was Peter Tressler, who moved to the area in 1887. His son Wellington started the Sinclair gas station in 1923 on the southwest corner. On the left is Lydia Tressler, who did the cooking for the Ramble-Inn service station. Skeels actually was named after the second settler, Simon Skeels, who came in 1888 and built a log cabin and started farming on the northwest corner. Mail originally came through the nearby Meredith post office, but that closed when the railroad pulled out in 1892. Because Skeels was a Civil War veteran, the U.S. Postal Service moved a post office into his cabin and began calling the location Skeels. Mail was picked up from Gladwin first twice a week and then three times a week. Then in 1912, the government started the rural route system and took the post office out. Simon Skeels eventually donated the land where the Skeels Northern Christian School sits today, and the Ramble-Inn is long gone. (Courtesy of Stanley Smith.)

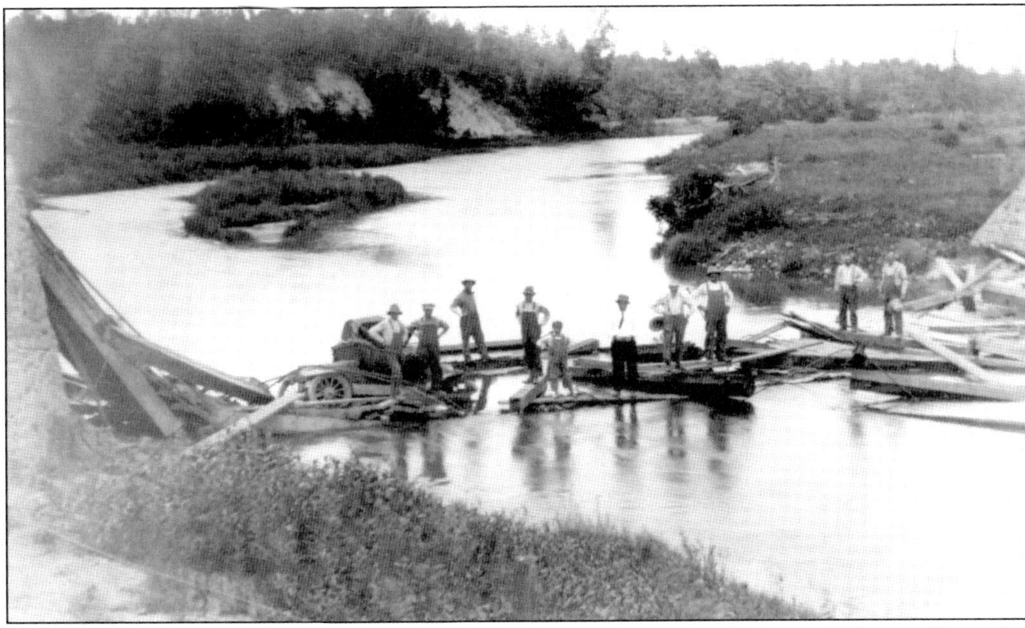

On June 30, 1914, the Dale bridge that crossed the Tobacco River in Tobacco Township unexpectedly collapsed. Notice the partially submerged car on the left. The bridge was in the process of being reinforced, but had no warning signs posted when Dr. Henry A. Barbour of Beaverton attempted to cross. He made it half way. He broke his hand in the accident and was disabled for the rest of his life.

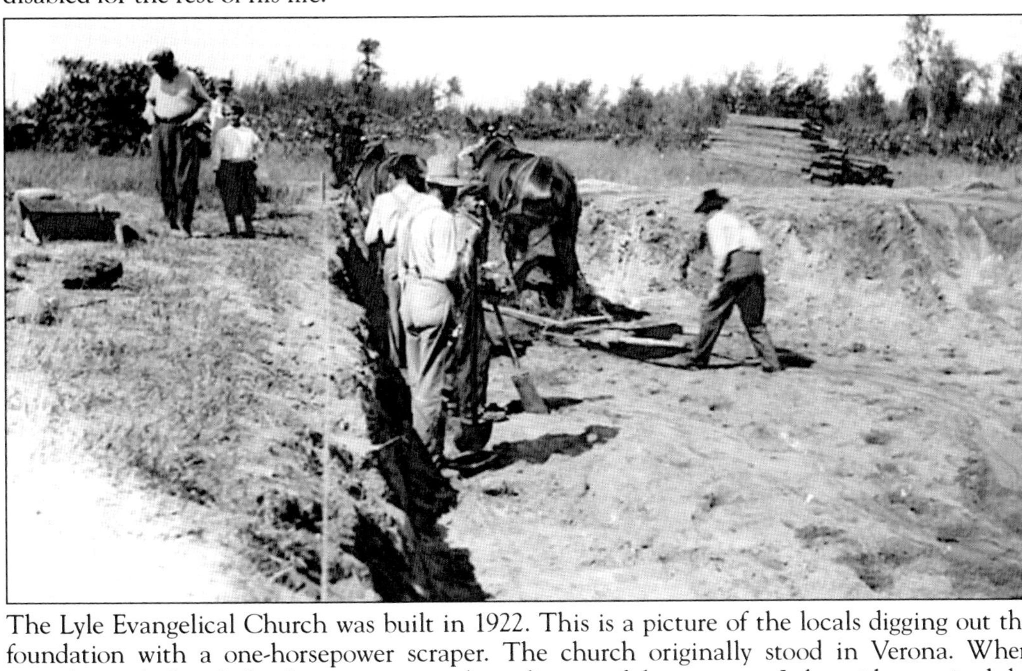

The Lyle Evangelical Church was built in 1922. This is a picture of the locals digging out the foundation with a one-horsepower scraper. The church originally stood in Verona. When attendance declined, the decision was made to dispose of the property. Lyle residents seized the opportunity to acquire the church. It was disassembled in Verona and put on a train for relocation in Lyle. Putting the Verona church back together was a community affair. The cornerstone was laid on August 20, 1922. (Courtesy of Inez Soldan.)

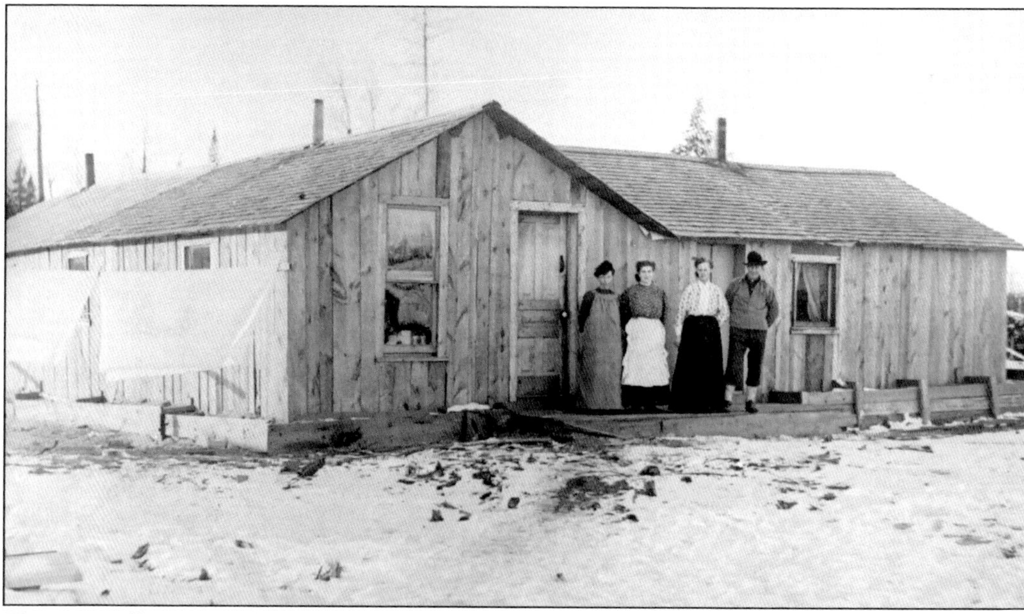

The post office was Edith Howard's boardinghouse in Bowmanville from 1880 to 1904. The town also had hotel called Highwood House, a community church, a store, and a school. The Michigan Central Railroad routed a spur initially for logs, but by 1899, four passenger trains provided passage to Gladwin.

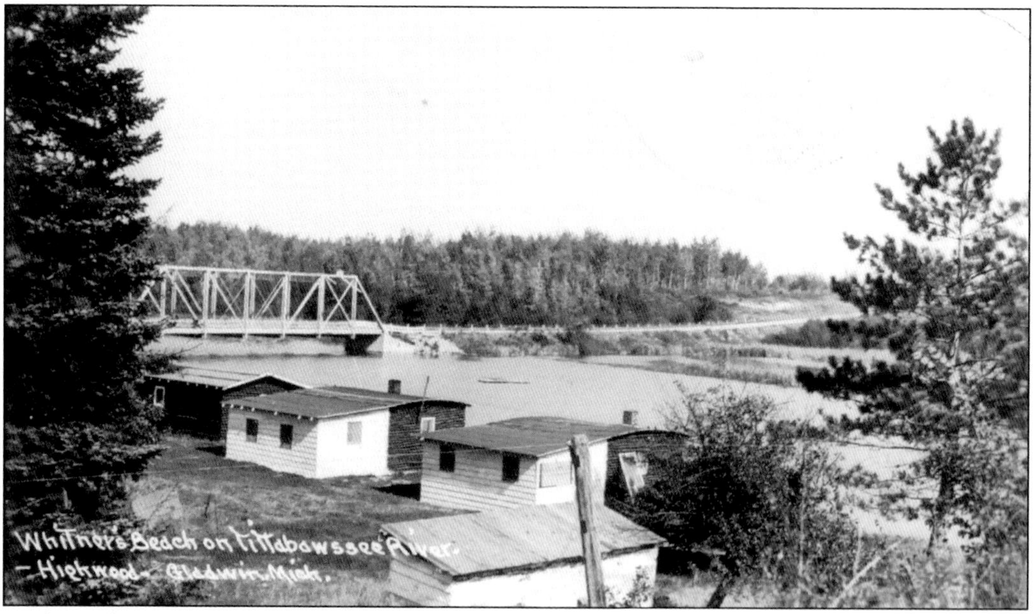

Highwood, so named because of the abundance of tall timber in the area, had one of the largest logging operations in Gladwin County. There was a shingle mill, two sawmills, and a number of lumber camps. The 1880s were booming years for Highwood.

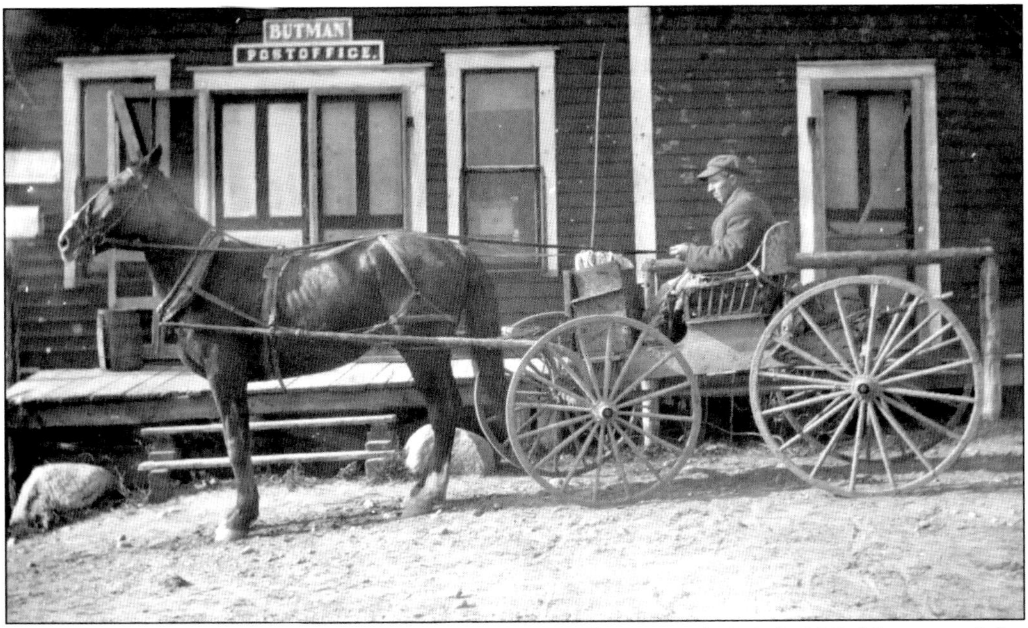

This is a picture of the Butman Store in Butman Township around 1910. L. V. Soldan owned the store at the time. Butman Township was organized in 1883 and was prime timber country. It is difficult to pinpoint the location of Soldan's store and the town of Butman because it changed multiple times over the years. (Courtesy of Inez Soldan.)

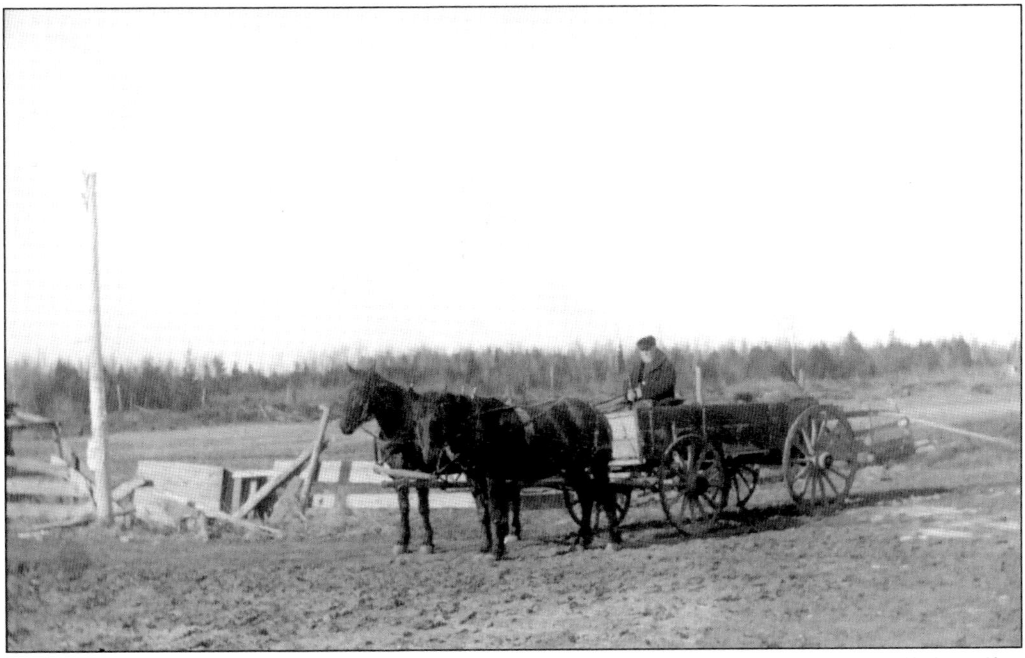

Here is Soldan getting ready to go to Gladwin to get supplies for the store. It was an all-day affair because it was approximately 28 miles round trip. Round Lake Road (F-19) was no more than a rutted wagon wheel path. What is now Michigan 18 was an improved road, but it was not paved for almost half a century. (Courtesy of Inez Soldan.)

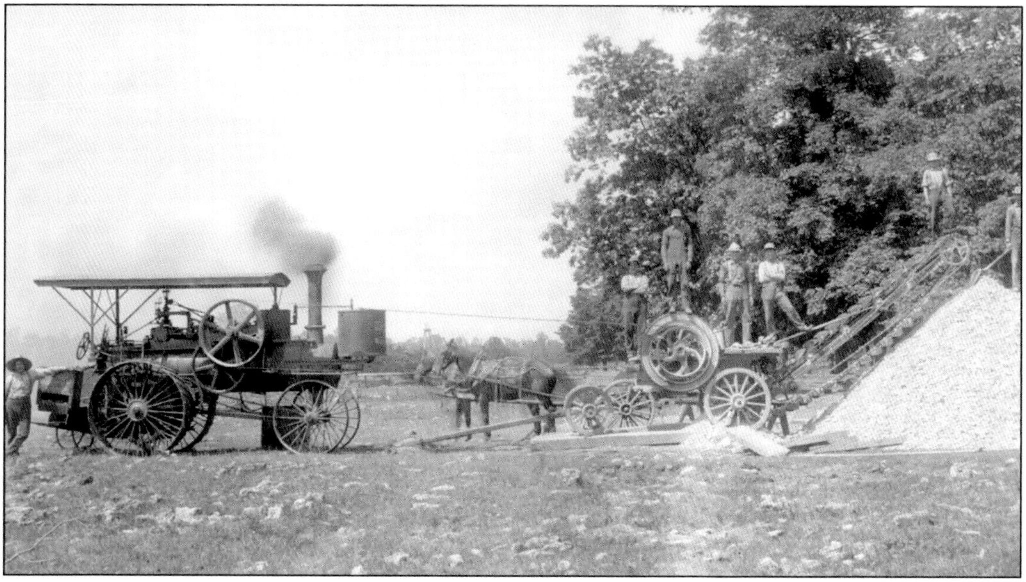

Pictured above is one of the essential pieces of equipment in the development of Gladwin County—the crusher. The rocky field and oil well in the background suggest this might be Beaverton Township. Many farmers improved the path to their farms by bringing the rock-crushing machine in to make gravel. The county waived their tax debt if the gravel was used to upgrade the road.

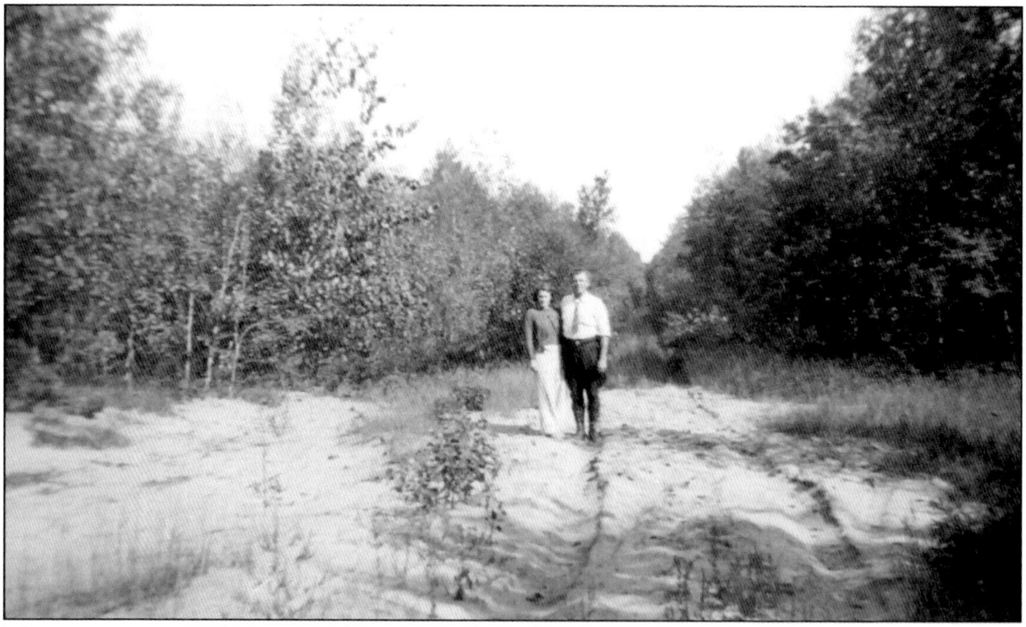

This is a picture of the corner of Drummond Road and Cedar Lake Road in Clement Township in the 1960s. Today Drummond is still a gravel road, but Cedar Lake Road was paved in 1999. Over the years, the number of automobile shocks damaged and the amount of dust accumulated in the few homes on these roads is hard to imagine. The only complaint about paved roads comes from the snowmobilers. (Courtesy of Nancy Nakkula Prescott.)

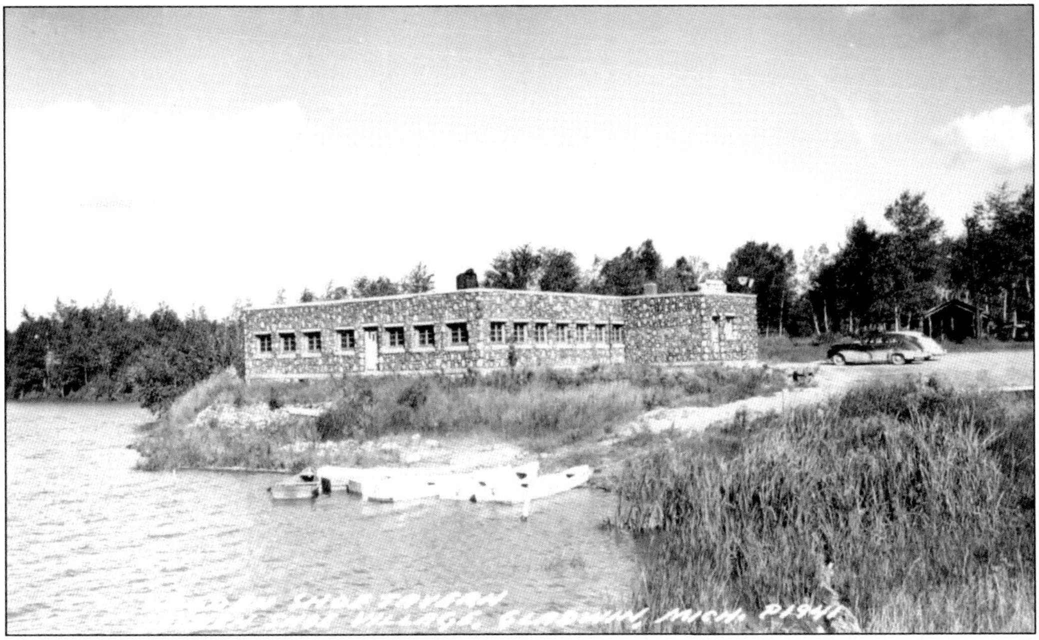

Wooden Shoe Tavern is located in the village of Wooden Shoe in Hay Township, which separated from Buckeye Township in 1909. The Wolverine Power Company built the Smallwood Dam just a mile southeast of the tavern's location. Originally, Michigan 61 went south of the building. The new bridge was built, and the highway now runs on the north side.

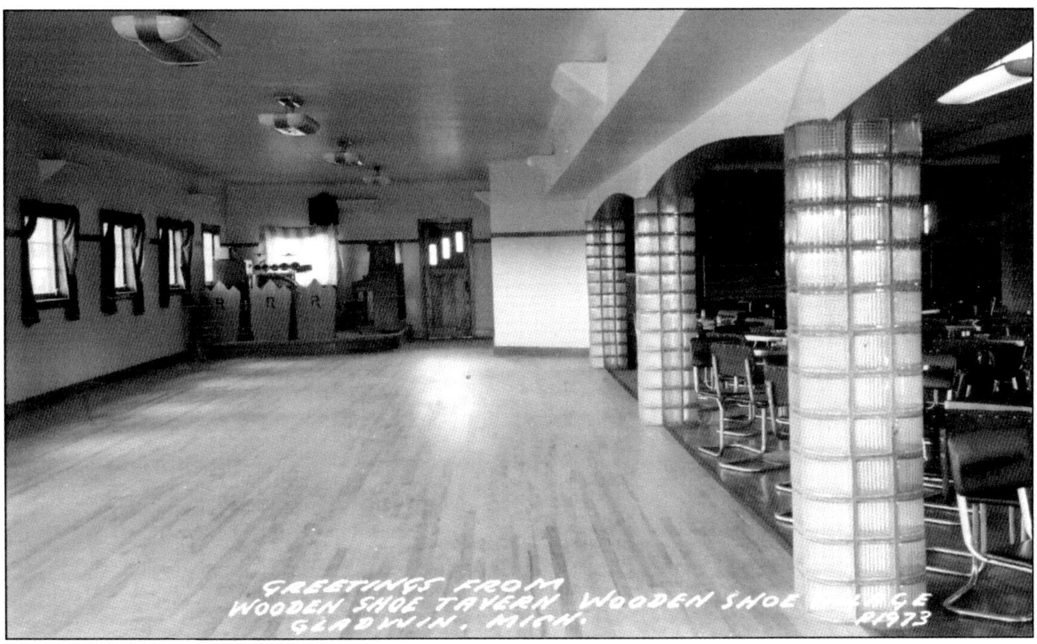

The Wooden Shoe Tavern has been remodeled several times. It always manages to maintain an atmosphere that attracts people interested in good food and having fun. The dance floor is plenty big enough for entertainment. With the addition of a large docking area on the backwaters of the Tittabawassee River, many resort residents utilize the waterway to get there.

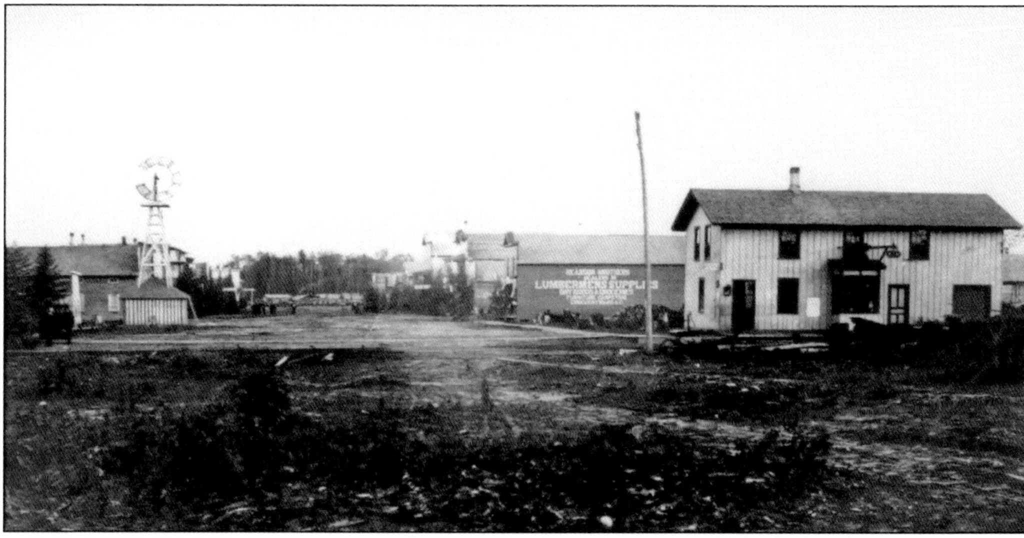

In 1883, rails were laid from Harrison to what became known as Meredith. The town has the unique distinction of literally straddling the county line between Clare and Gladwin. Also Meredith quickly gained a reputation of rivaling the Wild West. Stories of a town full of rowdy lumberjacks made the newspapers statewide. Some examples from articles in March 1891 include a bride being arrested after her wedding for polygamy, two prize bulldogs battling it out on Main Street, and a preacher being arrested while attempting to elope with one of his flock. (Courtesy of Robert Greaves.)

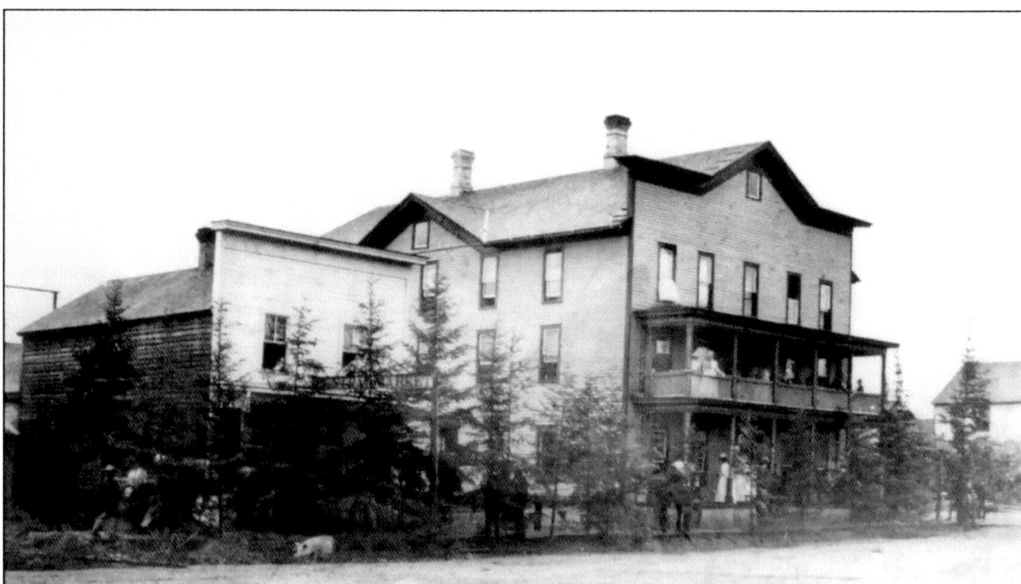

Freeman Black built the Corrigan House in 1890. The hotel and merchant building in Meredith was one of the most expensive buildings constructed north of Bay City, costing more than $5,000 for the bar. It had one of only a few two-story railroad depots in Michigan at the time. By 1910, the town of Meredith had virtually disappeared. (Courtesy of Robert Greaves.)

Nine

Dam the Waters and Recreation

Gladwin County is blessed with an abundance of water. The logging industry took full use and abuse of it to transport the logs to milling operations downriver. But this took a lot of water, so a system of dams was built, originally to float the logs and later to generate power. Of course, water can be a curse as well. Dams have been known to fail, as the Chappel Dam and Schultz Dam did several times. Flooding has also been a major problem throughout Gladwin County's history. The spring runoff made many county roads virtually impassable. The Wolverine Power Company created a power dam system in the 1920s that included Edenville, Smallwood, and Secord Dams. This, in addition to producing electricity, created several large lakes, such as Wixom, Albright Shores, and Secord. In turn, resorts and recreation areas created economic opportunities after the lumbering days were over. Gladwin has always been blessed with excellent hunting and fishing. Large tracts of state forest are ripe with game animals, and the streams are prime for sport fishing.

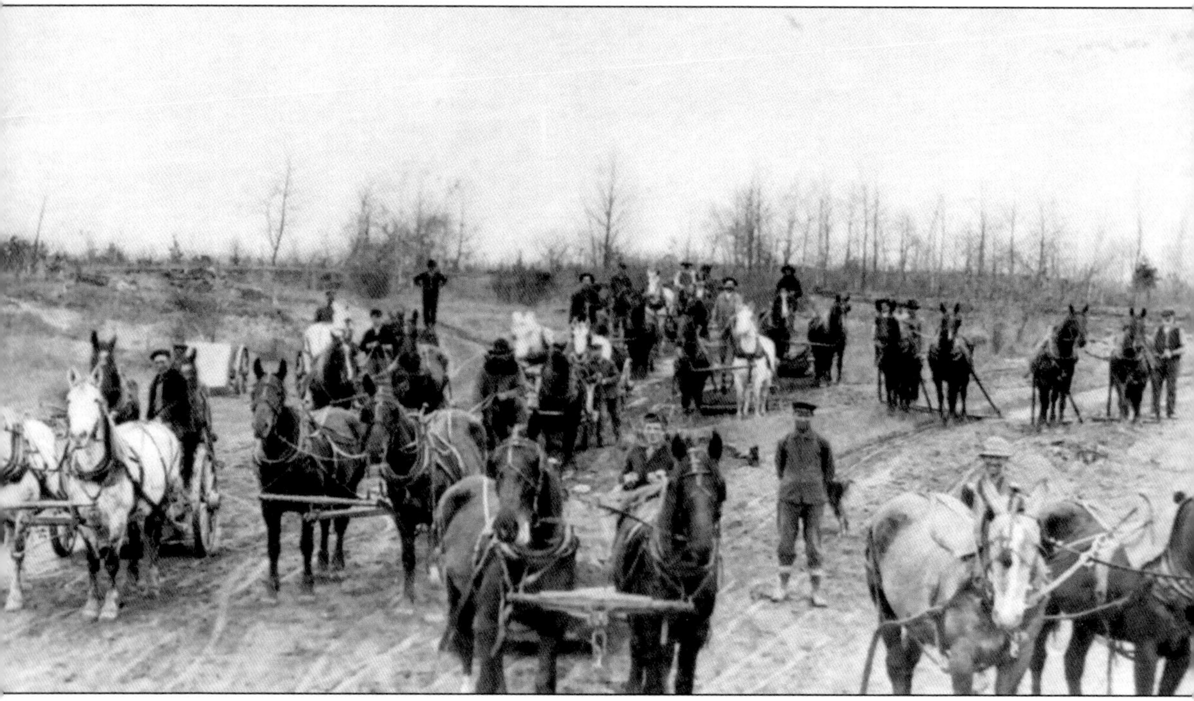

The locals bring their team of horses to scrape up the land for Chappel Dam in 1912.

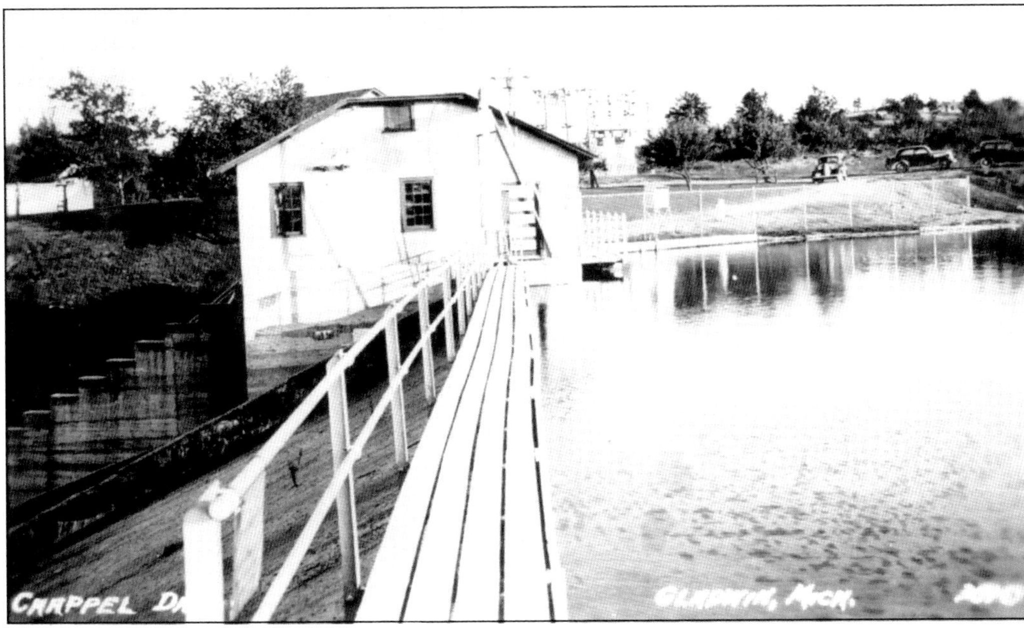

Chauncey Chappel built a dam in the 1880s for the purpose of floating logs downriver. In 1912, Consumers Power built another, more effective dam, seen here, on the other fork of the river for the purpose of generating power. The dam was later sold back to Gladwin County for the cost of $1.

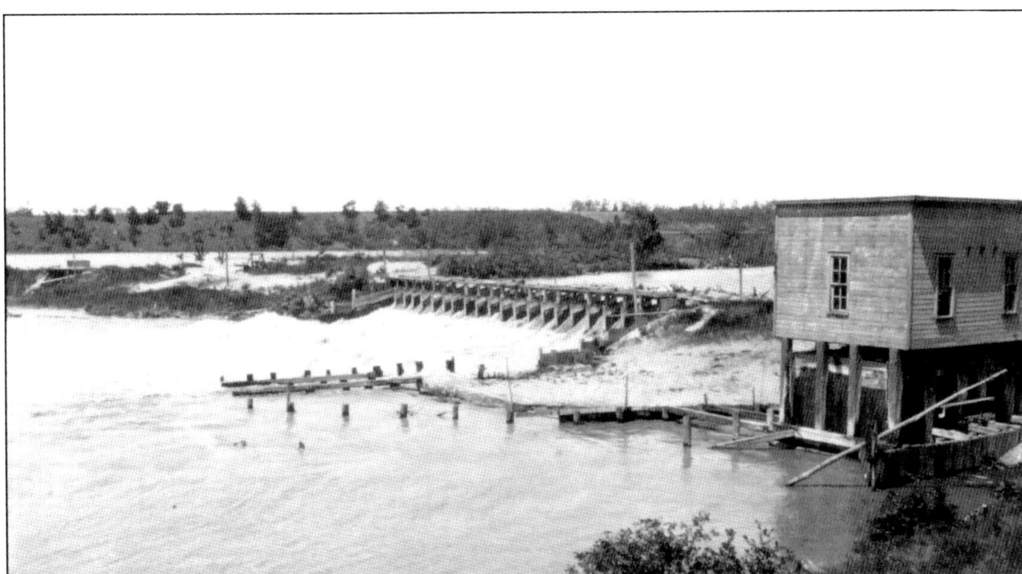

Joseph Schulz was invited by local merchants to establish a flour and gristmill in 1889. He constructed a dam on the Cedar River in the area behind Gladwin's current city hall to furnish waterpower for the mill until 1900. At that time, he and Frank Prindle put in an electric power wheel to generate electricity for the city of Gladwin. The entire structure was wiped out for a second and final time by floodwaters in 1929.

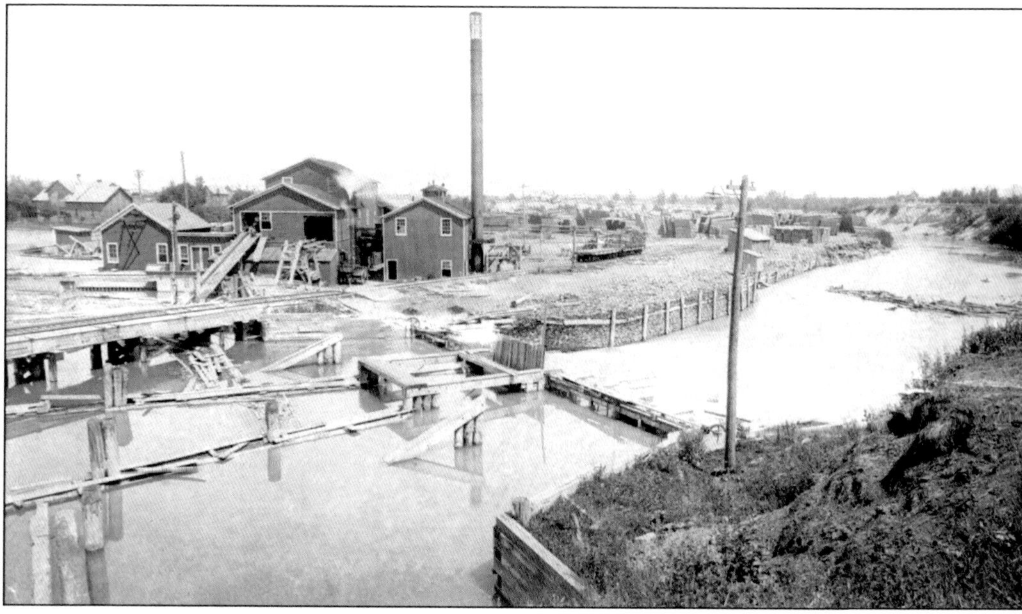

The Ross brothers built the first dam in the spring of 1891 after the Sapling Paving Block mill was constructed. This photograph of the Bandsaw Mill, nicknamed the "Big Mill," clearly shows the mechanism in the middle of the river that was used to allow logs to pass through and continue downriver during the spring. The band sawmill is in the background.

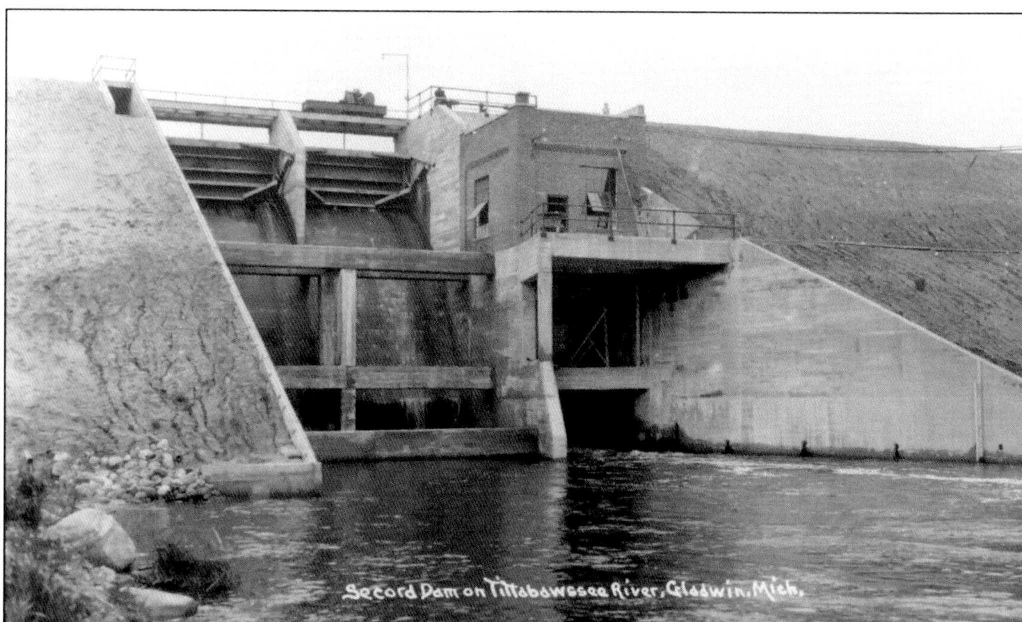

The Secord Dam is the northernmost dam in a chain of a four-dam system created in the 1920s. It is located east of Michigan 30 and is four miles north of Michigan 61 on Secord Dam Road. Although a large amount of energy was immediately produced, none of the local residents benefited, as the power was converted into high-voltage electricity and sold to Bay City. It was many years before the local homes received electric power.

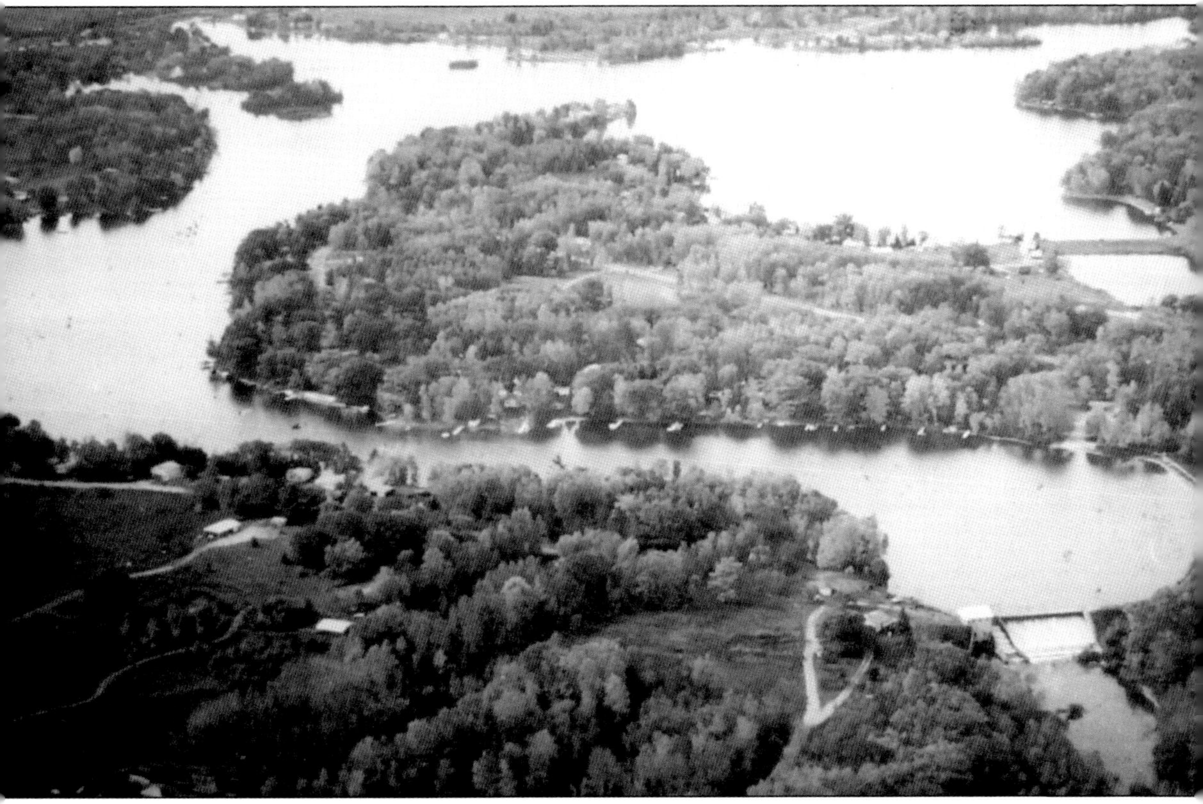

Wiggins Lake was formed from the backwaters of the Chappel Dam, seen here near the bottom right. Now a dike, the original dam, seen at middle right, is where the settlement known as Gladwin City was located. From 1880 to 1900, there were at least four logging camps in the area and a population of about 100. A Wiggins Lake Property Owners Association was formed in 1963. (Courtesy of Fran Seebeck.)

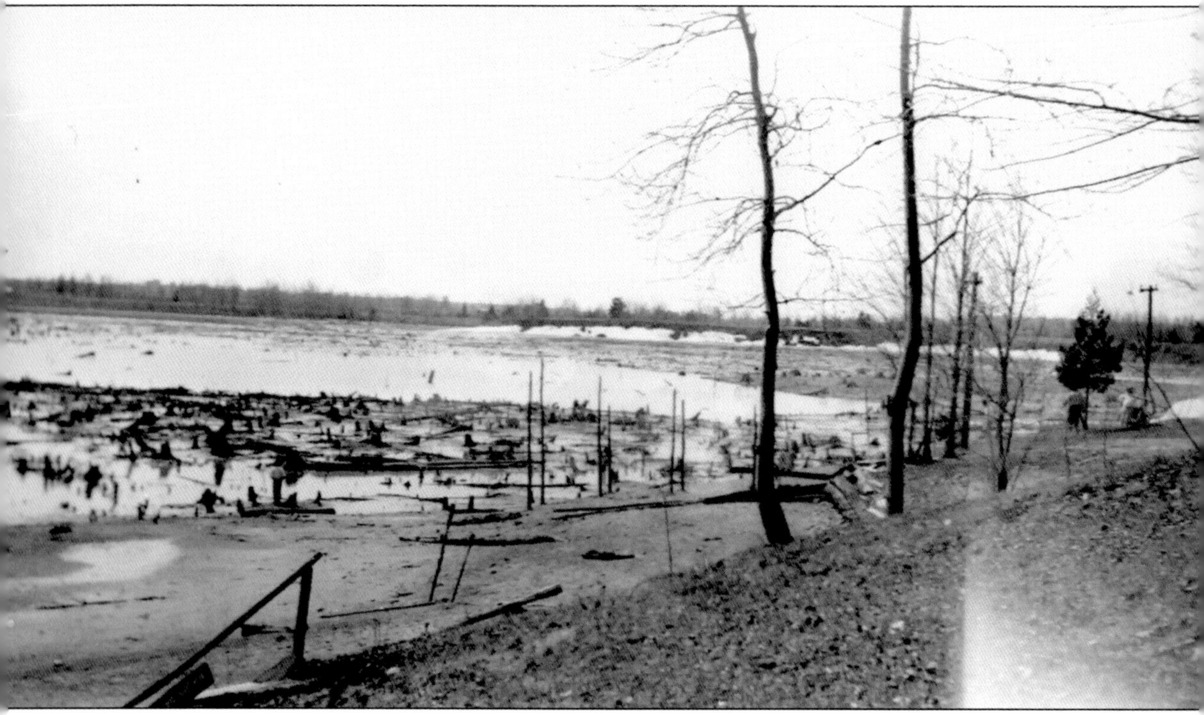

From time to time, the water in Wiggins Lake has been lowered to make repairs to the dam. Here is a picture from the early 1960s that clearly shows the emerging stumps. It makes for a great fishing habitat, but it is a little scary when boating and water skiing resumes after the lake refills. (Courtesy of Fran Seebeck.)

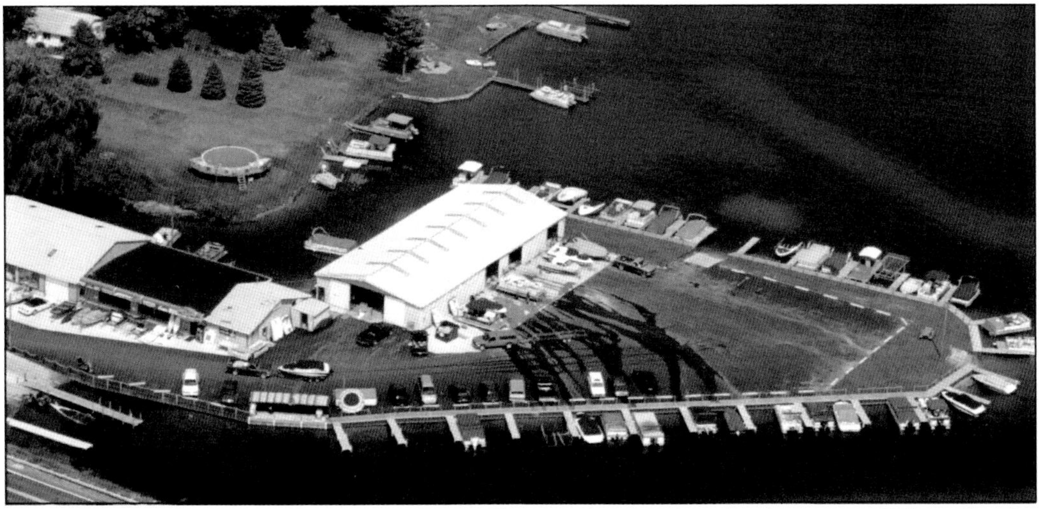

When the Tittabawassee River was dammed up at Camp 16, today known as Edenville, the backwaters created became Wixom Lake. As of 2008, Stryker's Marina has been located at the Michigan 30 bridge for 25 years. From there, boaters can go on the Tobacco River side north about nine miles to Beaverton or go 13 miles to Michigan 61 on the Tittabawassee side. (Courtesy of Greg Stryker.)

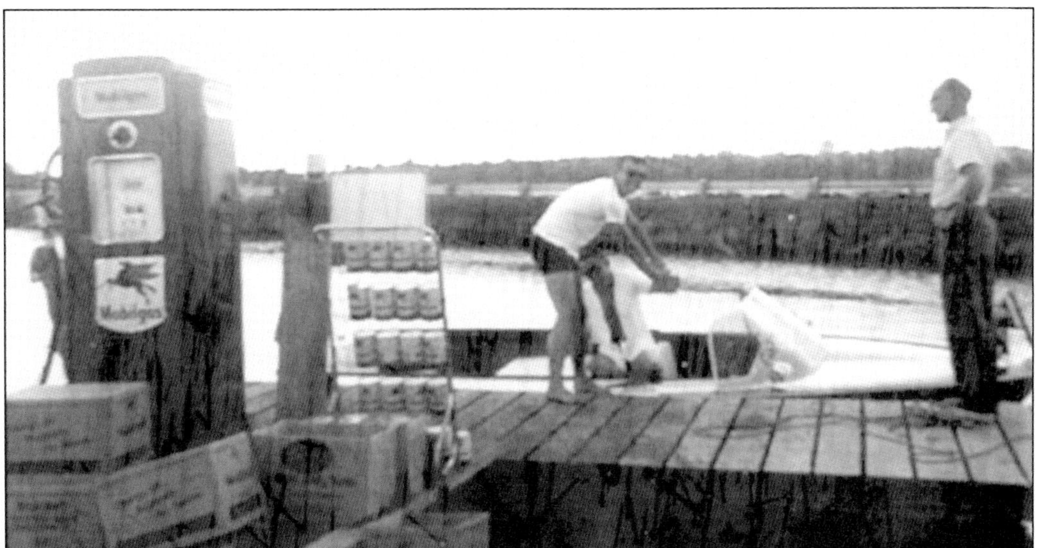

A recreational boat launch has been at the Stryker's Marina site since the late 1950s. Here is what the boat dock looked like in 1963. Immediately following the completion of the Edenville Dam, the legend of Wixom Lake began. People reported seeing a crane beneath the water on days the water was clear. The legend grew to include several railroad cars and an old steam engine. Every few years, there were rumors of divers spotting the equipment buried in silt. (Courtesy of Greg Stryker.)

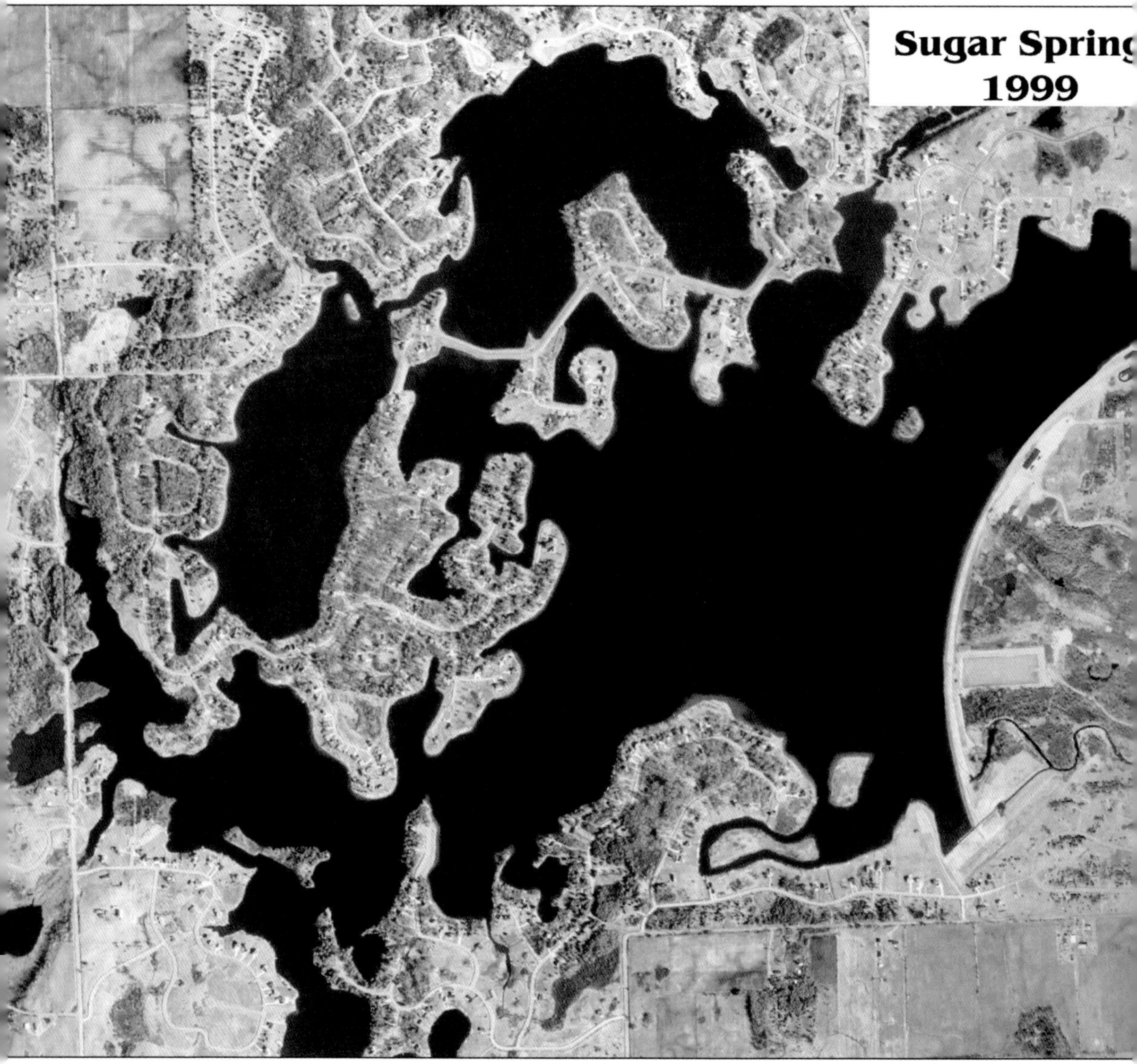

Sugar Springs Resort is known as "the best kept secret in Michigan." Located in Butman Township, it is no secret to Gladwin County. Approximately half of the almost 3,000 lots have structures and the population increases to over 6,000 in the summer months. The brainchild of N. E. Isaacson of Wisconsin, the development was begun in the late 1960s with the purchase of over 3,000 acres that were dissected by the Sugar River. By 1972, the first house was built on one of the many roads, and the river was dammed up to make two lakes— the smaller Lake Lancelot and the larger Lake Lancer. Notice Grass Lake Road, which dead-ends at the lake from the left. One of the locations of the town of Butman may be where the road intersected with Butman Road running north/south. That junction was first known as Shotgun Corners in the logging days. There are many old-timers who talk of an old settlement called Millsville, whose stores and cemetery remnants rest at the bottom of Lake Lancelot. (Courtesy of Robert Frei.)

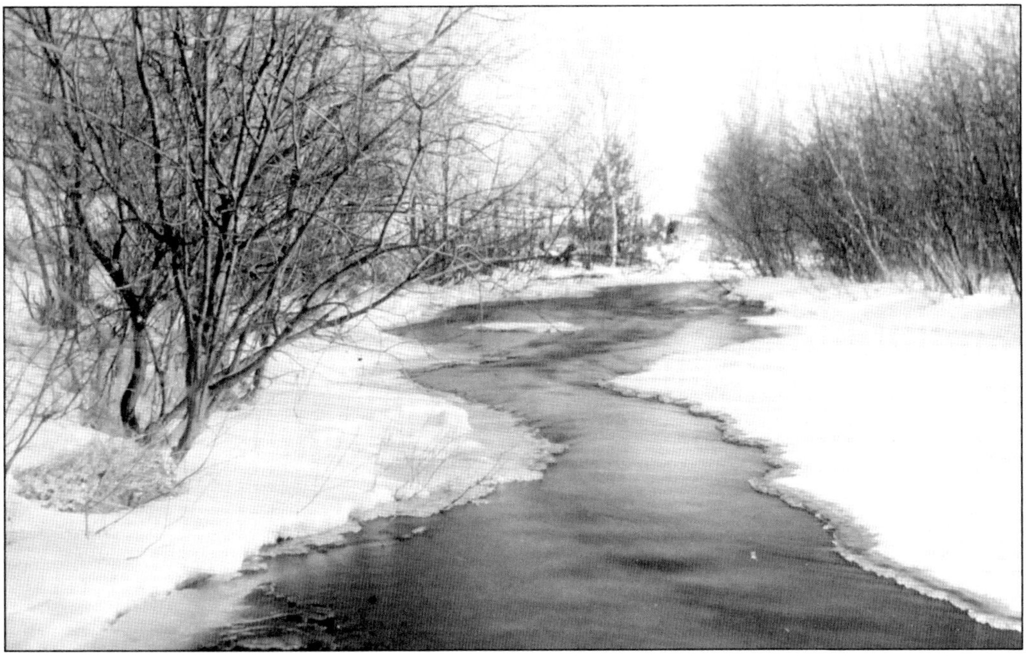

The Sugar River headwaters are in Roscommon County and flow into Butman Township. Not far from the one-time town of Butman, the river was dammed to form what are now the Sugar Springs lakes—Lake Lancer and Lake Lancelot. From there, it continues on to Secord Township to become part of Secord Lake and the old Wolverine Power Dam system.

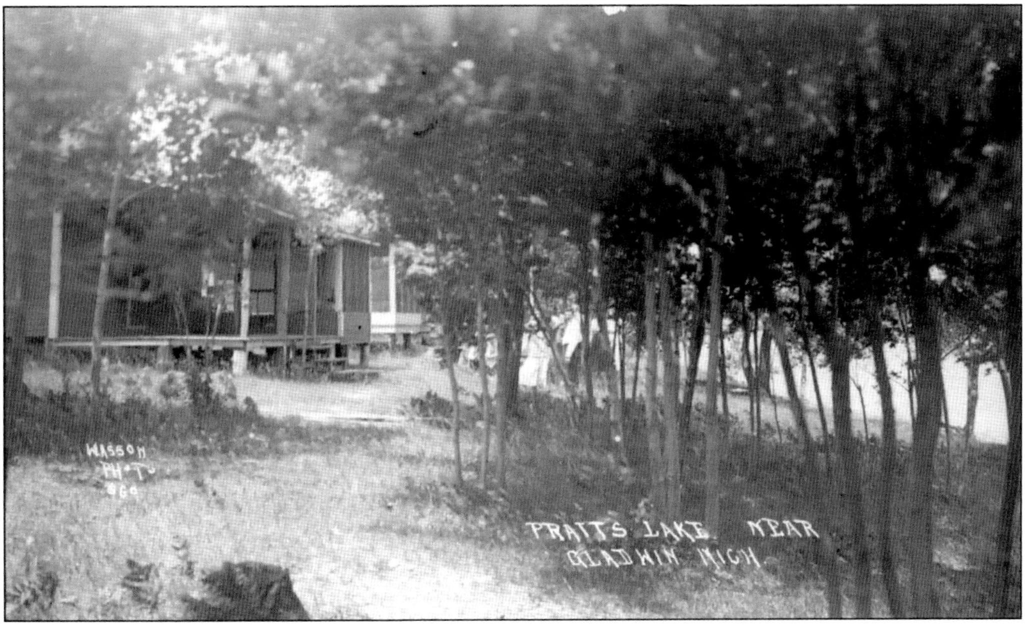

This postcard from the early 1900s clearly reads Pratts Lake. It is named after Edward Pratt, who stopped lumbermen from draining the lake by walking to Bay City and filing the proper papers. A popular resort area around 1900, Pratt Lake was located just a few miles northwest of Gladwin in Sage Township and is now almost completely lined with year-round homes. (Courtesy of John Rhode.)

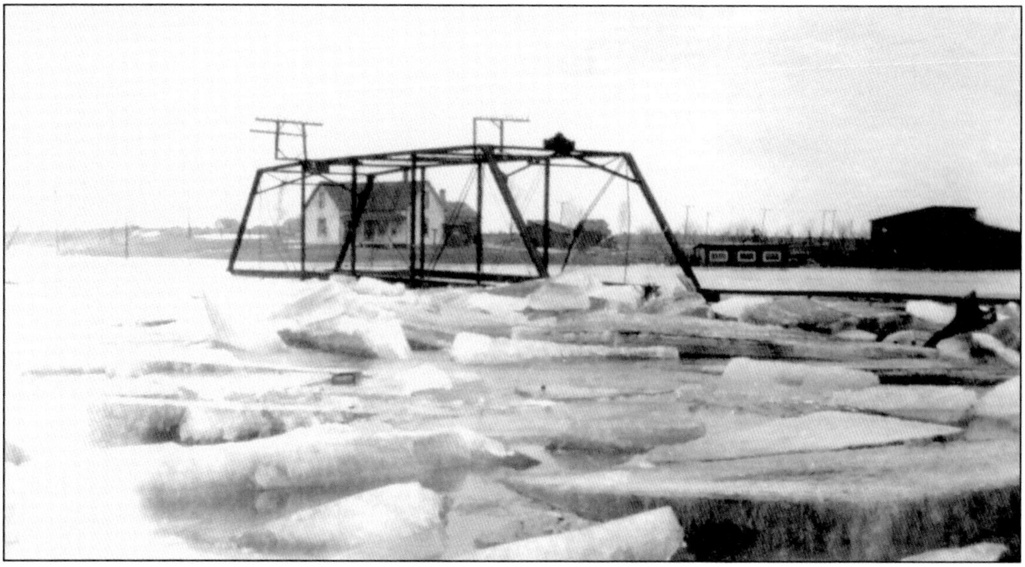

Floods have always been a problem in Beaverton. With spring runoff from the Tobacco and Cedar Rivers, ice jams, and dam failures, Beaverton experienced major floods in 1912 and 1917, as depicted in this photograph. This is also a good picture of the iron bridge across the Tobacco River that was built in 1899 by the Wrought Iron Bridge Company of Canton, Ohio, for the bid of $1,575.

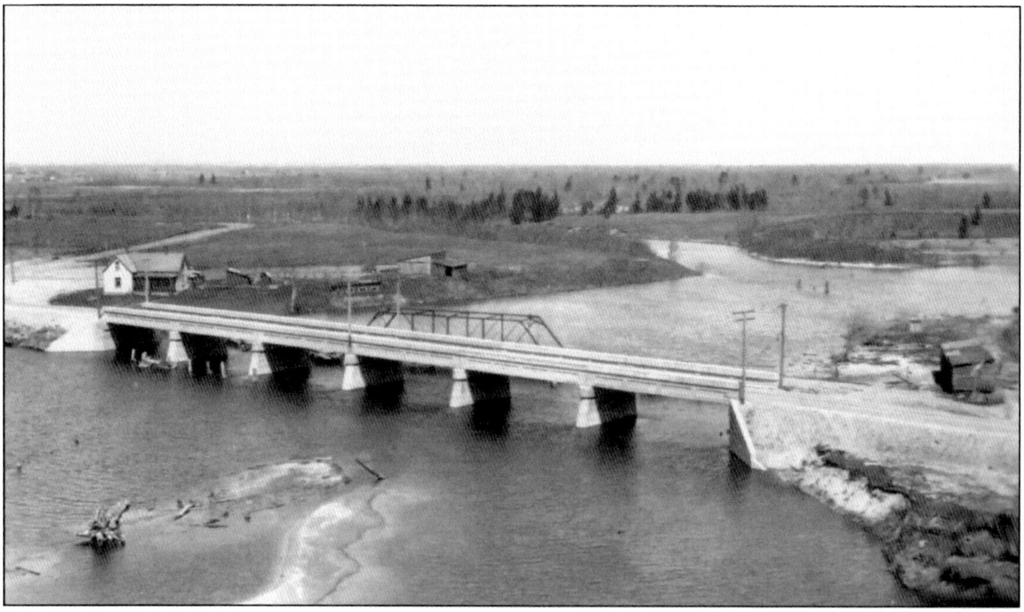

The new Michigan 18 concrete bridge over Ross Lake was completed and open for traffic in 1939. Notice the water level of Ross Lake just beginning to fill. This bridge replaced a narrower concrete bridge built by E. C. Nolan and Son in 1918. Prior to that, there was an iron bridge built in 1899, which replaced the wooden bridge built in 1891. (Courtesy of Clarke Historical Library.)

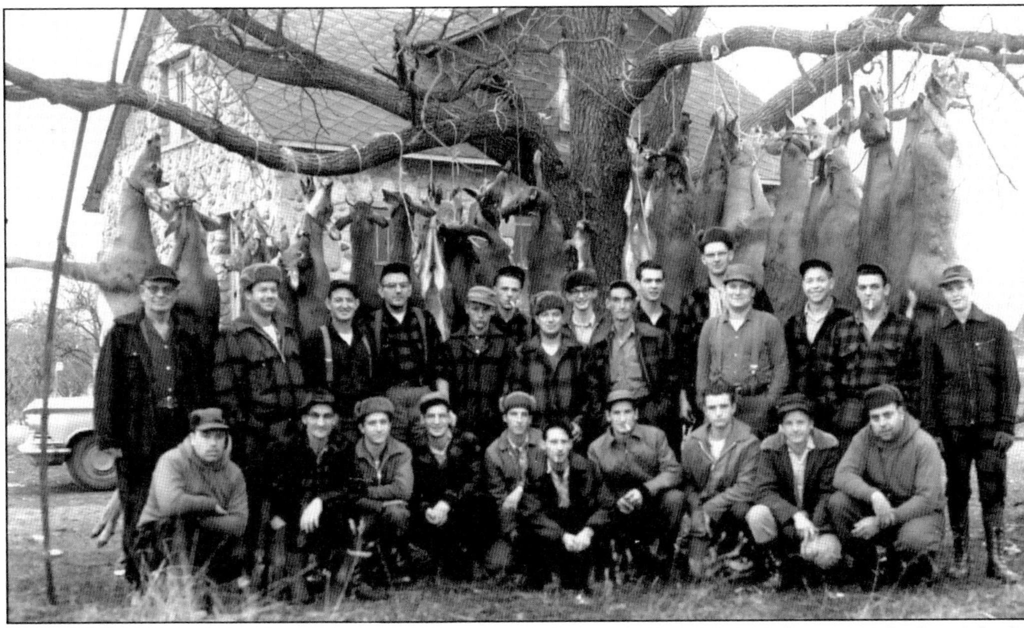

Gladwin County has long been known for its excellent hunting ground. Karen Corlew Mack's family settled in northern Butman Township, and Corlew Road runs west of F-97 and is within gunshot distance of the Roscommon County line. Here is a picture of the opening week of deer camp in 1963. There are 20 deer and one rabbit hanging from the Corlew "buck tree." (Courtesy of Karen Mack.)

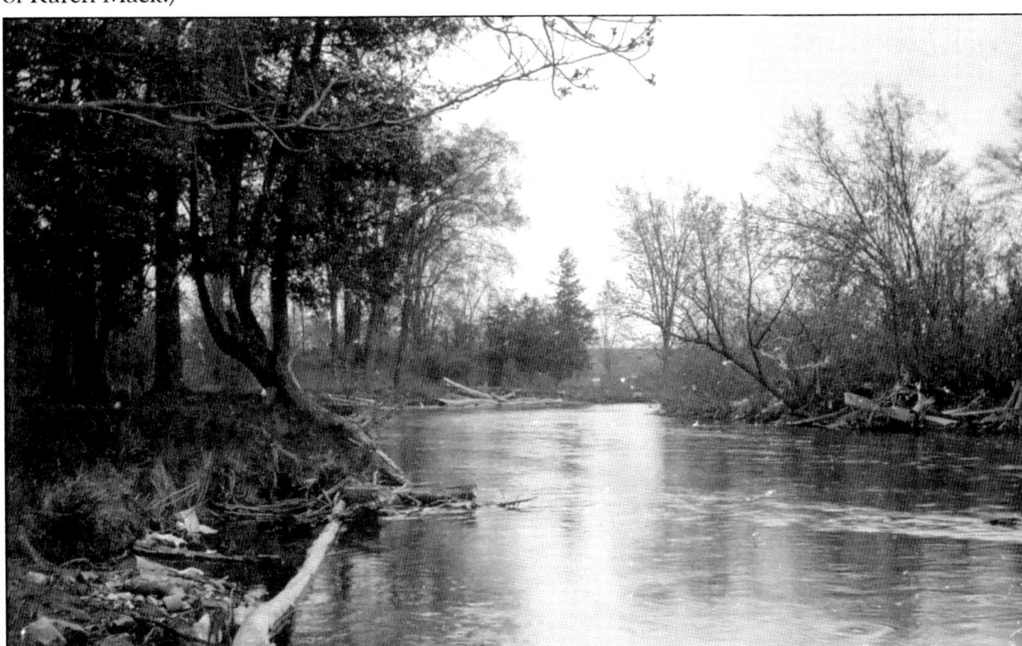

From the picture above, it is obvious why the Cedar River was useful in shepherding the logs downstream. The headwaters of the river start in the Meredith area on the northern edge of Gladwin County. Three branches merge near the city of Gladwin, ending at Ross Lake and the Beaverton Dam.

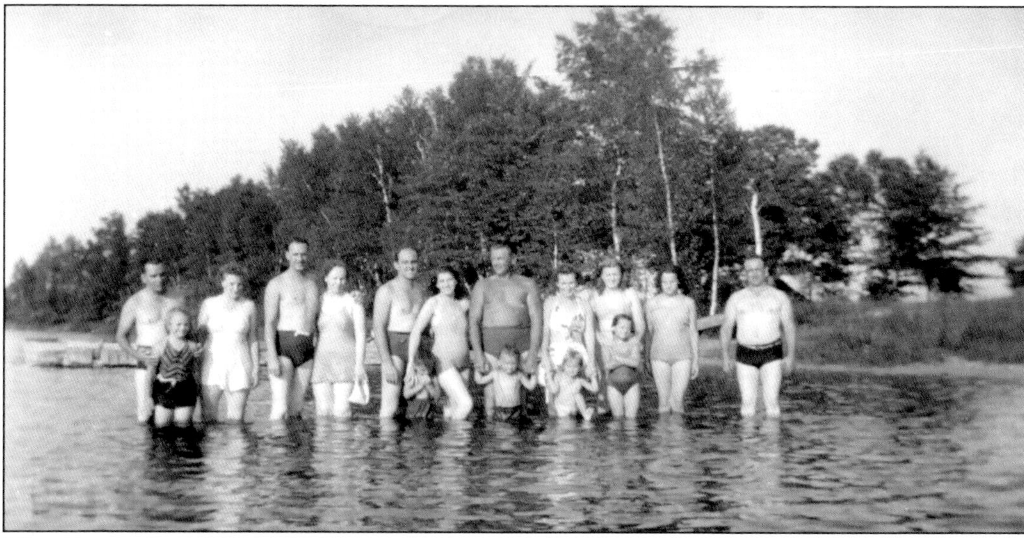

This is a picture of a Fourth of July outing on Indian Lake in the 1950s. At the time, there were only a few dozen summer cottages. Although everyone around referred to this area as a public beach, it was really just a path between two cottages down to a sandy beach area. Times have changed since those days. (Courtesy of Nancy Nakkula Prescott.)

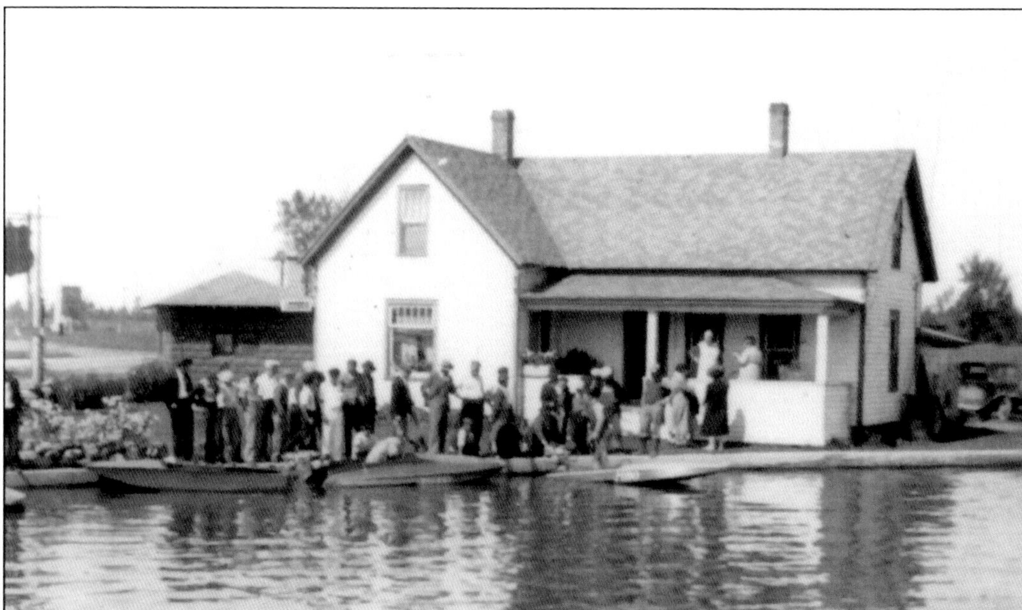

As soon as Ross Lake became large enough, it was an instant attraction for water activities and as a resort area. Here are cabins that were built to accommodate summer vacationers. The home in the background is still standing on the north side of the Michigan 18 bridge. Boat races were a common occurrence on Ross Lake and are still scheduled occasionally. (Courtesy of John Rhode.)

Ten

Roots Run Deep with People

It was Abraham Lincoln who once said, "This country . . . belongs to the people who inhabit it." Gladwin County is no different. The landscape changes, the boundaries change, and the economy changes, but the people's spirit in Gladwin has never changed. Wayne Ellis's Gladwin Township farm was the fifth in Gladwin County to reach centennial status in 1982. Elwood Gedney established the first centennial farm in 1871 on Gedney Road in Grout Township. Many others followed, including the Buzzells, the Brushabers, the McKimmeys, and the McIntoshs. Roads are named after people too, like Kerswill, Hockaday, McCulloch, and Blades. The original forests are gone but are replaced by more trees. Some of the roots were removed or plowed under, but many remained. John Blades is like many who chose to stay, and stated, "I am the first son of a first son of a first son whose father, Robert Blades, came here to establish roots." There have been good days, bad days, hard times, and fun times. The spirit of the Gladwin County people endures.

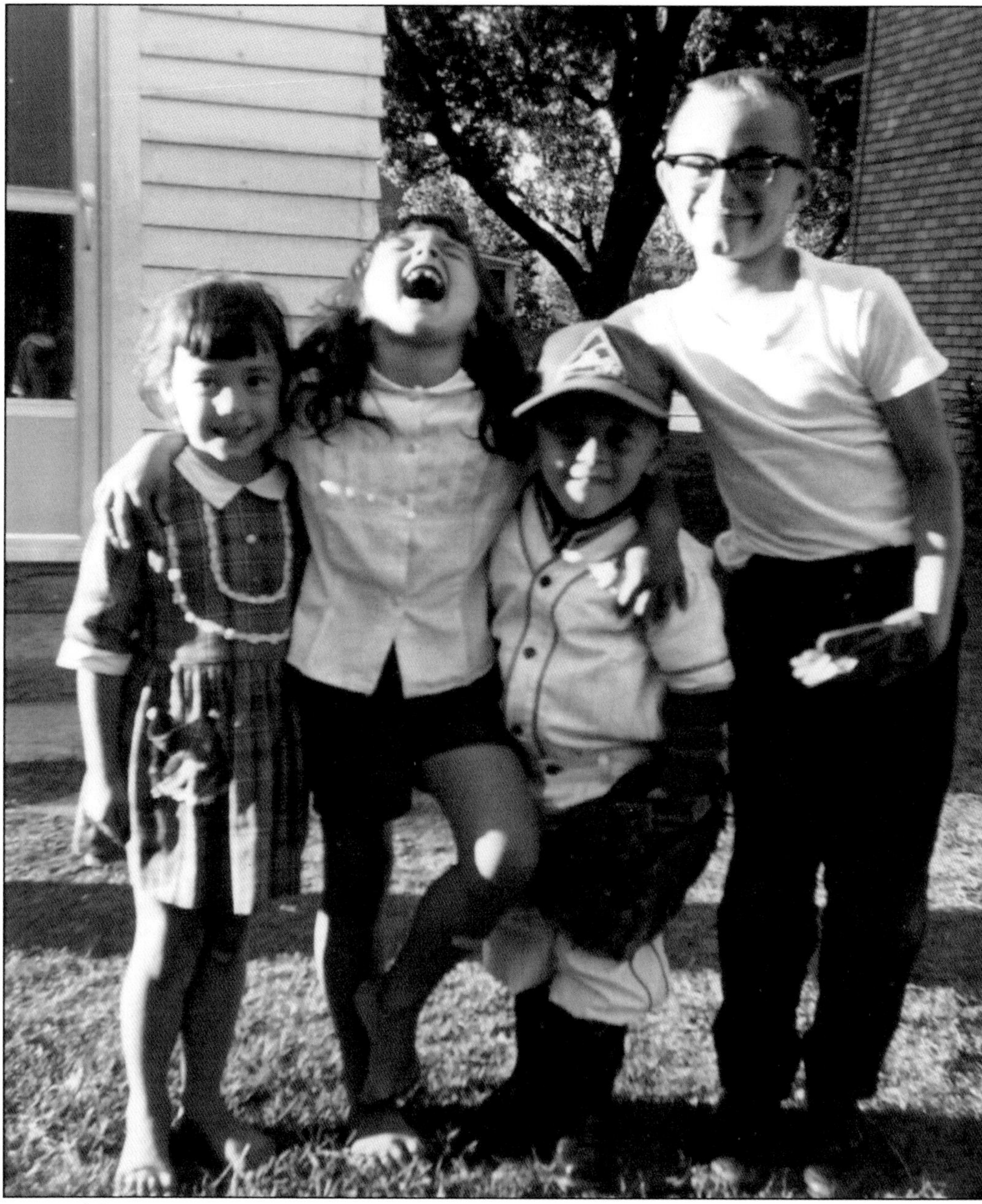

Pictured here in 1965, from left to right, are Julie Ellis, Cheri Ellis, Kevin Ellis, and David Hudson. They are headed for grandpa's backyard to play baseball. Julie is related to Wayne Ellis, who owned a centennial farm. (Courtesy of Julie Ellis.)

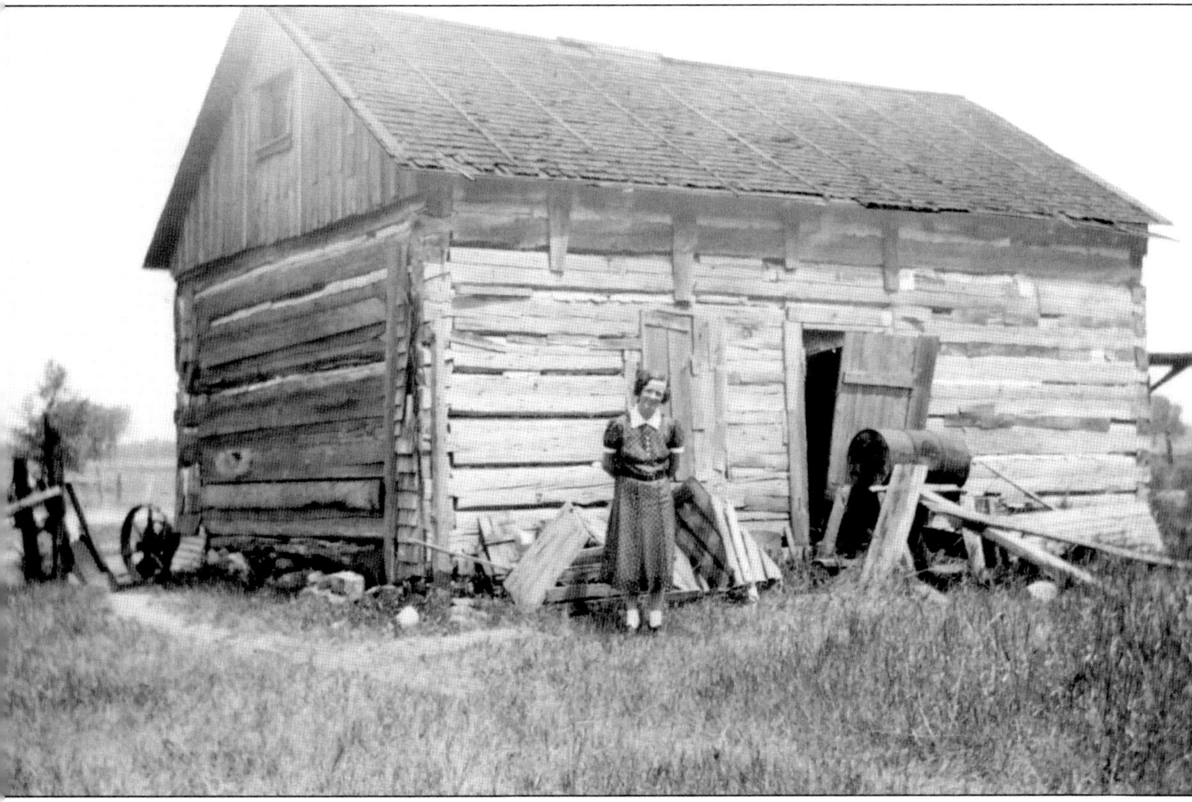

Nila Frei's great-grandfather Nils Carlson came to Clement Township from Sweden in 1901. His wife, Alfreda, and the kids came the following winter, arriving by train in West Branch to subzero temperatures. They packed up their belongings and arrived at the log cabin shown above. There was a big problem. Carlson and his uncle John Lunquist, who came to Gladwin and bought a farm in 1883, had been deceiving Alfreda. Her father had been a cook for the king of Sweden, and she was accustomed to the finer things in life. To convince the family to come to America, Lunquist had been sending pictures of the beautiful Victorian homes on Center Avenue in Bay City. Carlson continued the ruse. Alfreda never forgave him for the deception. Nila is currently the mayor of Beaverton. (Courtesy of Robert Frei.)

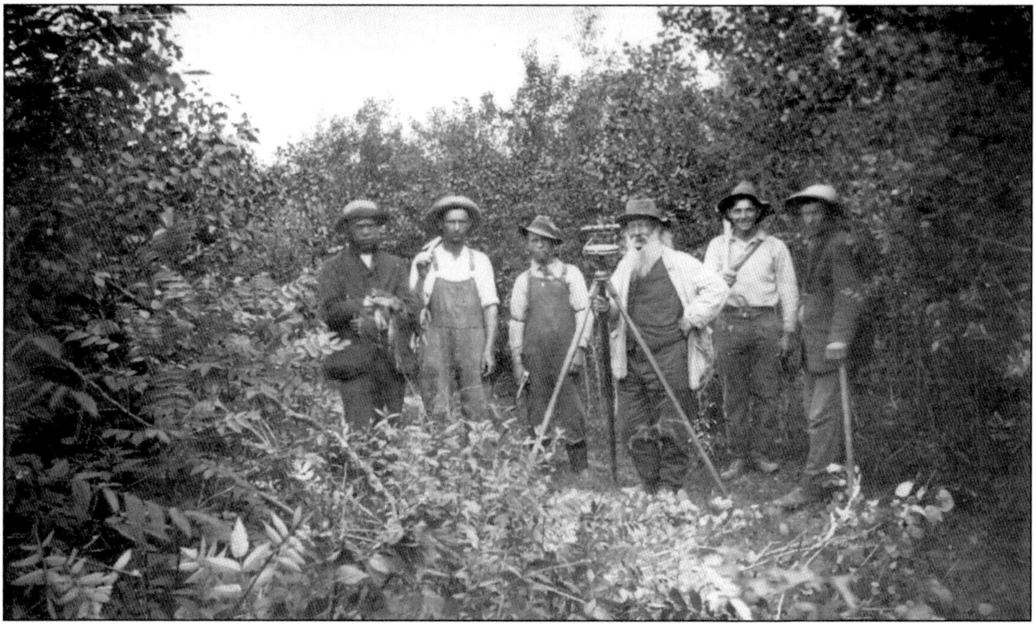

John Knox, a surveyor by trade, was responsible for establishing the major boundary lines in Gladwin County. Although he resided in Beaverton and had the Knox Store in the downtown area, he was seen in many parts of central Michigan doing his surveying work. The store is long gone, but Knox Road in Beaverton is a reminder today of the valuable work he contributed to the establishment of Gladwin County. (Courtesy of Inez Soldan.)

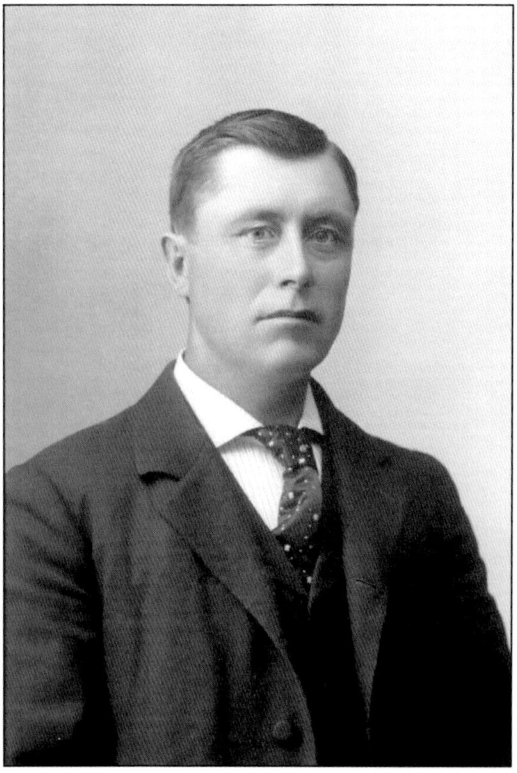

William Ross came to Beaverton with his father and brothers in 1889. Beaverton's first city elections were held in 1903, and he was elected mayor. While his brother Ronald was in charge of the elevator and feed mill, William was in charge of the Ross Brothers store. Known to be a very astute businessman, the lifelong bachelor was called "Uncle Bill" by most of the children in town. He died in Beaverton in 1939.

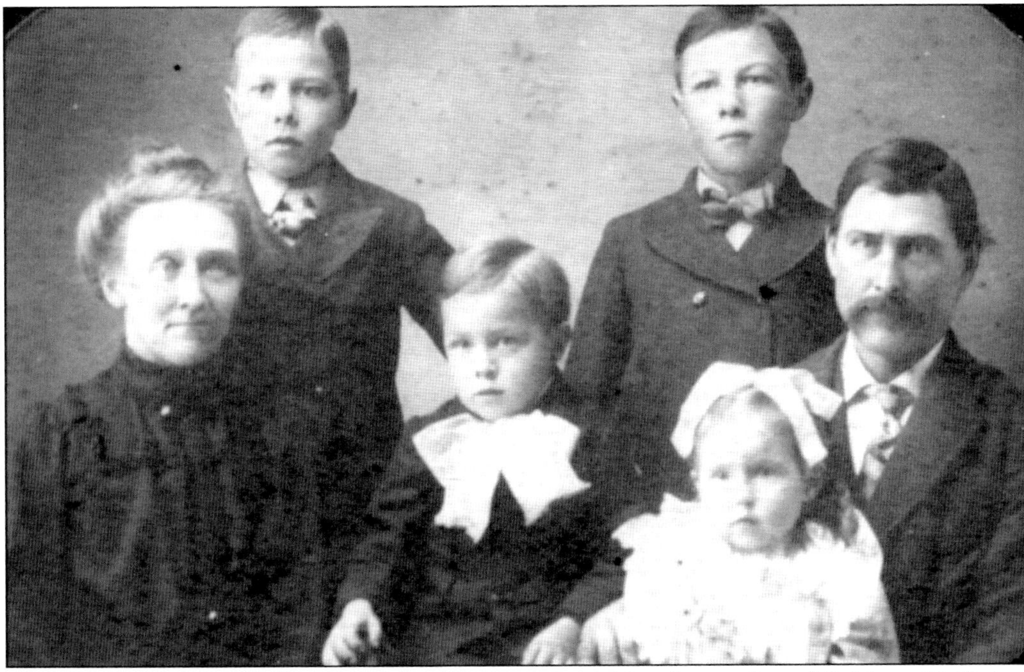

Blades Road is just a half mile south of Beaverton and heads east from Michigan 18. Robert Blades brought his family to this area and settled to farm in the late 1890s. This photograph of his family from about 1902 was the beginning of generations of Blades to follow. From left to right are Anna, Earl (born 1892), Dewey (born 1898), George (born 1890), Robert, and Elba on his lap (born 1900). (Courtesy of John Blades.)

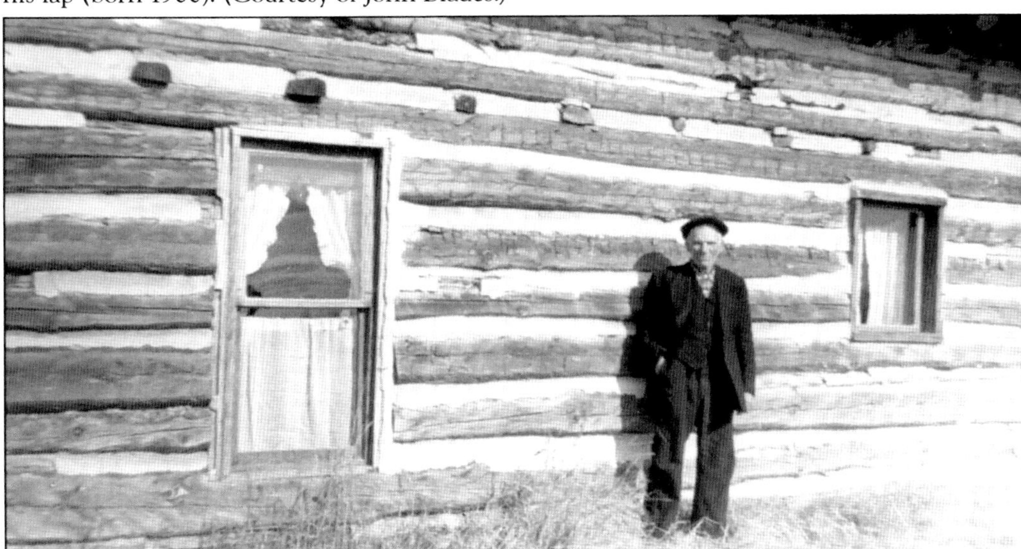

Ike Geesey came to Gladwin in the late 1880s from Pauling, Ohio. He settled in Clement Township, which separated from Gladwin Township in 1884. He sold a portion of his farmland to build the South Clement School. In addition to farming, Geesey was also the township highway commissioner. Another portion of his land is known as the Geesey Marsh, which is still considered prime hunting area today. (Courtesy of Gladwin County Historical Society.)

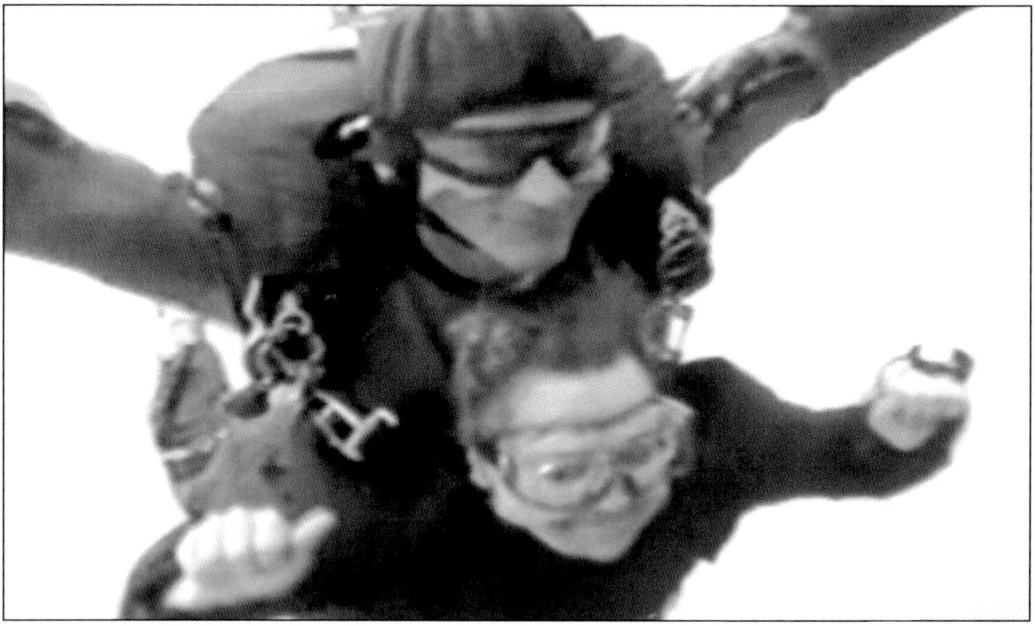

Joyce Swartzmiller has lived in Billings Township her entire adult life just eight miles from where she grew up. She and her husband, Frank, raised two children and now have eight grandchildren. They all live within a few miles of Beaverton. After over 25 years in the banking industry, she is the events coordinator for the Beaverton Business Association. She is the last person one would consider a risk taker. She is pictured tandem skydiving. (Courtesy of Joyce Swartzmiller.)

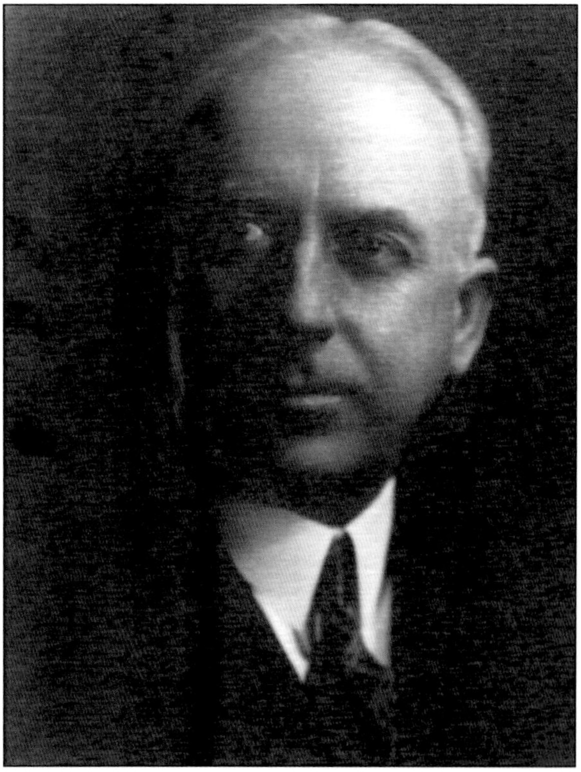

Floyd Armstrong was born and raised in Gladwin County and was a product of the Gladwin school system. After receiving his college degree, he returned to teach in Gladwin and eventually became the county commissioner of schools. Later he attended Harvard University for postgraduate work and became a professor there. (Courtesy of Gladwin County Historical Society.)

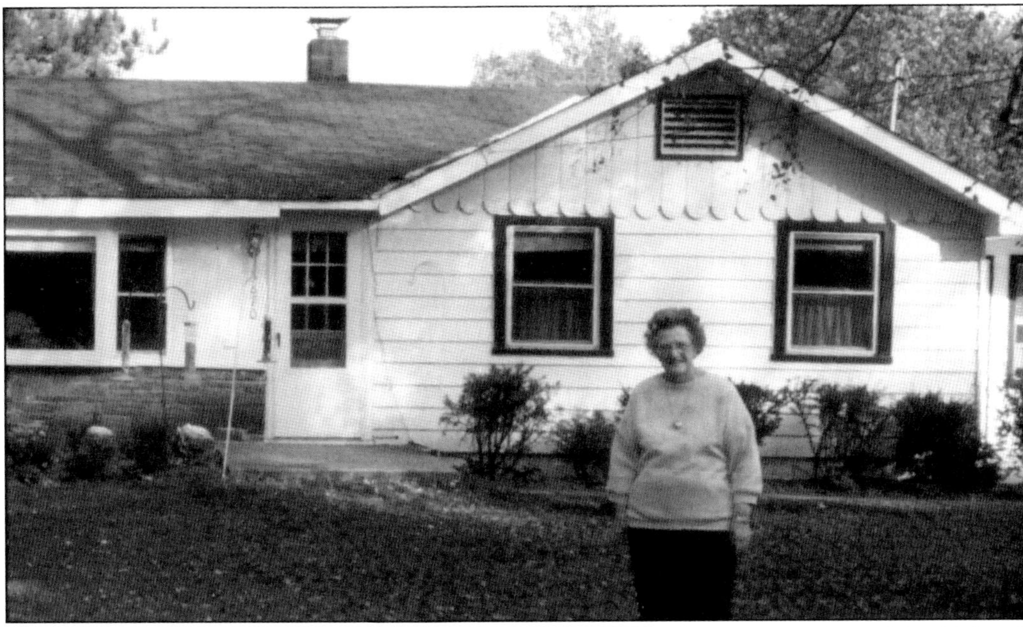

Julie Nakkula, shown in front of her home on Cedar Lake Road, was married to Walter Nakkula and had three children. They moved into what originally was an upgraded two-room log cabin. Most women would say that the happiest day of their lives were either the day they were married or the day their children were born, but not Julie. The happiest day of her life was April 30, 1949, at 4:00 p.m., when she got electricity in her home. (Courtesy of Nancy Nakkula Prescott.)

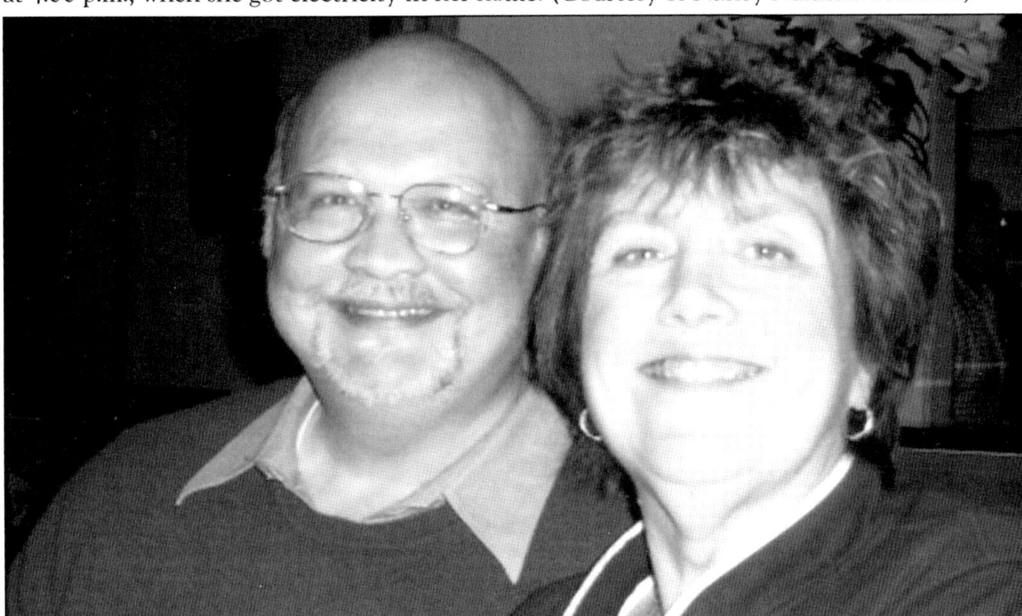

Here is a recent picture of Nancy Nakkula Prescott and her husband, Dave Prescott. They were married in 1976. What is unique about their relationship is that they met in Lansing while serving as pages for state representatives. To their knowledge and the records of the State of Michigan Legislative Retirement Bureau, they are the only two children of two state representatives in Michigan that are married. (Courtesy of Nancy Nakkula Prescott.)

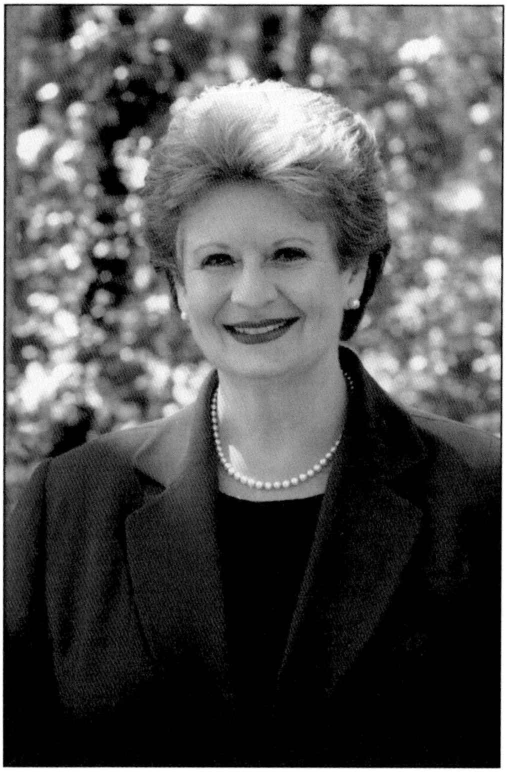

Sen. Debbie Stabenow of Michigan was born in Gladwin County. Although she now resides in Washington, D.C., and Lansing and was raised in Clare, she still considers Gladwin her home. She was born at the old Gladwin hospital as the oldest child of the Geer family and moved to Clare at age two. Stabenow earned a three-part bachelor's degree in criminal justice, psychology, and sociology. She went on to obtain a master's degree in social work at Michigan State University. For her, politics began with a local issue involving a nursing home that the county commissioner in her district was pushing to close. At age 25, she was elected to the Ingham County Board of Commissioners and served there until 1979. From there, it was on to the Michigan House of Representatives from 1979 to 1990. She served for four years in the state senate and another four years as a U.S. Representative from Michigan and is currently in her second term as the junior senator from Michigan. (Courtesy of the office of Sen. Debbie Stabenow.)

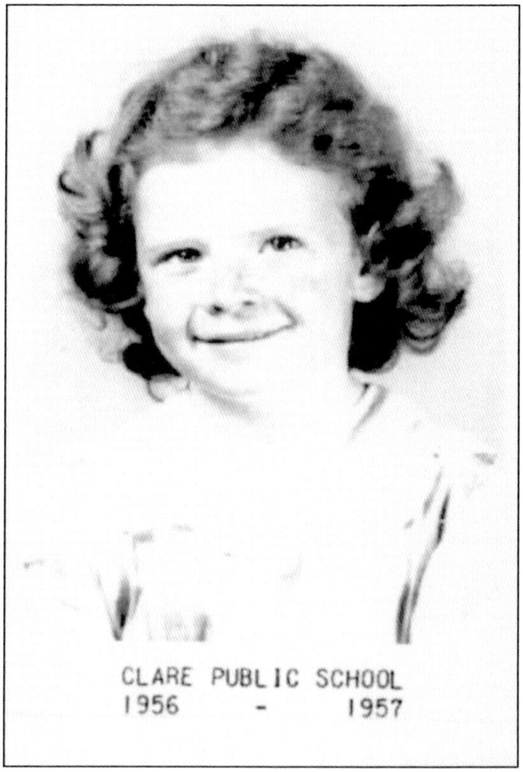

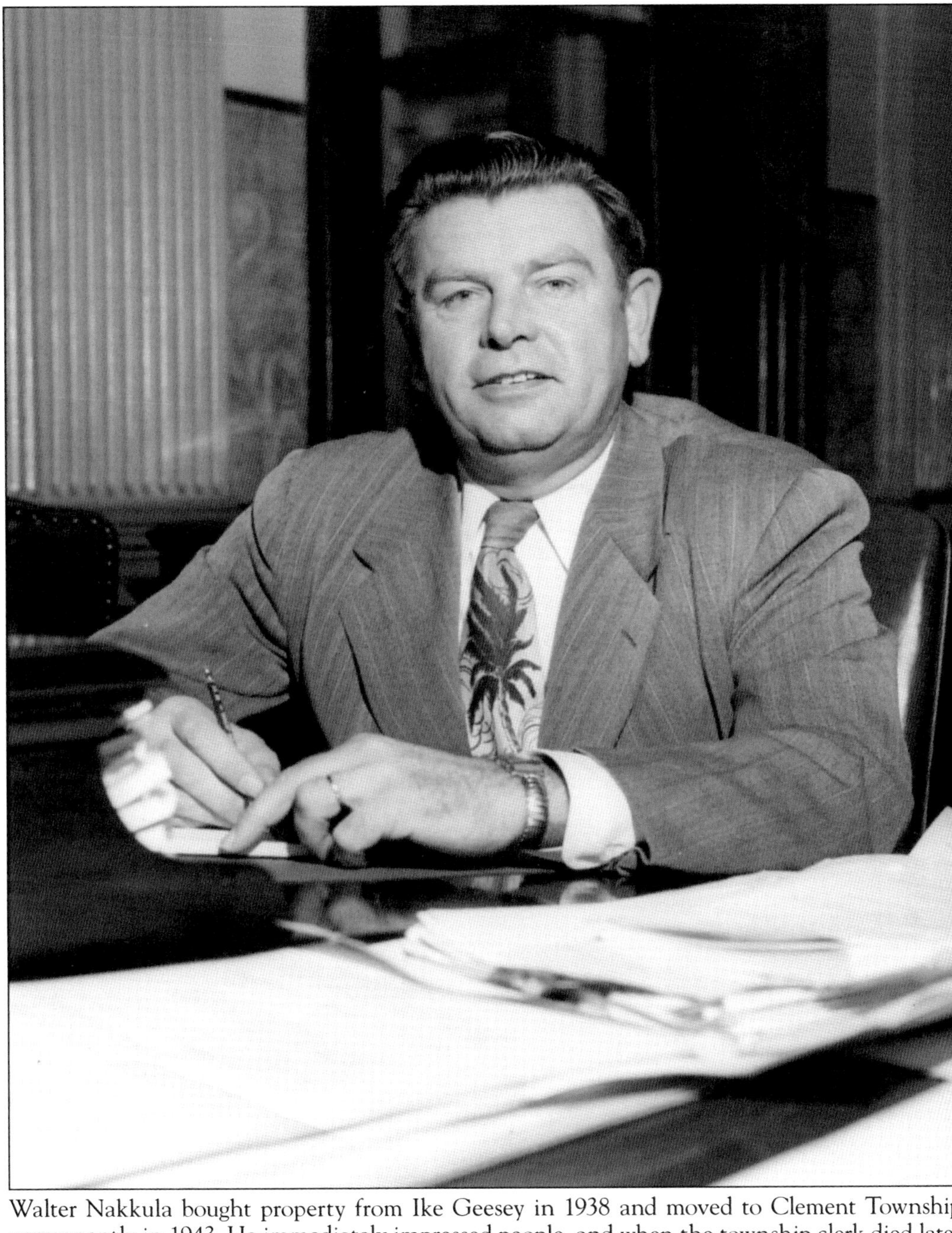

Walter Nakkula bought property from Ike Geesey in 1938 and moved to Clement Township permanently in 1943. He immediately impressed people, and when the township clerk died later that year, many of his newfound friends asked him to serve, which he did until 1949. Within a year of taking the position, he was the chairman of township supervisors. He made friends easily and politics seemed to be a natural, so when a group of local citizens asked him to run for state representative for the 35th district, he accepted. With the backing of the current representative, Nakkula won. He served 12 years as a state representative. After redistricting, he finally lost his seat and began serving as a liaison for Sen. Al Cedarburg. Nakkula passed away in 1971. (Courtesy of Nancy Nakkula Prescott.)

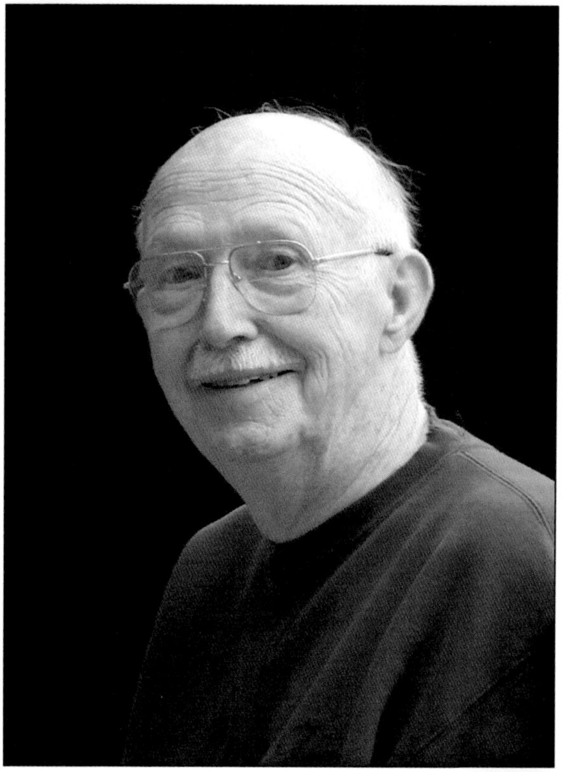

Ken Kerswill's roots are in Gladwin. His father, Lyman, came from Canada in 1892. His mother was a member of the Foutch family and was born and raised in Gladwin. His great-grandfather was David Foutch, Christopher Columbus Foutch's brother. A graduate of Gladwin High School's class of 1937, Ken became postmaster during Pres. Dwight D. Eisenhower's administration and stayed on the job for over 28 years. A great historian and storyteller, he is quite proud of never missing a Rotary Club meeting in over 50 years. (Courtesy of Robert Frei.)

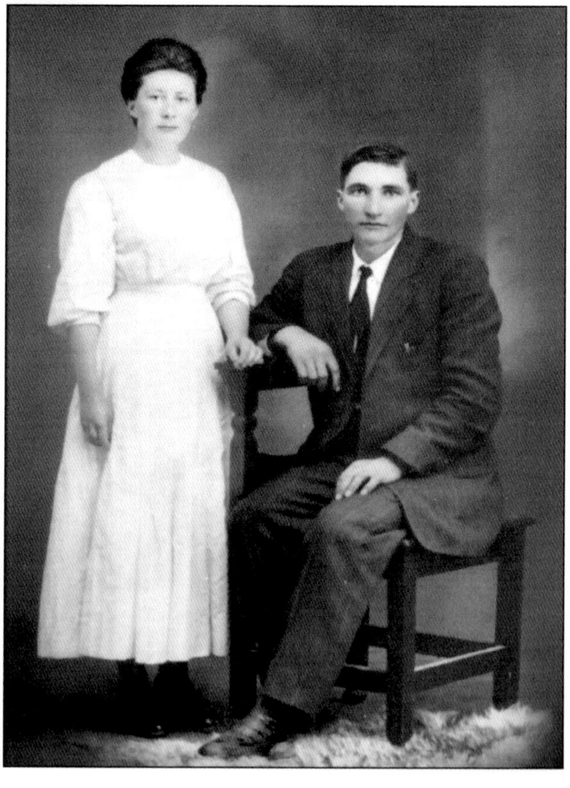

Parker Weaver was born in Gladwin in 1892. Ellen Wilson, his future bride, was also born in Gladwin one month later. They were married at age 18 in 1911 and had 10 children. Parker worked for the road commission and part of his land is the industrial park in Gladwin today. His granddaughter Linda Weaver Winarski has served on the school board for over 20 years and is married to Tom Winarski, the mayor of Gladwin. (Courtesy of Tom Winarski.)

The first Miss Beaverton contest was held in 1929 in conjunction with the Water Carnival. The first winner was Lorraine Budge. She went on to win the Miss Eastern Michigan contest, which made her eligible to attend the Miss America pageant in New Jersey. At that time, there was no state pageant to select a Michigan representative. Instead, Miss Michigan was chosen from the Michigan contestants in Baltimore. Later she said her reason for entering the Miss Michigan contest was because the winner received a free airplane ride. She did win and also got her first case of airplane sickness. In the Miss America pageant, she won the swimsuit contest but missed several other portions while recovering from her airplane ride. As Miss Michigan, she did spend the next year making many appearances all across the state. She also toured Michigan as the mistress of ceremonies in a variety show featuring Olympic champion Johnny Weismuller, who became famous for starring in the lead role of the Tarzan movies in the 1930s.

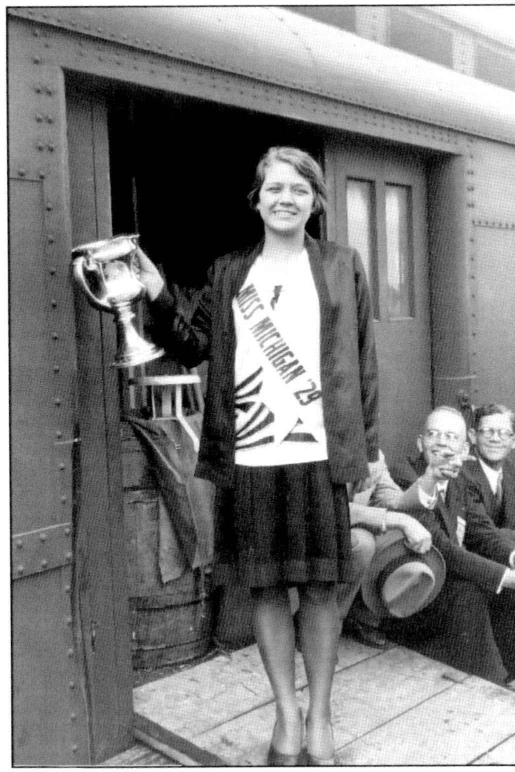

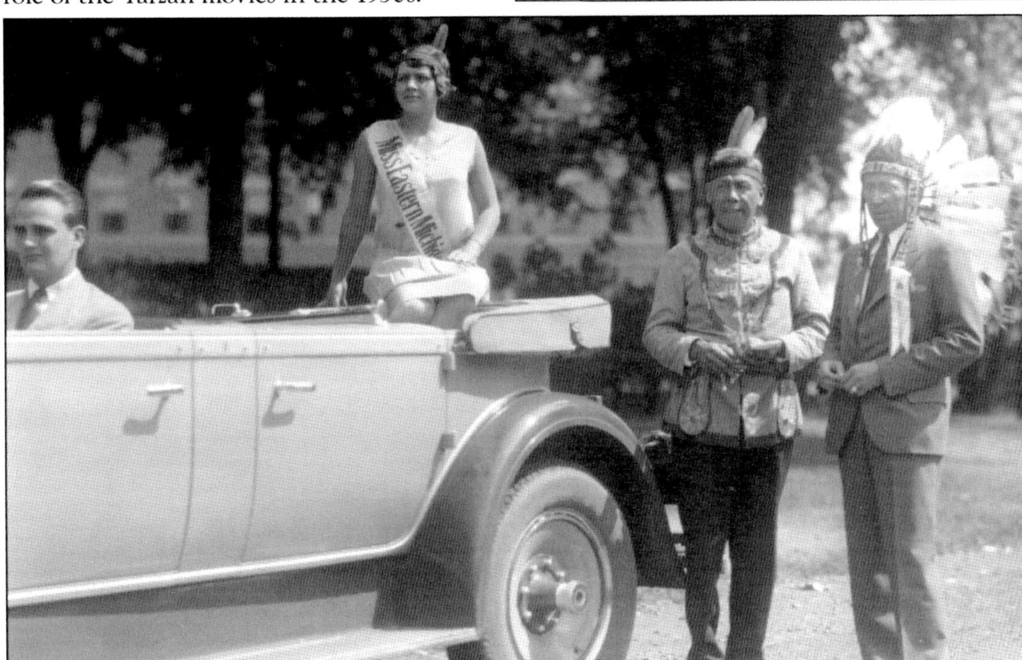

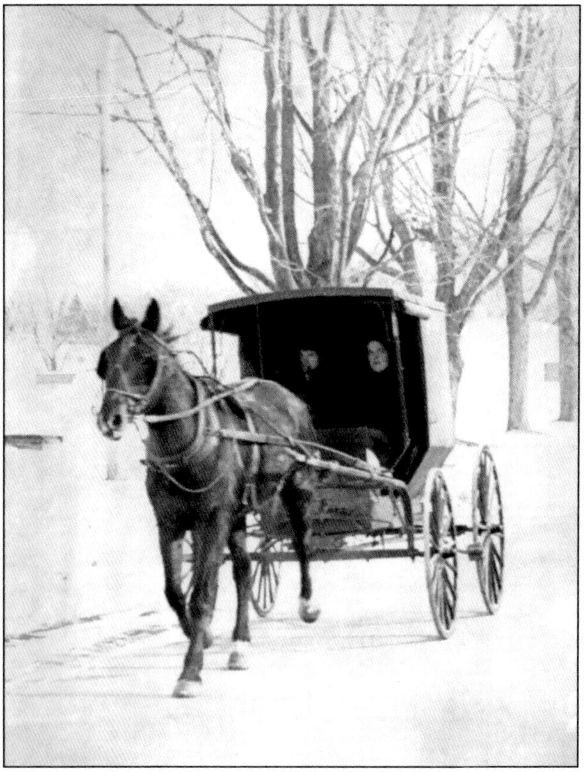

There is a very large Amish presence in Gladwin County. In the Beaverton area, Enos Swartzentrauber bought the Kerswill farm on Kerswill Road in 1979. He developed an Amish community referred to as the Swartzentrauber Order, which started in Holmes County, Ohio. There is another Amish order or community in the northern area of Gladwin County as well. Many people mistakenly think "all Amish are alike," but that is far from accurate. Within a 30-mile radius, there are at least three separate orders with three distinct levels of modernization. The Swartzentraubers use no electricity and will only ride in a motorized vehicle for emergencies. The Old Order Amish use electricity and have telephones in their businesses. The New Order Amish use electricity and are often seen with cell phones. In each case, the Amish and the rest of the county's population are working diligently to coexist in the 21st century.

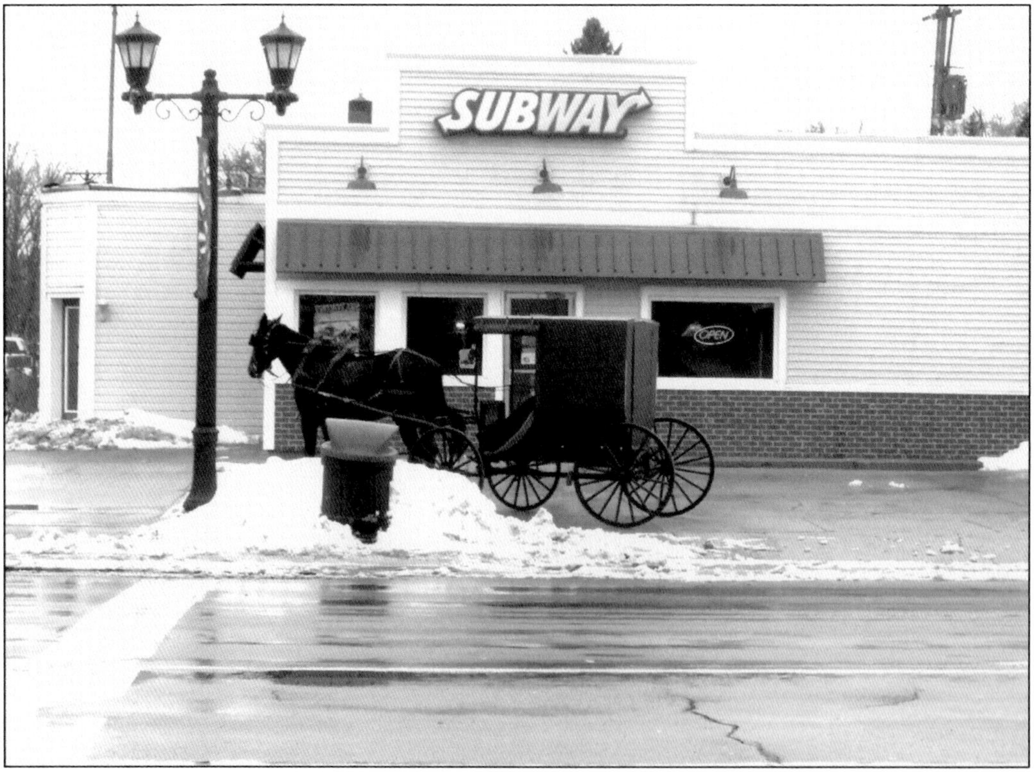

This picture shows four generations of Walker ancestry. Josephine Chatterton (right) showed true pioneer spirit and came to Gladwin on her own with her youngest daughter of 11 children in 1887. On the left is Harriett (Chatterton) Walker, Josephine's oldest daughter and the mother of Walter Walker, who is standing in the back. The little girl in the middle is Alice Walker, Walter's first child. (Courtesy of Ben Ball.)

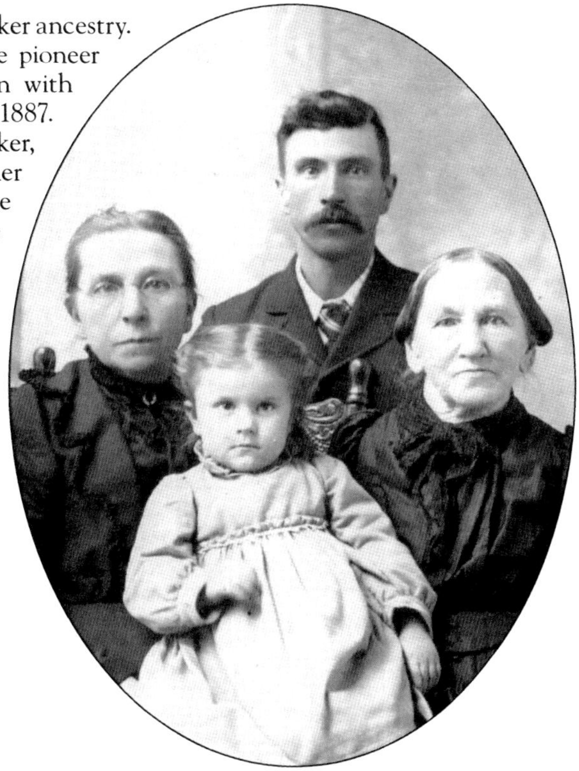

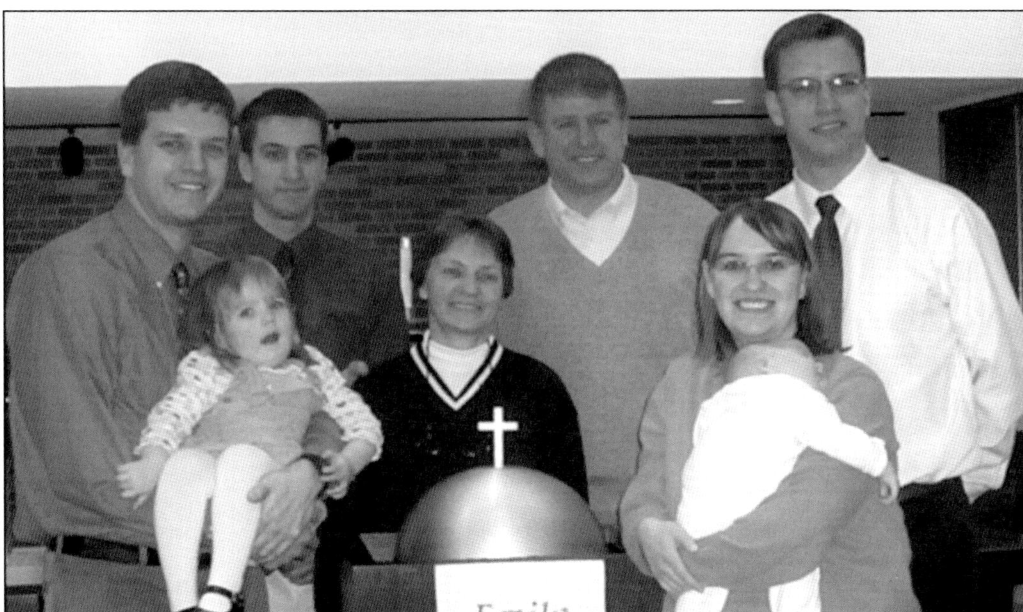

Ben Ball came to Gladwin from Isabella County to teach school and coach golf. He did that for 35 years and became part of the community. He met his wife, Lana, who has roots in Gladwin County as long as almost anyone. During their 35 years of marriage, they to raise three boys. Why is this special? Each one graduated as valedictorian for their respective high school classes. That is special in any county. Here is a recent picture of the Ball family. (Courtesy of Ben Ball.)

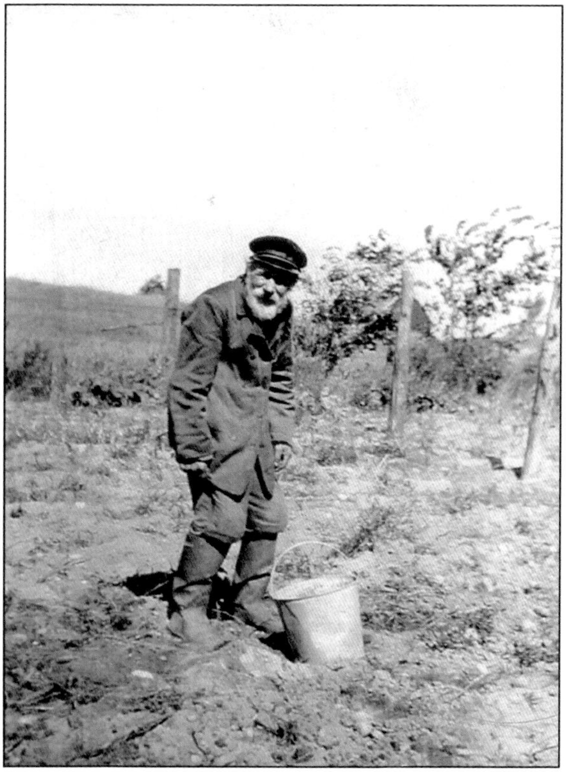

Ludwig (Louis) Schindel was born in Russian Poland in 1844 and came to America in 1904 aboard the *Carpathia*, the ship that came to the *Titanic* survivor's rescue in 1912. With his wife, Emilie, they moved directly to Sage Township, where they bought a farm on Michigan 18. They were the parents of 12 children. (Courtesy of Nadine Erdman Saiki.)

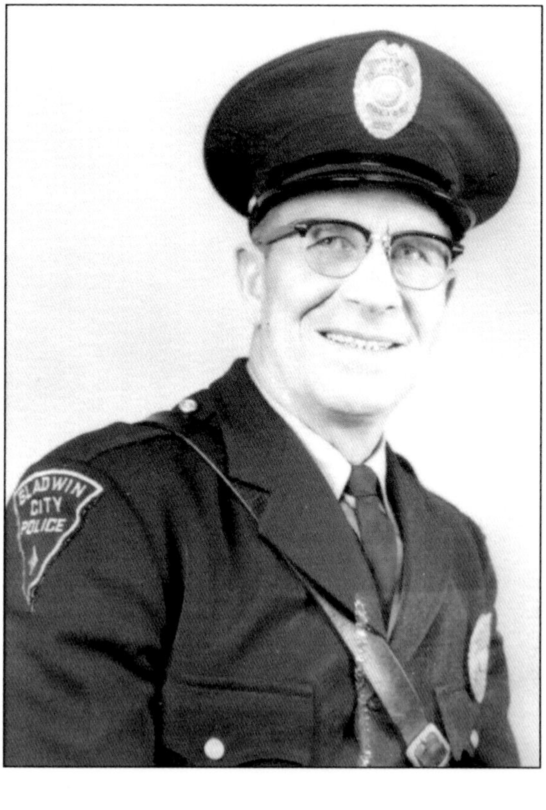

Albert Erdman was born in Clare County in 1907 but was a resident of Gladwin County for almost his entire life. He married Martha Schindel in 1927 and was quite a squeeze box player. In addition to farming, owning a business, and doing carpentry work, Erdman was chief of police in the city of Gladwin from 1957 to 1967. (Courtesy of Nadine Erdman Saiki.)

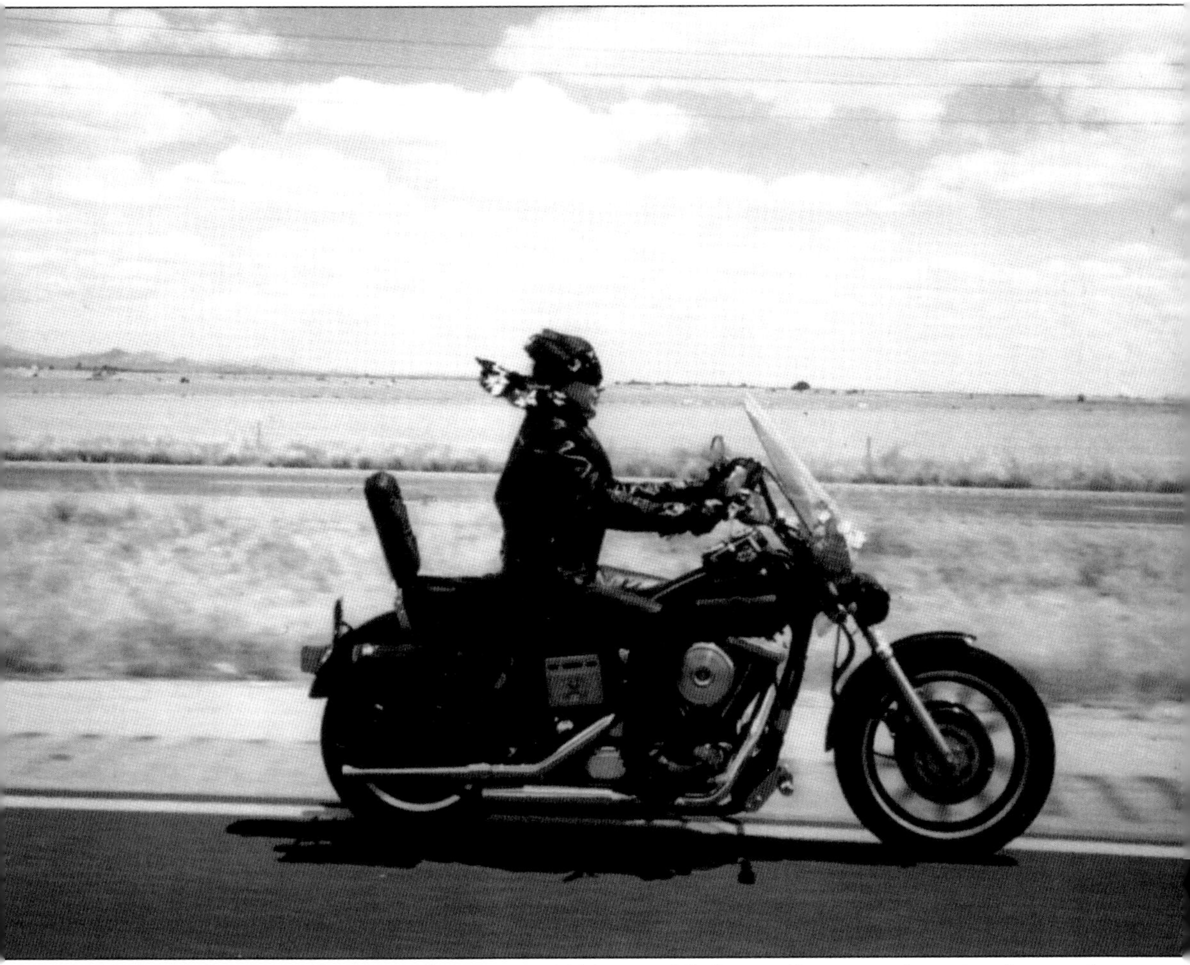

Nadine Erdman Saiki was born in 1946 in Gladwin County, the daughter of Albert and Martha Erdman. She went to the one-room Sage school and graduated from Gladwin High School in 1964. That year, she was the senior representative on the homecoming court. The following year, she finished second runner-up in the Miss Detroit contest representing Bloomfield Hills. For many years, she had a career as a professional model. After working as an office manager in the automotive industry, she took a job managing the clothing and accessories line for a large Harley Davidson dealership. As the picture above shows, she loves her Harley. (Courtesy of Nadine Erdman Saiki.)

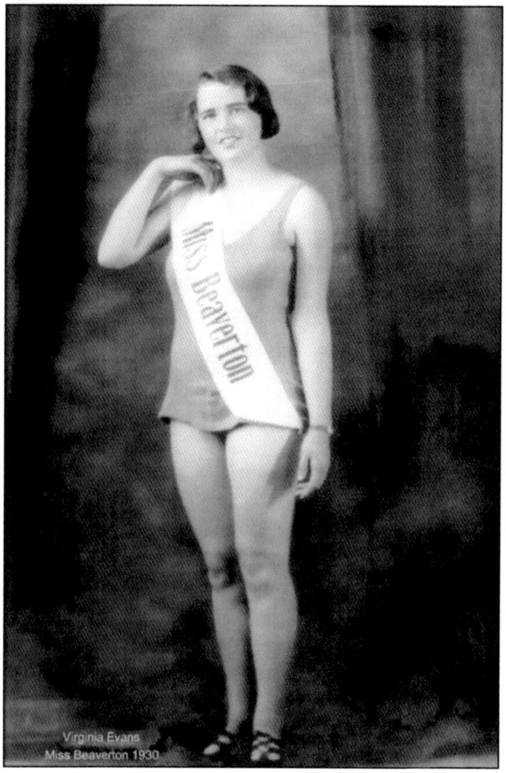

Virginia Evans McCulloch moved to Lyle from Ohio in 1915 when she was two years old. She won the 1930 Miss Beaverton contest in its second year of competition. It is true that her father, A. C. P. Evans, would not look at her wearing her bathing suit, because according to Virginia, "he thought it was too risqué." (Courtesy of Virginia Evans McCulloch.)

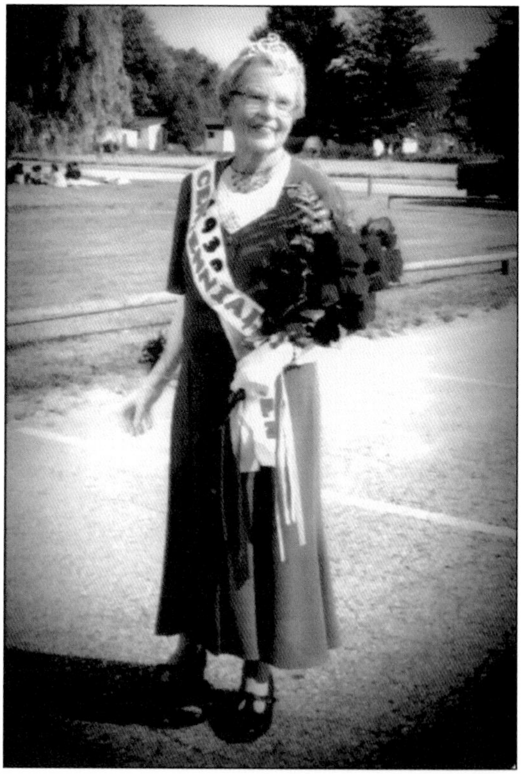

McCulloch was chosen Miss Centennial of Beaverton in 2003. She is now 95 years old and proud of it. At age 58, she went to college to learn to be a hearing technician. Now a great-great-grandmother, when asked if she felt old, she said it never even occurred to her until someone pointed out that her son was a great-grandfather. (Courtesy of Virginia Evans McCulloch.)

Minnie Foutch, the sister of Christopher Columbus (C. C.) Foutch and David Foutch, was the first businesswoman in Cedar/Gladwin. She owned a store that was built in 1877 and operated it for many years. Also an avid hunter, she lost an eye in a hunting accident from a buckshot.

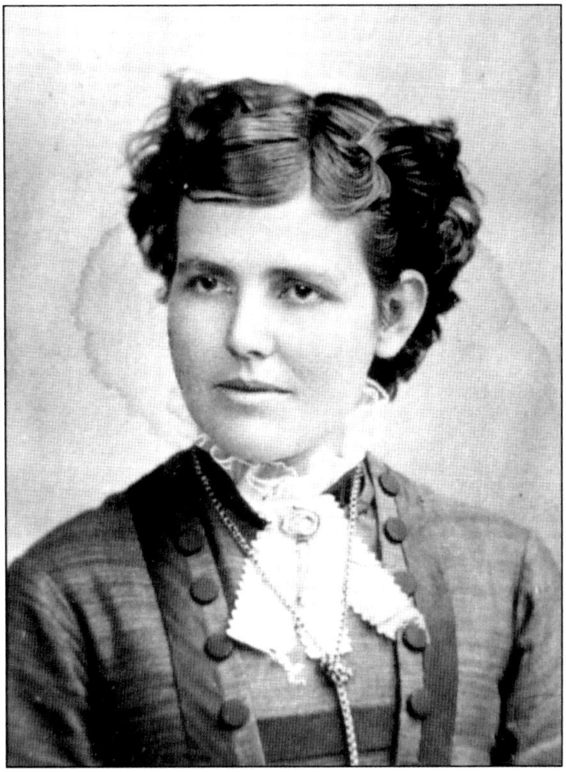

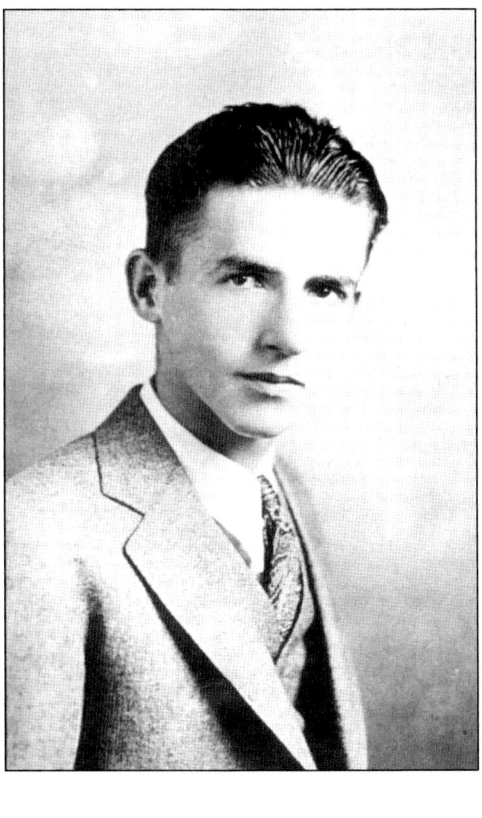

Dr. Floyd Myers was one of the veterinary practitioners in Gladwin who operated a vet clinic one block north of Cedar Avenue on Maple Street and Antler Street. He served as mayor from 1929 to 1931. His son Ralph, shown here, was also elected mayor. In his mid-20s, Ralph was also the youngest mayor, serving from 1942 to 1945. (Courtesy of Betty Myers.)

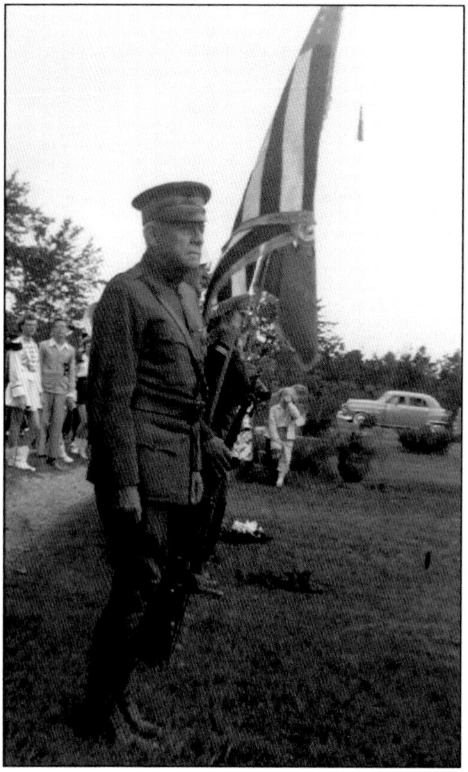

Laurin Budge moved to Beaverton to work in Pierce's Drug Store in 1902. He soon received his pharmacy credentials from Ferris Institute (now known as Ferris State University) and bought his own drugstore. During World War I, he served as a first lieutenant. After serving three terms as Beaverton's mayor, Budge was elected as a state representative to the Michigan Legislature and served two terms. Because of his distinguished military service, he was the founding commander of Beaverton's American Legion Post. This picture shows Budge commanding an honor guard in 1955.

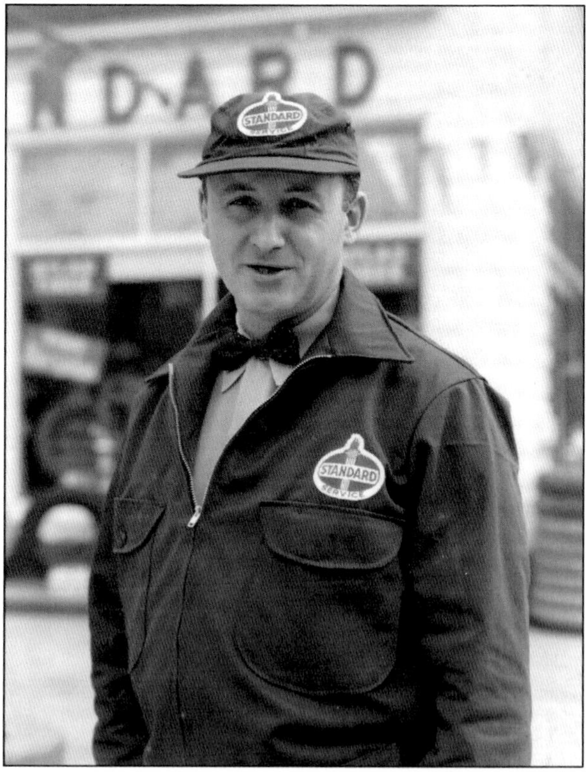

Adolph Presidio came to Beaverton in 1947 and along with his cousin took over the Standard Oil service station on Ross Street. He eventually turned that into the Presidio Ford dealership. Always civic minded, he served as mayor of Beaverton for 17 years and then was a Gladwin County Commissioner for 27 years. (Courtesy of Gladwin County Historical Society.)

George Taylor came to Beaverton as a young man and was one of the first mail carriers. A teacher by trade, he excelled as he worked his way through the system to eventually become the superintendent of schools in Beaverton. He went on to Gladwin as the county superintendent of schools, where he worked for the next 30 years. His love for music and children prompted him to organize a county band, a county-wide music program, and an all-county-wide spelling bee contest. (Courtesy of Stanley Smith.)

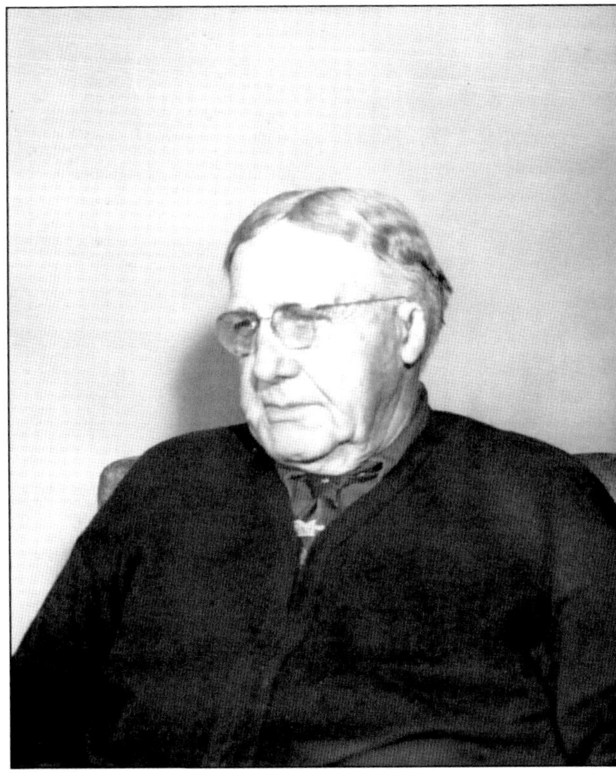

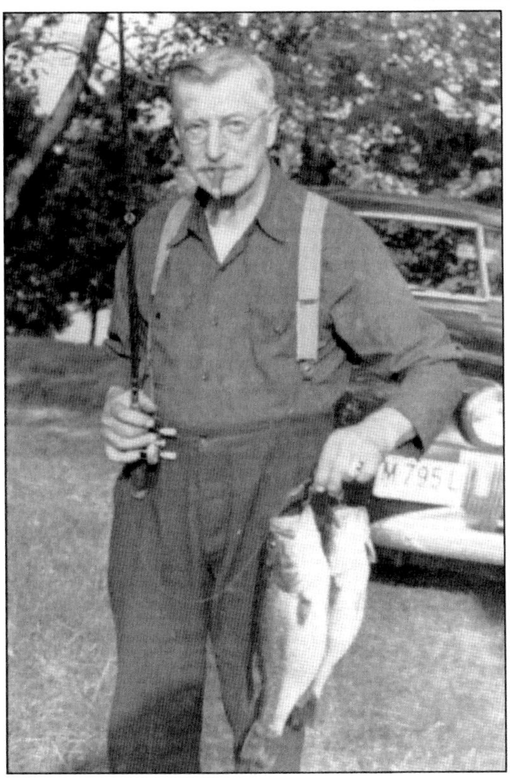

Willis Smith came to Gladwin as a young man from Cleveland, Ohio. He worked on many of the buildings in the city, including the Powell building and the Masonic temple and had a reputation for fixing anything. His love for hunting and fishing prompted him to build the first summer cottage on Wiggins Lake. He was hired to survey the lots there and was offered the opportunity to buy each lot for $35 during the Depression. His taxes were $6 a year. (Courtesy of Stanley Smith.)

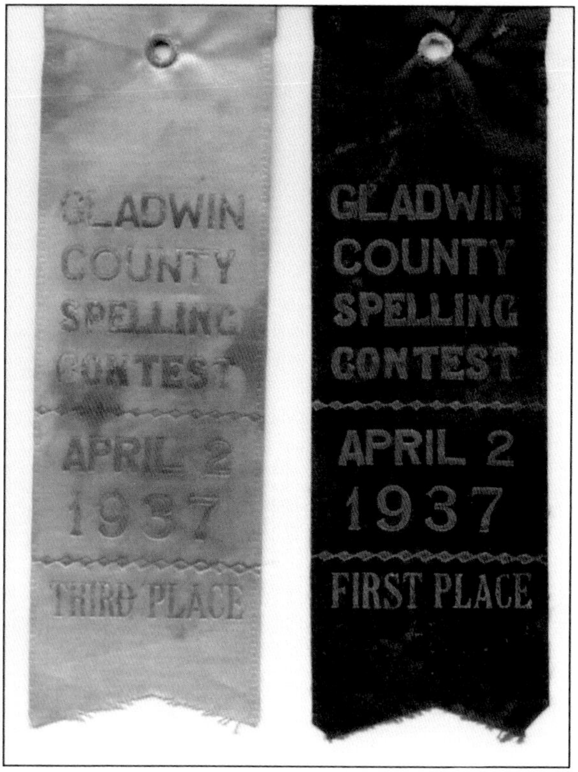

Stanley Smith is the grandson of George Taylor and Willis Smith. He remembers the days of working the fields on his father's 80-acre farm on Butman Road. Stanley took up the Taylor trait and went into education. He worked at the intermediate school and then taught fifth grade until he retired. One fond memory he recalls is participating in the spelling contest. Seen here are the ribbons he and his brother won. When asked who won, he said, "I honestly can't remember, but let's say I did." (Courtesy of Stanley Smith.)

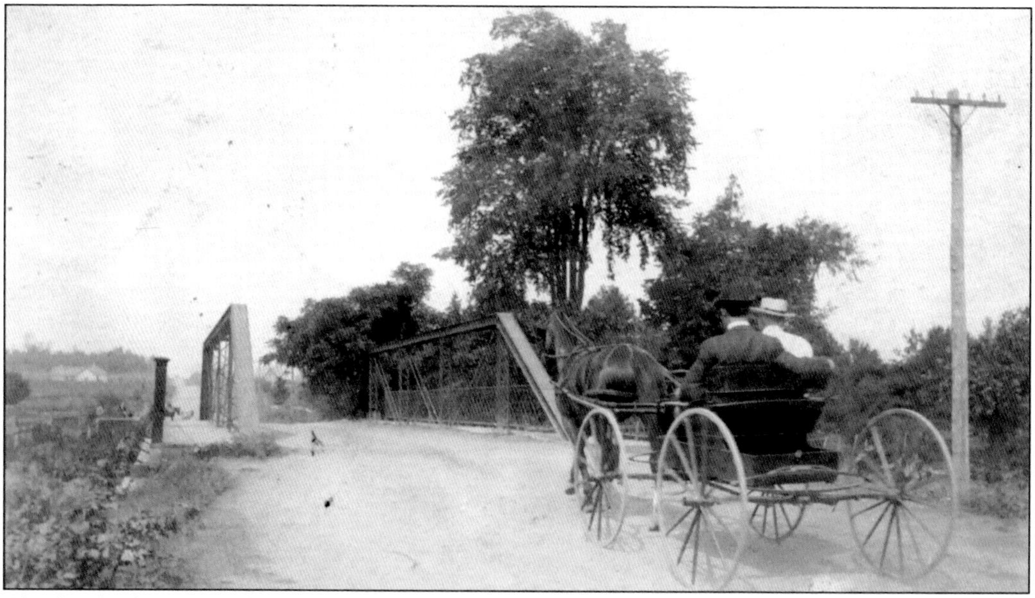

The first bridge across the Cedar River was built in 1885. Shown here, a single, one-way iron bridge replaced it in 1893. The bridge was significant because it connected the newly incorporated city of Gladwin with Grout Township and the western half of the county. Josephine Steele recalled getting the wagon hitched to go into town for Saturday shopping. The trip from their house in Grout Township took about a half hour. But when their horse, "ole Pat," hit the metal bridge at the edge of town, "we were home in about ten minutes."

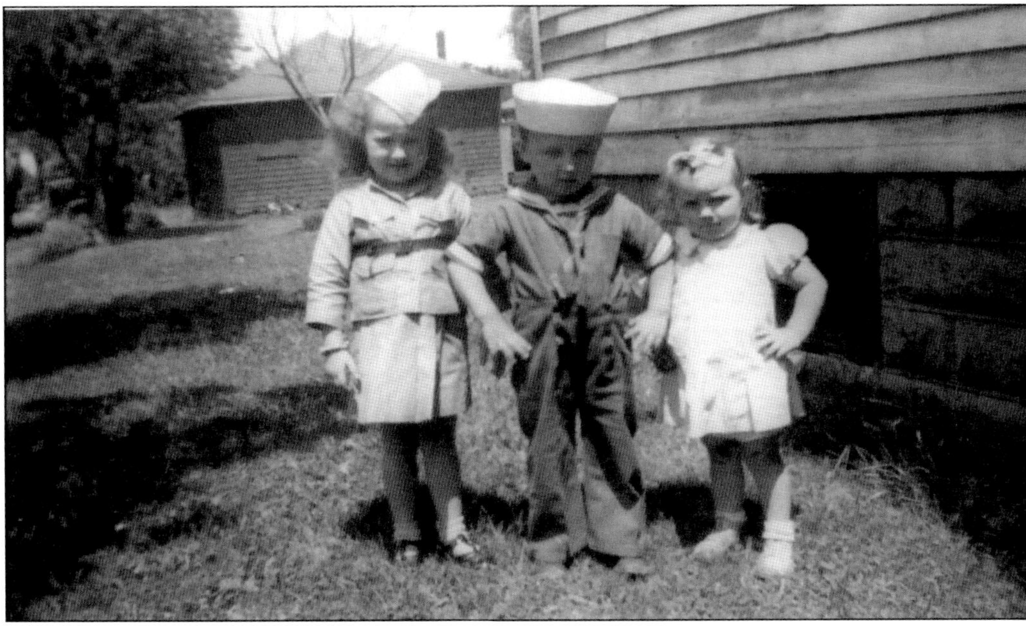

Fran Seebeck is the middle child in the picture above, and it fits because for most of her adult life she has been in the middle of almost every charitable activity in Gladwin County. She and her husband, Dick, are in the 18th year of owning the Oak Outlet Furniture Store, which is just off Cedar Avenue in Gladwin. Her seven grandchildren are on an advertising billboard somewhere along Interstate 75. (Courtesy of Fran Seebeck.)

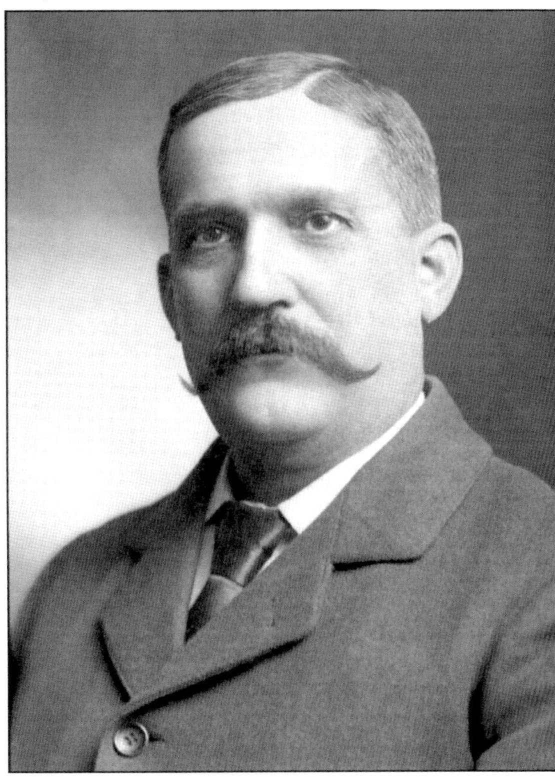

John Shaffer came to Gladwin in 1881. He was a very influential and important businessman and contributed greatly to the development of the growing community. In addition to being credited with building the first and many of the prominent brick structures in town, Shaffer was also on the first village council, served as county treasurer, and chaired the railroad commission that brought the railroad to Gladwin.

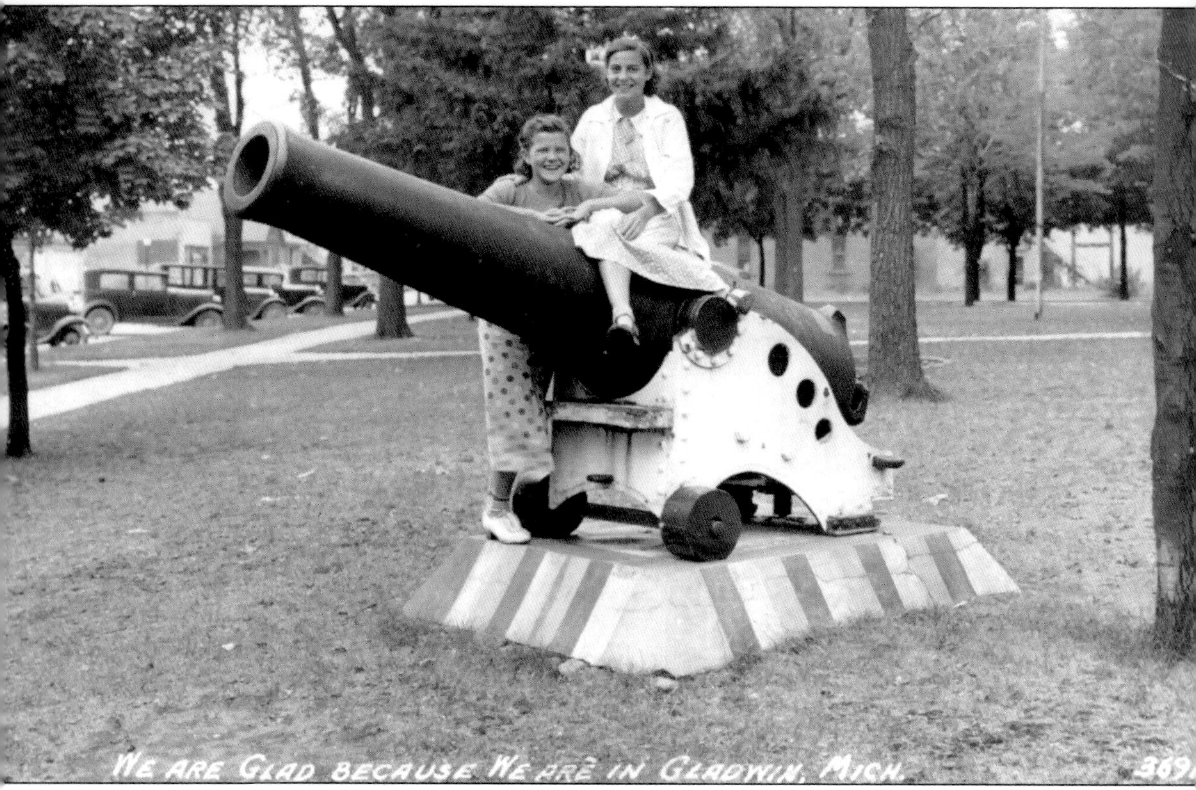

"We are glad because we are in Gladwin" is from a 1937 postcard. The cannon was one of two Civil War cannons guarding the courthouse until they were melted down for metal in World War II. Here are excerpts from a newspaper account of an interesting event involving the cannons: "Recalling November 11, 1918 when Armistice was signed . . . some of the fellows took up a collection and bought gun powder to fire one of the old cannons on the courthouse lawn. When touched off every front window in the *Record* office was shattered. . . . Someone asked Ike Foster, of the *Record*, is he was going to make the pranksters pay for the broken windows. Ike said, 'No, I don't think we will. I think I gave the boys most of the money to buy the gun powder.'" On the left is Emma Lou Rogers and the girl on the right is unidentified. (Courtesy of John Rhode.)

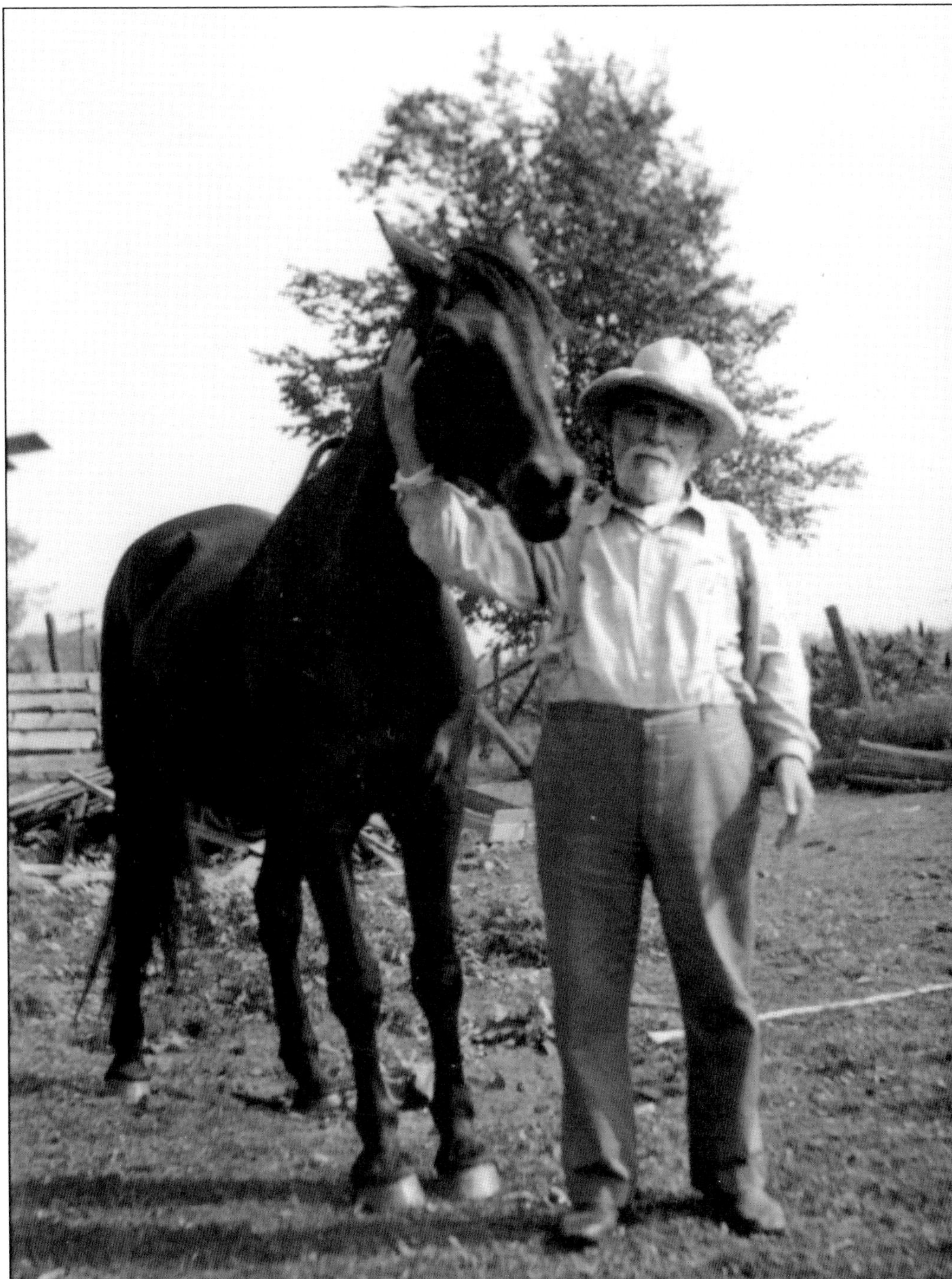

L. V. Soldan was a lay minister, a farmer, and a storekeeper. He had the store in Butman first then took over the store in Lyle. However, the real star in the Soldan family was their horse Comet. He was named because he was born in 1910, the year Halley's Comet appeared in the summer sky. Comet took Soldan to town, pulled a plow, was the girls' transportation to school, and was the envy of children in two townships—Butman and Beaverton. (Courtesy of Inez Soldan.)

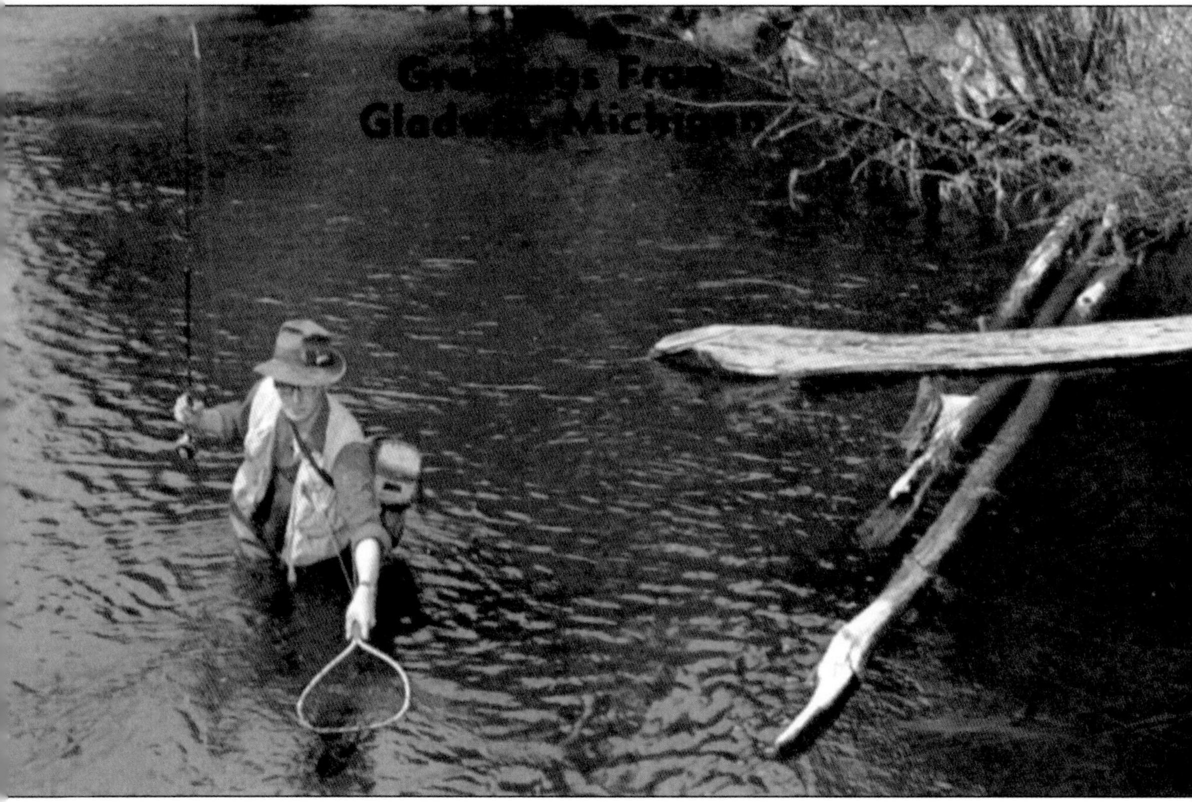

This is a stock postcard from about 1953 that states, "Greetings from Gladwin." Although the fisherman pictured is most likely not in a Gladwin river, the county is blessed with an abundance of excellent fishing rivers and lakes. Michigan does boast of being a "water wonderland," and Gladwin fits that description. An interesting note about the postcard—it has a 2¢ Jefferson stamp on it. (Courtesy of Clarke Historical Library.)

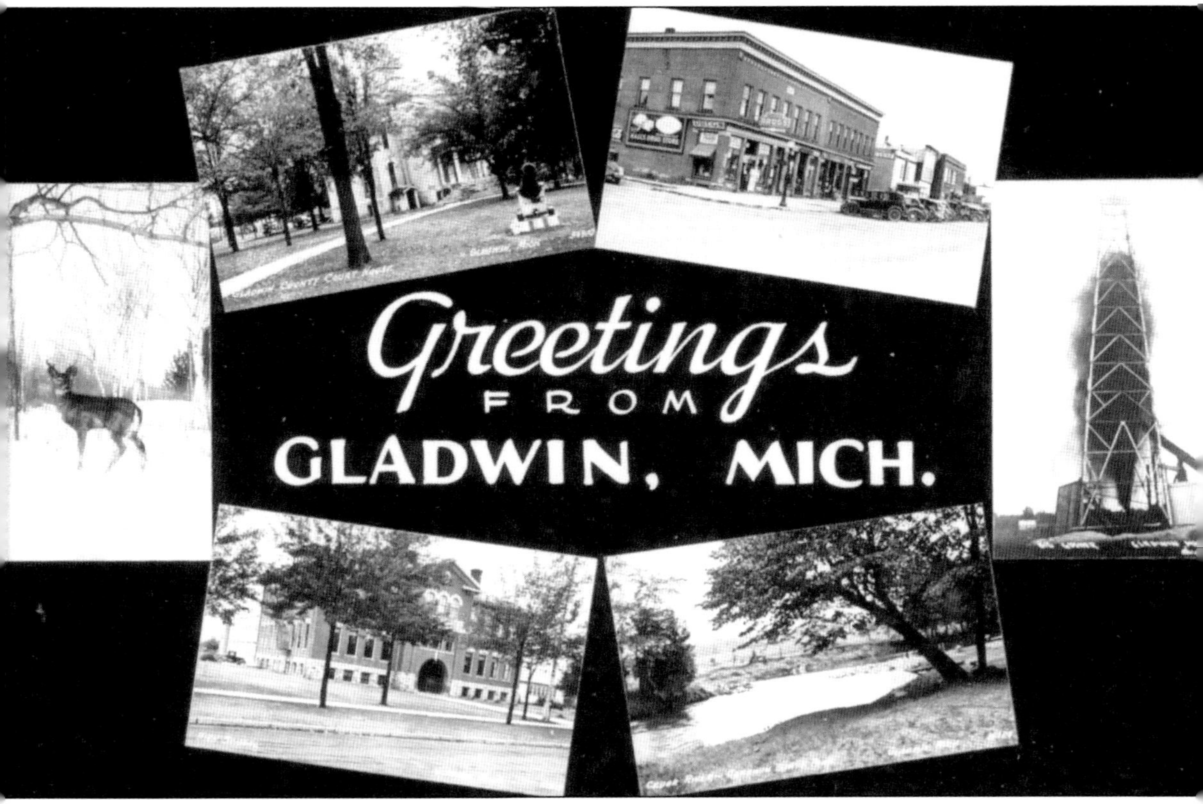

Here is a 1937 postcard that states, "Greetings from Gladwin, Michigan." This card gives a brief review of the highlights and an insight into what people thought were important aspects of the county in the 1930s. Shown clockwise from the left is a white-tailed deer for the great hunting, the courthouse for safety, a thriving downtown area, the oil boom for prosperity, the scenic Cedar River for fishing and relaxation, and finally the school building for a quality education. (Courtesy of John Rhode.)

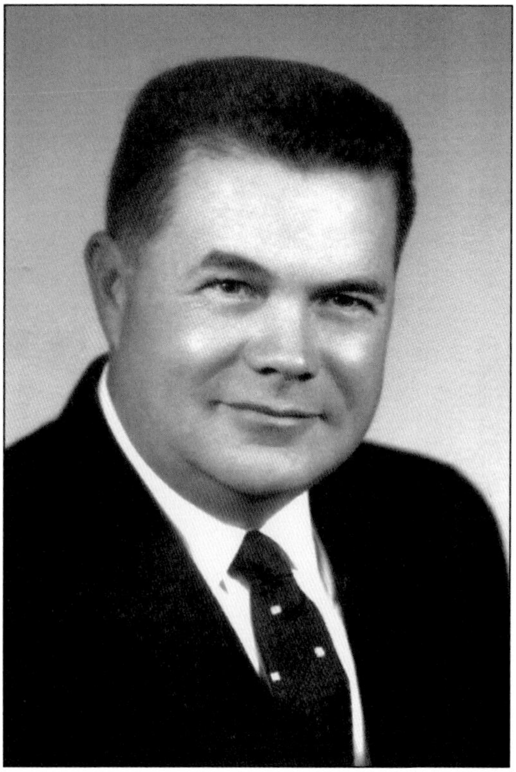

Gaylord Brown invented the machine that rolled the edges of plastic cups. Many of the disposable plastic cups and food containers used today are made with machines produced at Brown Machine in Beaverton. If there is such a thing as "the king of thermoforming," Brown wore the crown until he passed away in 2002. (Courtesy of Brown Machine.)

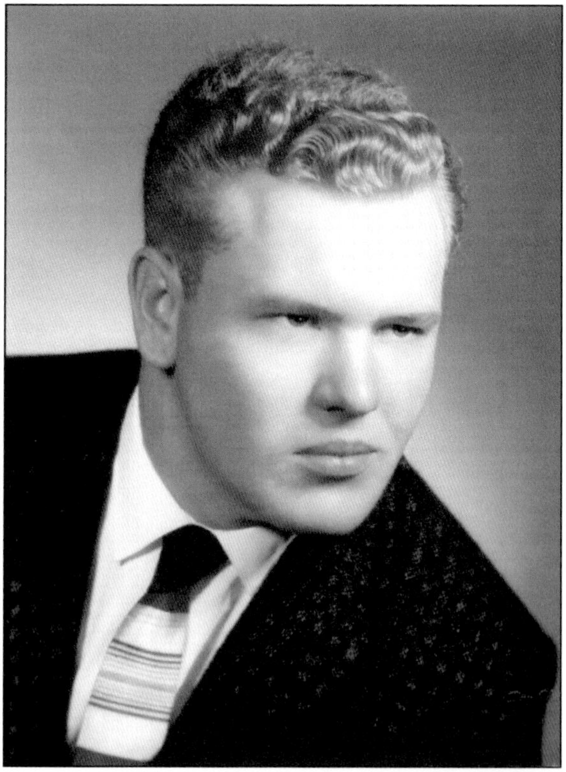

Don Hetherington was born and raised in Gladwin on his father's farm in Secord Township. His relatives homesteaded much of the property when Marvil Secord created his settlement. Hetherington, like many typical small town kids, "couldn't wait to get outta here." After high school, he went to California to become an engineer. He worked there until he retired. Then, like so many, he decided to return to his roots. The saying, "you can never go home," is not true, and he is living proof. (Courtesy of Don Hetherington.)

Bibliography

Beaverton 1902. Beaverton, MI: Beaverton City Centennial Committee, 2002 reprint.
Frei, Robert. *Beaverton: A Century in the Making*. Beaverton, MI: self-published, 2003.
Rhode, John. *Gladwin Illustrated*. Gladwin County Record, 1991.
Gladwin County Historical Society. *The Gladwin County First Settlers Centennial*. Second edition, Gladwin County Record, 1990.
The First Years. Gladwin County, MI: Gladwin County Centennial Corporation, 1991 reprint.
Gladwin History Then & Now. Gladwin County, MI: Gladwin County Historical Society, 1990.
Sigsby, Rick. *Discovering Hidden Treasures: Interesting People and Places in Mid-Michigan*. Coleman, MI: Dreambuilder Publications, 2007.

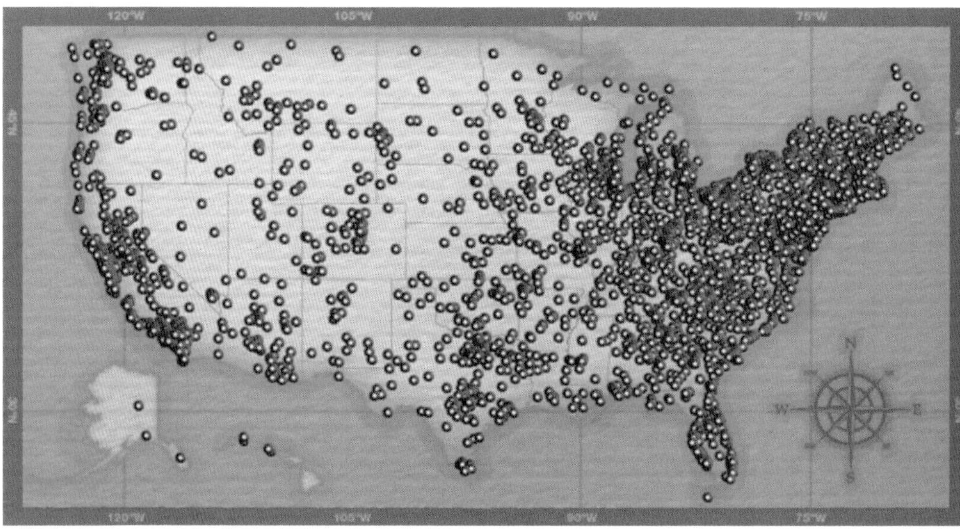

120°W
105°W
90°W
75°W
N
W
E
S